THE INDUSTRIAL WORKER

1840–1860

THE

INDUSTRIAL WORKER
1840–1860

*The Reaction of American Industrial Society
to the Advance of the Industrial Revolution*

by

NORMAN WARE

With an Introduction by Thomas Dublin

THE INDUSTRIAL WORKER, 1840–1860. Copyright © 1924 by Hart, Schaffner and Marx. New edition copyright © 1990 by Ivan R. Dee, Inc. Introduction copyright © 1990 by Thomas Dublin. This book was originally published in 1924 and is here reprinted by arrangement with the Hartmarx Corporation. All rights reserved, including the right to reproduce this book or portions thereof in any form. For information, address the publisher at 1332 North Halsted Street, Chicago 60622. Manufactured in the United States of America.

Library of Congress Cataloging-in-Publication Data
Ware, Norman, b. 1886.
    The industrial worker, 1840–1860 : the reaction of American industrial society to the advance of the Industrial Revolution / by Norman Ware ; with an introduction by Thomas Dublin.—1st Elephant pbk. ed.
        p.   cm.
    Reprint, with new introd. Originally published: Boston : Houghton Mifflin, 1924.
    Includes bibliographical references.
    ISBN 0-929587-25-1
    1. Working class—United States—History—19th century. 2. United States—Social conditions—To 1865. I. Title.
HD8070.W3   1990
305.5'62'097309034—dc20   89-25736
                                                CIP

CONTENTS

Introduction to the 1990 Edition v

Introduction xv
I. The State of the Nation 1
II. The Immigrant and the Homes of
the Poor 10
III. "The Spirit of the Age" 18
IV. The Degredation of the Worker 26
V. The New Power: The Factory
Controversy 71
VI. The New Power: The Dangers of
Paternalism 101
VII. The Degradation of the Operative 106
VIII. The Ten-Hour Movement: Industrial,
1840–50 125
IX. The Change of Personnel 149
X. The Ten-Hour Movement: Political,
1850–60 154
XI. The Reformers: Associationists 163
XII. Land Reform 180
XIII. Coöperation 185
XIV. The Labor Movement: Defensive,
1840–50 198
XV. The Labor Movement: Aggressive,
1850–60 227
Selected Bibliography 241
Index 250

INTRODUCTION TO THE 1990 EDITION

I DISCOVERED *The Industrial Worker, 1840–1860* almost twenty years ago in a graduate seminar on American Economic History. Norman Ware's voice was a breath of fresh air amid arguments I did not accept but whose logic I had been unable to counter to my own satisfaction. With the ascendancy of consensus historiography in the 1950s and '60s, conflict in American history seemed to disappear. Jacksonian Democrats became "venturesome conservatives," and ideological conflict was banished from most accounts of historical change.[1] For many, the study of capitalist industrialization in the United States became a search for the determinants of sustained economic growth. Wage and price levels and annual rates of economic growth became the focus of sophisticated research once labor protest, ideological differences, and class consciousness had been effectively banished from the historical landscape.

Norman Ware wrote *The Industrial Worker, 1840–1860* in 1924, well before the ascendancy of consensus historians, and offered a rather different view of the Industrial Revolution in the United States. Conflict was central to his perspective. As he noted in his introduction: "While this revolution in its later results is pleasing enough in modern eyes, it was repugnant to an astonishingly large section of the earlier American community."(xvi)* That the Industrial Revolution in the United States entailed a dramatic restructuring

*References to pages within *The Industrial Worker* appear in parentheses after quotations. Other citations appear as endnotes below.

of values and social practice is a major theme of *The Industrial Worker*, one that has been taken up and elaborated upon by numerous labor historians in the past fifteen years.[2] It is particularly appropriate, then, that Norman Ware's classic work should be reprinted at this time.

Norman Ware was born in Canada in 1886 and earned his B.A. degree at McMaster University in Hamilton, Ontario, in 1908 and his Ph.D. at the University of Chicago in 1913. A child of the Progressive movement, Ware worked after graduation as the head of the University Settlement in Toronto. After a period of military service in World War I, he moved permanently to the United States in 1919 and became a naturalized citizen in 1924. In 1928 he joined the Department of Economics and Social Sciences at Wesleyan University, an appointment he held until his death in 1949. Throughout this period he also held a variety of state and federal government jobs, among them chairman of the Connecticut State Board of Mediation and Arbitration and a regional head of the National War Labor Board.[3]

The Industrial Worker, 1840–1860 was Ware's first book; his successive publications built upon its treatment of early labor history. *The Labor Movement in the United States, 1860–1895* (1929) examined the continued growth and development of organized labor in the next thirty-five years, with particular emphasis on the Knights of Labor. *Labor in Modern Industrial Society* (1935) carried this story into the twentieth century with most of its emphasis on the history of organized labor and labor law, from the founding of the American Federation of Labor to the passage of the National Industrial Recovery Act (NRA) in the 1930s. Ware's final work, *Wealth and Welfare*, appeared in 1949, the year of his death, and placed the devel-

opment of American capitalism within a broad framework of economic history stretching from the early
middle ages to the mid-twentieth century.

Throughout this body of work, Norman Ware was
notable for his willingness to stake out positions and
make judgments. He did not hide his opinions behind
a veneer of seemingly objective prose. In *The Industrial Worker* he displayed impatience with utopian
reformers whom he felt often misled the working class
with idealistic schemes. Of the failure of Fourierist
phalanxes in the 1850s, he wrote: "A new society
cannot be created overnight according to plans and
specifications drawn up in the study."(174) He found
the land reform scheme of George Henry Evans
wanting: "It sought not a solution, but an escape."(180)
He viewed Evans as "the most rigid doctrinaire in a
period of doctrinaires."(182)

Labor leaders came in for their share of criticism in
Ware's writings. Of the head of the Knights of Labor,
he wrote: "Powderly was a land crank. . . . Powderly
made long speeches on the land question but little
attention was paid to them." Ware described the
strategies employed by Adolph Strasser and Samuel
Gompers to maintain control of the cigarmakers union as "unconstitutional, unfair, and high-handed."[4]

Ware knew the writings of Marx and was sympathetic in his appraisal of Marx as an organizer and
social critic, but he maintained a critical respect. He
acknowledged the tremendous impact of Marxism on
working-class movements in the nineteenth and twentieth centuries, but he would not have considered
himself a Marxist.[5] Nevertheless, Ware had a clear
understanding of the dialectical nature of social and
economic change in this period. That insight is evident in the subtitle of this book: "The Reaction of
American Industrial Society to the Advance of the

Industrial Revolution." The work explored both the objective advance of industrialization and the subjective responses of workers and reformers.

Ware's key insight in *The Industrial Worker, 1840–1860* was his understanding (which he shares with more recent Marxist labor historians) of the social character of the Industrial Revolution in the United States. More was involved than simply the adoption of machinery and the utilization of water and steam power. He expressed this added dimension in his introduction as "the social revolution in which sovereignty in economic affairs passed from the community as a whole into the keeping of a special class."(xvii) In the book itself, he explored the nature of this revolution in class relations and the protest it stirred up. Anticipating his broader argument, he noted, "For every protest against machine industry, there can be found a hundred against the new power of capitalist production and its discipline."(xvii) Ware understood that workers objected principally to capitalist relations of production more than to industrialization itself.

While examining the American Industrial Revolution within a framework compatible with a Marxist analysis, Ware was committed to approaching this period of tremendous social change on its own terms and as it was experienced by contemporaries. He took strong exception to those—Marxist and non-Marxist alike—who would study the period simply for its contribution to some broader social process. Like E. P. Thompson writing forty years later about the English working class in a similar period, Ware sought to "rescue" American labor reformers of the 1840s and '50s from the "enormous condescension of posterity."[6] He took the words of these social critics seriously and resurrected their moral vision for more sophisticated (but also more jaded) twentieth-century readers:

> Much of the language of these protests is hackneyed enough to-day. The ever-recurring contrast between the rich and poor leaves moderns cold. But even clever men in the forties were not deterred by the danger of platitudes. To them the poverty of the growing cities was new, alien, and wrong—a thing to be extirpated before it fastened itself irrevocably upon American civilization.(21)

Ware understood the growing class divisions that appeared in industrializing America at mid-century and permitted voices of protest in that period to be heard.

Another strength of Ware's analysis was his sensitivity to the breadth of work experiences during the early Industrial Revolution. He did not articulate this insight explicitly, but he did treat separately the experiences of male artisans such as ironworkers, printers, hatters, and shoemakers and those of female factory workers in textiles. Moreover, he also explored urban outwork in handloom weaving and the needle trades. We come to understand the overall impact of the growth of capitalist industry as the sum of rather different effects in these varied realms of production. Ware had a nuanced vision of the complexity of the industrializing process.

Finally, Ware offered an interpretation of the labor movement between 1840 and 1860 which continues to influence labor historians today. He argued that the labor movement of the 1840s was integrally intertwined with broad reform activities in that decade and attempted to defend against the assault of industrial capitalism in social, economic, and political realms.

Setbacks in the 1840s led, in Ware's view, to a narrowing of vision in the next decade and the emergence of craft-based, aggressive trade unions which fought for workers' economic interests within a framework that accepted industrial capitalism. Ware's interpretive framework has proven extremely durable and has reappeared in only slightly modified form in the work of a number of later historians.[7]

Despite its many strengths, *The Industrial Worker, 1840–1860* will appear dated in some respects to the contemporary reader. On the most general level, Ware's methods are not entirely adequate to his argument. In describing working-class living conditions, for instance, he relied primarily upon contemporary observers whose comments are not always entirely trustworthy. This method means that Ware was on less solid ground describing actual wages or working conditions than when discussing workers' perceptions of those conditions.

His treatment of Lynn shoemakers provides a case in point. "Nearly all" Lynn shoemakers, in his view, owned their homes and had vegetable gardens. "Almost every family kept a pig and many had their own cow."(39–40) Paul Faler has since shown that at no time in this period did a majority of Lynn taxpayers own real property; moreover, the proportion of Lynn taxpayers owning pigs declined from less than 20 percent in 1832 to 7 percent in 1849.[8] Utilizing surviving tax records, Faler showed quite conclusively that Lynn shoemakers were far more dependent on their wages than Ware suggested. Ware's reliance on contemporary published accounts evidently led him astray.

A similar difficulty arises in Ware's discussion of factory discipline. His treatment of the regulation of operatives' behavior in the Lowell textile mills relied entirely on printed regulations and contemporary

testimony.(107–109) He tended to take written regulations at face value while in fact there was considerable discrepancy between actual practice and stated
ideals. Before the entry of the Irish famine migrants
there was such a steady shortage of mill operatives
that the textile corporations commonly winked at
violations of their printed rules. My own analysis of
turnover in the workforce of the Hamilton Manufacturing Company in the 1830s, for instance, revealed
that the corporation simply was not enforcing its
stated requirement that operatives work a year at the
company and give two weeks' notice before leaving.[9]
As with his treatment of property ownership among
Lynn shoemakers, there are points here where Ware
was misled by contemporary literary records and a
more systematic, quantitative analysis of primary
sources provides a needed corrective.

It should not surprise us, however, that portions of
Ware's analysis appear dated today. The work of
economic and social historians in the intervening decades has superseded Ware's relatively unsophisticated
discussion of the levels of wages and profits. These
issues, however, in no way detract from Ware's note-
worthy accomplishment. Sixty-six years ago he had
the vision to see the growth of industrial capitalism in
the United States in the broadest conceptual terms.
During a period in which the institutional perspective
of labor economists of the Commons school held sway,
Ware did not limit his study to a treatment of organized labor's response to the Industrial Revolution.[10]
While at times critical of the role of intellectuals in
the labor movement, Ware understood that one could
not isolate the labor movement of this period from
broader reform movements and still do justice to its
history. He understood, as well, that the workers'
responses to industrial capitalism had economic and

political dimensions, and that the two were inseperable. Many of the insights we commonly attribute today to recent research in the new social history are evident in Ware's analysis. He stood out among labor economists of his generation, and *The Industrial Worker* still has considerable value as an overview and synthesis of American labor in the early Industrial Revolution. Despite the passage of time, there is really no synthesis for this period of comparable breadth or clarity of argument. Its republication will make accessible once again a major contribution to our understanding of the working-class response to the growth of industrial capitalism in the United States in the decades before the Civil War.

THOMAS DUBLIN

Binghamton, New York
December 1989

I would like to acknowledge critical readings of drafts of this introduction by Melvyn Dubofsky, Paul Faler, and Kathryn Kish Sklar.

  1. The term was employed in Marvin Meyers, *The Jacksonian Persuasion: Politics and Belief* (Stanford, 1957); for a rather different argument which also banished class or ideological concerns from the center of Jacksonian politics, see Lee Benson, *The Concept of Jacksonian Democracy: New York as a Test Case* (Princeton, 1960).

  2. A sampling of more recent work that has built upon Ware's essential insights includes Alan Dawley, *Class and Community: The Industrial Revolution in Lynn* (Cambridge, Mass., 1976); Thomas Dublin, *Women at Work: The Transformation of Work and Community in Lowell, Massachusetts, 1826–1860* (New York, 1979); Bruce Laurie, *Working People of Philadelphia, 1800–1850* (Philadelphia, 1980); Paul Faler, *Mechanics and Manufacturers in the Early Industrial Revolution: Lynn, Massachusetts, 1780–1860* (Albany, 1981); Jonathan Prude, *The Coming of Industrial Order: Town and Factory Life in Rural*

Massachusetts, 1810–1860 (Cambridge, England, 1983); Sean Wilentz, *Chants Democratic: New York City and the Rise of the American Working Class, 1788–1850* (New York, 1984); Mary H. Blewett, *Men, Women, and Work: Class, Gender, and Protest in the New England Shoe Industry, 1780–1910* (Urbana, Ill., 1988).

3. Biographical information in this paragraph is drawn from Ware's obituary, *New York Times*, December 29, 1949, p. 25.

4. Norman Ware, *The Labor Movement in the United States, 1860–1895* (New York, 1929), pp. 365, 264.

5. See in particular Norman Ware, *Labor in Modern Industrial Society* (Boston, 1935), chap. x.

6. E. P. Thompson, *The Making of the English Working Class* (New York, 1966), p. 12.

7. A similar shift between more utopian opposition to capitalism and a more narrow, economistic trade unionism has been discerned by most labor historians in the transition from the Knights of Labor to the American Federation of Labor in the post–Civil War decades. See especially Gerald Grob, *Workers and Utopia* (Evanston, Ill., 1961).

8. Faler, *Mechanics and Manufacturers*, p. 83.

9. Dublin, *Women at Work*, pp. 60, 265n.4.

10. For a useful overview and evaluation of labor history in the tradition of John R. Commons, see David Montgomery, "The Conventional Wisdom," *Labor History* (1972), 13:107–136.

INTRODUCTION

THE period 1840 to 1860 in American history has been regarded almost exclusively from the standpoint of the slavery issue; so exclusively, in fact, as to obscure social and industrial upheavals remarkable alike for their vitality and resource. There is no period in American history of greater individuality than the forties, and no more striking contrast than that between the decade preceding and the decade following the gold discoveries of 1849.

The impetus that carried America into the Civil War did not originate solely in the slavery agitation nor in territorial and economic antagonisms related thereto. Some part of it was a sublimation of other purposes that failed of achievement in the social ferment of the forties. It was inevitable that some one of the many 'causes' that agitated the minds of that generation should sooner or later take precedence and succeed to the motive power generated in the situation as a whole. It is unfortunate, however, that this sublimation tends to obscure those other vital issues that failed to emerge. The anti-slavery movement survived, not because it represented a more valid issue than others it enveloped, but because it of necessity involved territorial antagonisms. There was no Mason and Dixon line in industrial relations.

The aim of this study is to portray the social and economic conditions in which the revolts of the forties took their rise; to interpret the purposes of those involved, their reactions to the new industrialism; to trace the movements and experiments, working-class and reform, that emerged, and their transformation as the period advanced.

A community at any given time is a complex of group personalities, each striving to gain or maintain its place in the sun. Such a complex ordinarily involves a dominant and one or more subordinate groups, shifting both as to position and personnel. When the dominant group is at the beginning of its career, revolt tends to be of a defensive nature, seeking to ward off the subordination involved in the rise of a new power. When the new power is once fully established, revolt takes on an aggressive aspect seeking positive gains of a restricted sort, a 'practical' as opposed to an 'idealistic' programme. And, though this carries the analysis beyond our period, it is perhaps not out of place to suggest that, when the dominant power begins to decline, revolt is liable to return with more effective machinery to 'idealistic' purposes comparable to those of the first stage.

One of the major notes of American life in the forties and fifties was that created by the Industrial Revolution. Beginning about 1800, a process was set going, the direct physical achievements of which can now somewhat be seen, but whose social by-products are obscured by the passage of years and the perversion of vision. American life has had a turning over, not only in the methods of production and exchange, but in temper and ideals. And while this revolution in its later results is pleasing enough in modern eyes, it was repugnant to an astonishingly large section of the earlier American community.

It is commonly supposed that the dissatisfaction in the forties with the character and results of the Industrial Revolution was the result of purely temporary maladjustments. It is admitted that a temporary maladjustment lasting over one's working lifetime is sufficiently permanent for the one concerned. But it is claimed that, from the standpoint of history, the degradation suffered by the industrial worker in the early years of the Industrial Revolution can be discounted by his later prosperity. And this might be true from the calm standpoint of history if the losses and gains were of the same sort. But they were not. The losses of the industrial worker in the first half of the century were not comfort losses solely, but losses, as he conceived it, of status

and independence. And no comfort gains could cancel
this debt.

There were two aspects of the Industrial Revolution
closely related and supporting each other, but of quite different texture and meaning. One of these — the obvious,
new, dramatic aspect — was the application of water and
steam-driven machinery to production, and its concomi-
tant, the modern factory system. The other, not necessarily dependent upon machinery and not less revolutionary, though less regarded, was the social revolution in which
sovereignty in economic affairs passed from the community
as a whole into the keeping of a special class. It was this
social revolution that primarily affected the industrial
worker in this period and against which his protests were
made. Aside from a few riots in Pittsburgh, in which the
hand-loom weavers destroyed some of the new machines,
the American worker was not actively opposed to machinery. He was opposed to the method of its introduction, for
exploitive purposes, as he conceived it, in the hands of a
group alien to the producer. For every protest against
machine industry, there can be found a hundred against
the new power of capitalist production and its discipline.

There arose in the beginning of the nineteenth century
in a local, predominantly agricultural, little-specialized
economic society, not only a new technique of production,
but a new sovereignty in economic life, vested in a group
of owners of capital who had acquired their wealth, not
primarily as producers, but as distributors in foreign and
domestic trade. In a sense, the Industrial Revolution was
the apotheosis of the peddler, that unfortunate individual
who floundered amid the interstices of mediæval society,
hounded from manor to monastery, from peasant's cottage
to artisan's guild, bitten by dogs and fleas, welcomed only
by housewives with inhibited impulses toward conspicuous
waste. History is melodrama, the peddler Cinderella rising from the ashes of contempt to sovereign place and

power. And the resulting extension over production of the hegemony of the distributor, and the decline of the industrial worker as a person, constitute the general background for the revolts with which we shall deal.

During the period 1840–60 the industrial workers as a class were rapidly losing ground. As to wages, it is reasonably certain that no important group of workers made any advance beyond the increased cost of living until the effect of the gold discoveries was felt from 1850 to 1854. From 1850 until 1856 considerable wage advances were made by certain skilled groups, in the building trades especially. But the wages of factory operatives, shoemakers, clothing workers, printers, cabinet workers, hatters, iron workers, and, of course, the hand-loom weavers, did not, over the whole period, gain, but rather lost in relation to the cost of living. When wages are stated in relation to the rewards of capital, the loss is even more pronounced. Certainly the share of the worker in the general prosperity was not commensurate with that of the other factors in production.

A considerable reduction in the hours of labor had been achieved by mechanics outside New England before 1840, and in New England from 1840 to 1860. In the factories, hours were reduced during our period from twelve and thirteen to eleven and, in some cases, to ten, with corresponding reductions in wages. But these reductions do not represent a clear gain because the tendency of the new industrialism was constantly to speed up production and add to the effort and attention required of the worker. In the mills, for instance, the girls, toward 1850, were tending four looms where they had previously tended two and the speed of the machines was being increased as greater mechanical perfection was achieved. The older industrialism retained much of the leisureliness of its rural origin. It knew little of efficiency, in the sense of maximum output per unit of time and cost. And if the factory operatives had gained in the period a general reduction of the hours of labor to ten, which they did not, it is doubtful if they would have more than made up for the increased speed and discipline of their work. The old hours were appallingly long, but they were borne with better grace because the discipline was slack. When speeding up and driving became common, the shorter hour became a necessity. When to the discipline of the boss was added the severer discipline of the new industry, a change toward a shorter day became inevitable. The gain through shorter hours was a real gain, but it was not a net gain as is often assumed.

To the worker, the security of his tenure seemed greater under the older conditions of production, largely because the tenure of the mechanic and artisan was less dependent upon a single function than was that of the operative who succeeded them. This is seen most clearly in the case of the Lynn shoemakers who in the early years were able to weather repeated depressions in their trade because they were more than shoemakers. They were citizens of a semi-rural community. Each had his own garden, a pig and a cow. They were fishermen, more or less, and during a spell of depression in the shoe trade they could keep alive, at least, on sea-food, pork, and garden truck. The more highly industrialized this community became, the more completely the worker was divorced from these subsidiary sources of livelihood, the more unemployment became a specter where it had once had some of the characteristics of a vacation.

It is doubtful if the conditions of work were worse in the new factories than in the old homes and workshops. There was a great deal of criticism of the factories on the score of health and much of the controversy over the factory system turned on this point. On the whole this criticism was justified. The health of the operatives did suffer considerably, and it was only the constant supply of new blood and the short term of factory life that obscured the unfortunate results of the system. But the homes from which the operatives came, the shops of the non-factoryized mechanics and the schools of the period were, to say the least, by no means ideal in this respect. Sanitation was little understood or regarded, and Dr. Josiah Curtis, who made the only scientific study of the effects of the factories upon the health of the operatives, was well in advance of his profession and his time.

It was not primarily of these things, however, that the industrial worker and his friends were thinking when they spoke of the degradation they underwent in the Industrial Revolution. These things were a part of that degradation, but they were also indices of a psychological change that aroused the most fervid protests. This change was one of status, involving, in the opinion of the worker and his friends, a loss of dignity and independence: "The capitalists," they complained, "have taken to bossing all the mechanical trades, while the practical mechanic has become a journeyman, subject to be discharged at every pretended 'miff' of his purse-proud employer." [1]

This transition from the earlier to the later status was reflected in the terms of the labor contract. The old term for the remuneration of the mechanic was 'price.' It referred to his product rather than to his labor, for it was his product that he sold. When the producer, whether master or journeyman, sold his product, he retained his person. But when he came to sell his labor, he sold himself. The term 'wage' that displaced 'price' as the Industrial Revolution advanced had formerly applied only to day labor, and the extension of the term to the skilled worker was regarded by him as a symbol of a deeper change. As late as 1854, a little group of highly skilled pianoforte makers in New York declared that a daily wage was equivalent to slavery and hoped that "the day is far distant when they [the wage-earners] will so far forget what is due to manhood as to glory in a system forced on them by their neces-

[1] New York *State Mechanic*, September 10, 1842.

sity and in opposition to their feelings of independence and
self-respect. May the piano trade long be spared such ex-
hibitions of the degrading power of the day system." [1]

Two traditions, one religious and the other political, opposed the rise of the new power. Politically, Americans
were regarded as having equal basic rights; religiously, as
of equal personal value in the sight of God. In support of
these traditions there were, in the opinion of many of the
contemporaries of the Industrial Revolution, most of the
facts of the older local society in which men were more
nearly free and equal than the new discipline seemed able to
permit. The new discipline required a centralized control.
This was natural enough and necessary to the progress of
the Industrial Revolution. But it achieved, in addition to
this, a centralization of sovereignty that the workers and
the reformers claimed was neither necessary nor desirable.
It was not until the forties that any important section of
the community recognized the character of the change
already largely accomplished and it was out of this realiza-
tion that much of the unrest and agitation of the period
arose.

It cannot but strike every reflecting and observing man [de-
clared the mechanics of Baltimore in 1833] that a spirit unfriendly
to the standing and pursuits of mechanics is fast gaining ground
in this country . . . the result of which if not stopped in its onward
course will be to bring them to a state of servitude less enviable
than that of the vassals of the feudal lords and princes — because
they may hold the name but lose the rights of freemen. [2]

The rich are growing richer and the poor, poorer, and Mammon
is usurping sovereignty in all places. In proportion as railroads
and canals are constructed, these mammoth establishments in
tanning, shoemaking, saddlery, blacksmithing, and every depart-

---

[1] New York *Daily Tribune*, March 22, 1854. The term 'wage-slave'
had a much better standing in the forties than it has to-day. It was not
then regarded as an empty shibboleth of the soap-box orator. This
would suggest that it has suffered only the normal degradation of
language, has become a *cliché*, not that it is a grossly misleading characterization.

[2] Baltimore *Republican and Commercial Advertiser*, September 12, 1833.

ment of work and skill, send their productions and fabrics to distant parts of the country, and reduce smaller capitalists . . . constantly killing out their rivals and monopolizing the business to themselves.[1]

They [some of the shoe manufacturers] seem to think that the jours [journeymen] are designed for no other purpose than to be their subjects. . . . They seem to think it a disgrace to labor; that the laborer is not as good as other people. These little stuck-up, self-conceited individuals who have a little second-hand credit . . . You must do as they wish . . . or you are out of their books; they have no more employment for you.[2]

Wherever we turn our eyes we see insurmountable obstacles presented to our view. Here we see a moneyed aristocracy hanging over us like a mighty avalanche threatening annihilation to every man who dares to question their right to enslave and oppress the poor and unfortunate. If we take another view we find ourselves crippled and destroyed by human competition, and last, though not least, we see machinery introduced that will not only lessen but annihilate the last surviving hope of the honest mechanic.[3]

In the interpretation of these protests, it is necessary to guard against the danger of being misled as to their true character by the language in which they are couched. That the language is that of the agitator does not necessarily mean that the protest is of revolutionary intent. Essentially, the protests of the forties were conservative, defensive, in temper and purpose. Both the labor movement and the reform movements, including the so-called 'socialism' of Brisbane and the so-called 'agrarianism' of George Henry Evans, represented struggles to return to a past that had gone. Capitalism they regarded as the radical force, ruthlessly destroying the little liberties and amenities of another day, a new and alien power rising within the republican framework created by an earlier revolution.[4] "Is the system

[1] *Voice of Industry,* August 6, 1847.
[2] *The Awl,* August 21, 1844.
[3] *Ibid.,* January 8, 1845.
[4] A woman delegate from the Fall River strikers, at the New York Industrial Congress in 1851, protested that the operatives were the conservatives in that affair and the employers the 'revolutionists and levelers'

right or wrong?" demanded the Boston "Laborer." "Does it comport with the spirit of our free institutions? Is it republican? Is it American?" The workers' protest of the forties was to no inconsiderable degree against 'innovations.'

It is possible to approach the study of the period 1840-60 — any period for that matter — from either of two standpoints. One may fix attention upon the condition, activities, and ideas of the dominant group, or one may attempt to uncover the workings of those that were submerged or being submerged. The annals of the poor are short, but seldom simple. They are short, not because they are uninteresting, but because the poor are inarticulate. In the forties there were many voices speaking for them, but too often these self-constituted exponents had little appreciation of the necessities and compulsions of the poor themselves. It was this economic transcendentalism of the reformers, their denial of the necessity cf the industrial revolution that made them blind leaders of the blind. The workers, of necessity, were realists. For them there was no withdrawal into any inner sanctuary, Phalanx, Republican Township, or what not. And care must be exercised in distinguishing between the authentic voice of the worker and that of his advocate and advisor. G. H. Evans, the land reformer, is a case in point. It is often assumed that "The Working Man's Advocate," published by Evans in New York, was a 'labor paper' and represented the aims and attitudes of the workers.[1] In our period this was not the case. Evans had retired, after the political movement in New York in the thirties, to a farm in New Jersey. In 1844, he returned to New York and called together half a dozen kindred spirits among whom were John Windt, Thomas Devyr, James

who wanted to uproot the old order of things under which the factories had 'hitherto been conducted to their present flourishing condition.' (New York *Daily Tribune*, May 6, 1851.)

[1] Schulter, *Lincoln, Labor and Slavery*, and Professor John R. Commons's 'lower idealism' of the land reformers, in *Horace Greeley and the Working-Class Origins of the Republican Party.*

Pyne, James Maxwell, and Lewis Masquerier. These he organized as a band of speakers. They held meetings in the parks and at cross-streets uptown, "so as to catch the attention of the working-men on their return to their homes." [1] It is true that Evans did, to a certain extent, catch the attention of the workers, but that did not make him an accurate reporter of their protest. Evans was a propagandist, and the most opinionated of all the reformers.

Between 1840 and 1850 the industrial worker found himself in the difficult position of losing ground both as consumer and producer. His consumption gains, participation in the general advance of the community, lagged behind his production losses. The gold discoveries mark the point where consumption rewards, for the skilled workers at least, began to increase. It was the encroachment of industrialism upon his local freedoms with no material compensation — rather the reverse — that led to the remarkable labor revolts of the period and the reform waves that swept over the land. These revolts fall into two classes: the defensive movements of the forties aiming at the preservation of freedoms that were believed to be passing away or the return of freedoms already gone; and the aggressive movement of the fifties seeking positive gains of a material sort for special groups of workers more favorably situated than the common run. The latter was not so much a denial of the first as an acceptance of the facts. The older movement had underestimated the force that lay behind the Industrial Revolution. The later movement was possibilist.

A subsidiary conflict was involved in the mind of the worker with his own traditions. Among these, one of the most persistent was that of a 'community of interest' between the journeyman and boss. This 'community of interest' had actually existed in a simpler form of economic organization. But when the boss was ousted by the mer-

[1] Masquerier, *Sociology*, pp. 95–96.

chant capitalist and the absentee owner, it ceased in fact to exist. The journeyman, however, and the small master found difficulty in disentangling themselves from the tradition. This was particularly so with the skilled worker in the country as represented by the Mechanics' Association of New York State. It was less difficult for the mechanics and laborers of the cities, and it was among the factory operatives, especially the women, that the idea of 'community of interest' first gave way. The factory operatives had no strong traditions of this nature to overcome. They did not so much assert the opposite principle as simply ignore the tradition itself, partly because it had never been theirs and partly because the reality was more evident in the factories than elsewhere. The reformers were the least realistic of the lot. They steadily set their faces against a recognition of the permanence of the change that had come over the industrial situation. Not that they misunderstood it. They simply refused to accept it, insisting that the community retrace its steps, and return to the simplicity and localism of the past.

The break between the two points of view, defensive and aggressive, is clearly seen in the pronouncements of the National Typographical Conventions. In 1836, the National Convention, in an address to the printers of the United States, declared that "the interests of the employer and journeymen have been assimilated and we hope rendered permanent for the time to come." [1] But in 1850, after the experience of fourteen years of "assimilated" interests and a constantly declining standard of living, the same organization came to the conclusion that "It is useless for us to disguise from ourselves the fact that, under the present arrangement of things, there exists a perpetual antagonism between Labor and Capital . . . one side striving to sell their labor for as much, and the other striving to

---

[1] Bulletin of the Bureau of Labor Statistics, No. 61, appendix: "Address to the Printers throughout the United States."

buy it for as little, as they can." [1] With this latter declaration one of the secretaries, Mr. F. J. Ottarson, refused to agree, and the New York society, which counted Horace Greeley among its members in good standing, did not hold strongly to that point of view.

When a condition begins to oppress, the first impulse is to escape. One of the most significant general ideas in American history has been the place of the frontier in the making of the national mind. But the frontier had a bigger place than is discoverable from a study of the frontiersman. A considerable part of the significance of the frontier lies behind the frontier. In one sense, the westward expansion of the American people was a flight from the new industrialism. This flight was the salvation of the individual worker, but it meant the destruction of his plans and organization. The constant breaking-up of the labor and reform movements was due primarily to the extreme instability of the industrial population, an instability created, on the one hand, by the frontier outlet and, on the other, by the inflow of the immigrant. All the reforms of the period involved, in their beginnings at least, an escape. They were transcendental as opposed to the little realistic programmes of the workers themselves and their later diluted applications. Robert Owen, the Associationists, the Land Reformers, insisted on a withdrawal in which the workers were unable to follow. They would have renounced the world in order to save it. Greeley would have every one leave New York but himself. Evans wanted every man under his own vine and fig-tree. It was only when this transcendentalism failed that a realistic approach was made, an attempt to challenge the new order on its own ground. The workers, by strikes and otherwise, tried to prevent the continued cutting of their piece rates. Their prolonged and only partially successful struggle for the ten-hour system was epic. They diluted Association to coöperative stores and,

[1] New York *Daily Tribune*, December 26, 1850.

with the assistance of philanthropists and without, they attempted producers' coöperation or 'self-employment.' By 1855 all these movements and agitations had subsided. With the gold discoveries, the appeal of the frontier made itself effective. The labor movement of the fifties sought increasingly trade gains, in wages and hours, for special classes of workers. What was left of the moral force of the reform agitations was swept into the slavery struggle.

THE INDUSTRIAL WORKER

1840–1860

· ·
·

CHAPTER I

THE STATE OF THE NATION

THE period 1840 to 1860 was peculiarly a unit in many respects. The depression of 1837–39 cut it off very completely from the thirties, while the depression of 1857 and the outbreak of the Civil War made a decided break with the decade that followed. In these two decades were concentrated to an unprecedented extent the social effects of the revolution in industry, accentuated by the fact that the westward movement lagged behind the European migrations. The result was a high degree of concentration of population accompanying factory production, great national prosperity, and a lowering of the standards of the industrial population.

By 1840, machinery had taken almost entire possession of the manufacture of cloth and was making rapid advances in the iron industry. The clothing and shoemaking trades were entirely revolutionized by the inventions of the period. The first sewing machine was patented in 1842, but was not put upon the market. In 1843, B. W. Bean, of New York, invented a machine for basting, but the first complete sewing machine for general use was patented by Elias Howe, Jr., of Cambridge, Massachusetts, in 1846.[1]

The sewing machine did not immediately affect the men shoemakers to any extent. Binding shoes had been all

[1] Bishop, *History of Manufactures*, vol. 2, pp. 43–44.

along the work of women, and it was not until 1860, with the invention of the McKay machine, that the men shoemakers' craft skill was supplanted. The character of the revolution in the shoe industry in our period was determined by the extension of shop work, the beginnings of the factory system, and concentration of production in the hands of the merchants. The same is true of the clothing trade. No machine could have made the condition of the needlewomen of the cities worse than it was.

A further characteristic of the period was found in the unprecedented and well-sustained prosperity. "There is general agreement among all writers as to the great industrial advance made in the United States during the period 1840–1860; it was a time of solid prosperity and steady, continuous progress." [1] This is a reasonable generalization. It makes no allowance for minor depressions like those of 1848, 1853–54, and 1857, nor for the two-year hang-over, 1840–42, from the panic of 1837. If five bad years are allowed in the twenty, the case for prosperity will not be overstated and a very decided preponderance will be left on the side of 'good times.' Sumner, in his free-trade enthusiasm, called the period from the Mexican to the Civil War the "Golden Age." "It was one of those happy periods when the nation had little history." [2] This judgment depends of course on what is meant by 'history.' If history means war, Sumner was right.

There are numerous indications of the general prosperity of the period. Capital invested in manufacture seems to have risen from 250 millions in 1840 to 1000 millions in 1860.[3] In the cotton industry the number of spindles increased from about $2\frac{1}{4}$ million to nearly $5\frac{1}{4}$ million; the number of bales of cotton consumed from nearly 300,000 to nearly 1,000,000; and the number of employees from 72,000

[1] Bogart, *Economic History*, p. 178.
[2] Sumner, *Protection in the United States*, pp. 54–55.
[3] Clark, *History of Manufactures*, p. 369.

to 122,000.[1] Imports per head of the population rose from
$4.66 in 1843–46 to $10.47 in 1856–60, and exports from
$5.22 to $9.45.[2] Railroad mileage increased from 2818 in
1840 to 30,635 in 1860.[3]

In 1840, money was scarce, credit destroyed, wages de-
preciated, and farm products had fallen fifty per cent from
the high point of 1836.[4] Imports for consumption had fallen
from 168 millions in 1836 to 88 millions in 1842. Per capita
imports for consumption, after rising from $6.25 in 1833 to
$10.93 in 1836, fell by 1842 to $4.87 and by 1843 to $4.20.[5]

By the summer of 1843 the end of the depression was
seen.[6] In August, "Niles' Register" noted: "The papers
indicate the gradual revival of trade and the consequent
relief of the people generally from a long agony of pecuniary
sufferings such as this country has seldom been subjected
to . . . business revives upon a firm basis . . . and a wholesome and comparatively happy condition of affairs is at
hand." [7] In September the same authority described the

---

[1] U.S. Census of 1860, *Manufactures.*

[2] Grosvenor, "Does Protection Protect?" in Taussig, *Tariff History*,
p. 122, note.

[3] Executive Doc. no. 1, pt. 5, 49th Congress, 1st Session, p. 68.

[4] Bishop, vol. 2, p. 428.   [5] *Ibid.*

[6] Professor Commons (*History of Labor*, vol. 1, p. 487) claims that the
depression following the panic of 1837 continued until after the gold discoveries of 1849 with only a slight recovery 1843–44, that was not sufficient to affect the general conclusion of fifteen years' hard times. Professor Commons's theory, that the labor movement swings from reformist
to trade purposes with the fall and rise of industrial activity, would seem
to have led him in this case to an exaggeration of the period of depression.
The years 1843–46 were among the most prosperous that America had experienced up to that time. The letting-up from 1846–48 as a result of the
Mexican War hardly affected industry at all, and the panic of 1848 was a
momentary affair having little to do with industrial conditions. Professor
Commons's thesis does not hold for this period. The reform wave and the
returning prosperity are exactly co-terminous, both beginning in 1843
and ending about 1850. The labor movement did not so much change its
form during the depression as die out altogether. It revived in the revival of trade and industry and the form it took in its revival depended
upon much beside.

[7] *Niles' Register*, August 26, 1843.

manufacturers as "actively employed obtaining a living
for themselves and affording employment to thousands who
have for a long time been out of employment. . . . The cotton factories especially are now busily employed, every
spindle twirling, and double sets of hands are being engaged so as to work night and day." [1]

In the iron industry, "furnaces and shops that had been
stopped, whose owners had in many cases been ruined,
were being repaired and would soon be in blast again." [2]
Iron production, which was less than 230,000 tons in 1842,
rose to 765,000 in 1846, and 800,000 in 1847, while the cost
of production fell nearly fifty per cent. The production of
domestic anthracite increased from 1,312,000 tons in 1843
to 3,200,000 tons in 1847; cotton consumption from 325,000
bales in 1843 to 531,000 in 1848; wool from 55,500,000
pounds to 81,250,000 in the same period. The number of
vessels built in 1842 was 1021, with an aggregate tonnage
of 129,084, compared with 1851 in 1848, with an aggregate
tonnage of 318,075. Railroad mileage in 1840 was 2380;
in 1847, 4249; and in 1849, 7000. [3]

The Mexican War, 1846–48, served somewhat to check
this expansion, but its effect on established business was
slight. The gold discoveries of '48 and '49 offset the tendencies toward a crisis and in the new decade the country
embarked on another long stretch of prosperity. The panic
of 1857 was much less severe and general than that of 1837.
It came suddenly, and recovery was as sudden. Like the
milder premonitions of its coming, it was chiefly of a financial nature. [4]

This general prosperity meant excellent profits for most
business enterprises over the greater part of the period.
In 1843, the Otis mills at Ware were reported to have
paid a November dividend of 10 per cent. [5] The Mer-

[1] *Niles' Register*, September 9, 1843.   [2] *Ibid.*
[3] Bishop, vol. 2, pp. 449–50.   [4] Burton, *Financial Crises*, pp. 283–84.
[5] *Niles' Register*, November 4, 1843.

rimack Company of Lowell paid 9 per cent in the same month.[1] The Middlesex Woolen Company declared a dividend of 25 per cent which was reported as an 'extra,' representing accumulated profits in addition to the regular semi-annual dividend.[2] In 1845, the Nashua and Jackson corporations paid semi-annual dividends of 10 per cent and the Hamilton and Appleton companies paid 6 per cent.[3] In the same year, the Merrimack Company was said to have paid 10 per cent 'as usual,' and its stock was worth 133, and scarce at that.[4] A steam-power mill at Newburyport was said to have paid $42\frac{1}{2}$ per cent for the year.[5] The Lawrence Company had earned, since its inception in 1833, an annual average rate of 10.26 per cent and had paid an annual average dividend of 7.93 per cent.[6] Some of the smaller concerns made very high profits.

A treasurer of one of the corporations protested that quotations of semi-annual dividends for single years were misleading, because factories that made 20 per cent one year might have gone for two or three years without any dividends at all. He then gave the following table of the dividends paid by all the Lowell corporations from the date of their organization: [7]

	AVERAGE DIVIDEND PAID PER ANNUM (Per cent)
Merrimack (20 years old).........	12½
Hamilton (17 years old)..........	10½
Appleton (16 years old)..........	9¾
Lowell (14 years old).............	9
Suffolk (11½ years old)...........	14
Tremont (11½ years old)..........	10½
Lawrence (11 years old)..........	7
Boott (6½ years old).............	8
Massachusetts (4 years old).......	5¼

[1] *Niles' Register*, November 4, 1843.   [2] *Ibid.*, January 6, 1844.
[3] *Voice of Industry*, July 3, 1845.   [4] *Ibid.*, December 26, 1845.
[5] *Ibid.*, October 2, 1845.
[6] Aiken, *Labor and Wages*, p. 14.
[7] Carey, *Profits on Manufactures*, p. 8.

In 1845, Charles F. Lester, who had been commissioned by the Treasury Department to obtain information as to business conditions, reported that the manufacturers of Connecticut had refused to assist him, but that he was confident that their profits were equal to 40 per cent per annum.[1] From 1846 to 1850, the cotton mills controlled by Boston capital averaged profits of 14 per cent per annum. In 1853, out of 40 New England manufacturing corporations, 36 declared dividends ranging from 4 to 10 per cent. In 1855, out of 40 textile and textile machinery companies in New England, 12 passed their dividends. The following year, 10 out of 41 passed their dividends, the remainder paying from 3 to 11 per cent, while the York Company, of Saco, Maine, was paying 20 per cent. During the fifties the Boston Company, which had paid 18.75 per cent during the first ten years of its life, earned barely 6 per cent.[2]

Profits in leather, lumber, paper, and pottery ran from 10 to 25 per cent in 1846.[3] But in the iron industry nearly one third of the manufacturers were said to have failed between 1840 and 1850,[4] though from 1843 to 1848 iron production rose from 230,000 to 800,000 tons per annum.[5] During the fifties some iron works were said to have earned their cost in a single year. The dividends of the Hudson Iron Company were at the rate of 40 per cent per annum, and the Pennsylvania Iron Works earned 60 per cent per annum between 1857 and 1860.[6]

It is a demonstrable fact that during this period of prosperity the industrial worker was losing ground, absolutely in the first decade and relatively in the second. "Our city of New York," said Greeley in 1845, "is now enjoying an unusual degree of thrift and prosperity, growing and ex-

---

[1] Senate Doc. 62:1, no. 72, pt. 3, p. 1749, note.
[2] Clark, pp. 375–76.   [3] Ibid.
[4] Ibid., p. 373.   [5] Eckel, Coal, Iron and the War, p. 39.
[6] Clark, pp. 377–78.

panding on all sides, increasing in population, in business and in wealth. Her working classes are probably as well employed as ever before . . . a rapid yet continual increase of buildings, ships, etc., gives employment to carpenters, masons, joiners, laborers, to an extraordinary extent. And yet it is our deliberate estimate, the result of much inquiry, that the average earnings of those who live by simple labor in our city — embracing at least two thirds of our population — scarcely, if at all, exceed one dollar per week for each person subsisting thereon. On this pittance, and very much less than this in many thousands of instances, three hundred thousand persons within sight of Trinity steeple must pay city rents, buy their clothing, and obtain such medical attendance, religious consolation, mental culture, and means of enjoyment as they have." [1]

Hardly a day passed but "The Tribune" received applications from printers and others for work, "on any terms that would keep starvation at bay." In July it was estimated that there were 20,000 unemployed in the city alone. The shoemakers' wages had fallen "lower and lower" until the great majority were working at rates that did not bring them an average of five dollars a week. The average earnings of a journeyman printer were said to have fallen below six dollars a week or $300 per annum. The regular pay of day laborers was one dollar a day which, at four days per week throughout the year, would give them an annual income of about $200. Of the 50,000 women workers in the city, one half were teachers, house servants, etc., who averaged less than two dollars a week, while thousands could not, with steady work, earn as much as $1.50 a week.

A table quoted from the "Daily Commercial" showed the movement as to wages, profits, output, etc., from 1844 to 1845,[2] of eleven Lowell mills:

[1] New York *Daily Tribune*, July 9, 1845.
[2] *Voice of Industry*, July 19, 1845.

	1844	*1845*
Capital....................	$10,500,000	$11,000,000
Number of spindles........	192,376	204,000
Number of females employed	7,430	7,000
Wages per week...........	$2.00	$1.75
Yards of cloth per week....	1,435,450	1,500,000
Dividends................	4½%	12½%

In this year, the invested capital, number of spindles, output of cloth, and dividends increased, while the number of women operatives declined and wages fell off 12½ per cent. "This," said the commentator, "is the natural result of the state of things in New England. The more wealth becomes concentrated in a few hands, the poorer the great mass becomes."

The Massachusetts mills in 1846 declared a semi-annual dividend of 10 per cent on a capitalization of $1,200,000. "Only one half that sum is actually invested in the mills," said the editor of the "Vox Populi," of Lowell, "so it is seen that the actual profit of this concern is 40 per cent per annum, or $240,000, being upwards of $65,000 per annum more than is paid to all the hands of the corporation for labor and board." [1]

Under the title, "Two Pictures," the "Voice of Industry" in 1846 noted that the Merrimack Company had just declared a semi-annual dividend of 10 per cent and its profits for the previous six months had been 13 per cent. "Some years since it made a dividend of one third of its capital at one dash and now it puts its cash funds to a use that will earn 25 to 30 per cent annually." The Boott Mills "stand so well that 25 per cent advance is asked and for Suffolk 40 per cent," while the wages of many of the operatives employed in one of the largest woolen mills in the city had been greatly reduced — those who received one dollar a day "now get seventy-five cents and generally the reduction is in this ratio." [2]

[1] Quoted in the *Voice of Industry*, January 30, 1846.
[2] *Voice of Industry*, July 17, 1846.

Perhaps the clearest evidence of this discrepancy between the reward of labor and of capital is seen in the statements of the manufacturers themselves in reply to questions sent out by the Treasury Department in 1846 to secure information as to the state of industry under the tariff of 1842.[1] The replies constitute a mine of information as to profits, prices, wages, hours, etc. Under the question as to the cost of production there are occasional indications of the respective shares paid in wages and in profits during the four years of operation of the protective tariff of 1842. In these cases wages are seen to have fallen or remained stationary, cost of production declined, while prices were maintained and profits increased.[2]

[1] Senate Doc. 62:1, no. 72, pt. 3.
[2] *Ibid.*, pp. 1766–77; 1764–65; 1690; 1716; 1706–07; 1713; 1717–18; 1760–63; 1808; 1873; 1816; 1752.

CHAPTER II

THE IMMIGRANT AND THE HOMES OF THE POOR

THE whole contribution of the immigrant to the industrial situation of the forties and fifties is not assayed when it is noted that he brought with him lower standards of living and a more docile spirit than those of the American workers. The alien of this period was not seldom the rallying point of the labor movements. And if he sometimes prejudiced the workers' cause by his manner and previous record, he often provided the only leadership available. This was true of John Cluer in the Ten-Hour agitation in New England in the forties and of the German socialists of the fifties. But when all allowance is made for the contributions of the immigrant in the way of leadership, it is still true that the net effect of immigration was to lower the standards of the American worker and render the solidarity necessary to effective organization impossible of achievement.

It is difficult to realize to-day the proportions of the task set the community of the forties of assimilating the 'new immigration.' Never before or since have the numbers of immigrants been so great in proportion to the population. The alien stream rose constantly and rapidly from 143,439 in the period 1821–30, to 599,125 1831–40, to 1,713,251 1841–50, and to 2,598,214 1851–60.[1] The number of immigrants in 1854 was 427,833, a figure that was not reached again for twenty years.[2]

But the crude numbers do not portray the real significance of the influx. It is necessary to take into consideration also the population that received them. Thus, taking

[1] Hall, *Immigration*, Appendix, p. 339.
[2] No allowance is made for emigration that was of some importance in this period, though far less than it later became.

the numbers of immigrants per year, per 10,000 of the population, we find the figure rising from 41 in 1839 to 162 in 1854. From that point it fell to 47 in 1860. The highest figure, at a later date, was 150 in 1882. The number of immigrants per 10,000 population went over the hundred mark only five times from 1855 to 1901, while in the period 1840–60 it went over the hundred mark for eight successive years (1847–54).[1]

It is not correct to say, however, that immigration was the major cause of the distresses of the workers of the forties. The inflow of immigration did not begin in earnest until 1846, after the labor movements and reform agitations of the forties had almost spent themselves. It was more effective in breaking up the mass movements of the period and in dispersing the incipient organizations. In 1847, after participating in the labor movement in New England for four or five years, the editor of the "Voice of Industry" wrote from Boston, "I regret that the tide of immigration has seemed to throw many of our mechanics out of employment, as I have heard since I came to Boston, and they tell me it is the cause of these 'hard times,' and if we mean our paper should live we must take hold of Native Americanism."[2]

A considerable part of the new immigration had little direct effect upon the status of the industrial worker. The Norwegians, who sailed in great numbers from Le Havre in 1843,[3] many of the peasants from Alsace and Switzerland, the 30,000 Lutheran subjects of Prussia from the borders of the Baltic, many of large fortune among them, and the German nobles whose pedigrees were said to date back to the thirteenth century,[4] went directly to the West and settled on the land. They came with some capital and often with some organization among themselves. But from 1838 to 1842 the number of farmer immigrants increased only

[1] Hall, pp. 10–11.   [2] *Voice of Industry*, June 11, 1847.
[3] *Niles' Register*, July 15, 1843.   [4] *Ibid.*

from 6667 to 12,966, while the number of mechanics and laborers increased from 8327 to 29,072. From 1847 to 1853, the number of laborers increased from 36,000 to 83,000; the number of farmers from 44,000 to 56,000, and the number of mechanics declined from 25,000 to 17,000.[1]

This new immigration of English and Irish laborers and mechanics fitted into the industrial régime that was growing up in the Eastern cities. Coming to America with little or no capital, they remained in the seaboard cities and began to show the markings that warned the native mechanics of the dangers of a permanent pauper population like that of the older lands. But the pauper populations of the growing cities of the seaboard were not entirely created by the immigrant. Employers in country districts hired few fully trained journeymen mechanics. The farmers' boys were put out as apprentices in the trades, and when these apprentices became journeymen their places were taken by other apprentices and they wandered off to the cities in quest of work. There they tended to herd and swell the multitudes of the poor who existed somehow in the dark and filthy alleys of Boston, New York, and Philadelphia.[2]

From 1840 to 1860, the population of Philadelphia increased from 360,000 to 670,000, and that of New York from 410,000 to 910,000. The number of cities of over 8000 inhabitants rose from 44 to 141, and the urban population from 8.5 per cent to 12.5 per cent of the whole. In the North Atlantic States the population density increased from 41.7 in 1840 to 65.4 in 1860. The total population for the whole period increased 36 per cent, while the city population increased 90 per cent from 1840 to 1850, and 75 per cent from 1850 to 1860.[3]

The result of this rapid growth was a condition of con-

---

[1] Bromwell, *History of Immigration*, pp. 135–36.
[2] *Voice of Industry*, August 6, 1847.
[3] U.S. Census, *Population*, I, lxxx–lxxxiii; I, xxx.

gestion in some of the Eastern cities that is almost inde-
scribable. In Boston, in 1849, Dr. Henry Clark found in
Half-Moon Place a house with a triple cellar:

> The first cellar from the street was occupied in one corner by a
> bar for the sale of refreshments, and served as a kitchen and a
> parlor. The second, into which two beds were crowded, served as
> a family sleeping-room, whilst the third, a dungeon six feet square
> and the same in height, with no aperture for the admission of air
> save the narrow door, which was closed at night, served to ac-
> commodate boarders.
> The landlord said the tide came through the floor of his rooms
> but rarely! One cellar was reported by the police to be occupied
> nightly as a sleeping-apartment for thirty-nine persons. In an-
> other, the tide had risen so high that it was necessary to approach
> the bedside of a patient by means of a plank which was laid from
> one stool to another; while the dead body of an infant was actu-
> ally sailing about the room in its coffin.[1]

Half-Moon Place was a semicircular group of buildings
in the rear of Broad Street formed by an excavation into
the side of Fort Hill. The houses were built either up
against the hill or separated from it by only a few feet. The
place was entered by two alleys and a stair called "Jacob's
Ladder."

> To the right of "Jacob's Ladder" is a cluster of six privies situ-
> ated nearly in the center of the place. At the time of the [cholera]
> epidemic these were greatly out of repair and the ground about
> them was covered with their overflowing contents, removed only
> by evaporation. At the foot of the drain are two more clusters of
> privies, six in number. The open space likewise presents three
> cess-pools intended to carry off dirty water; but they were
> choked by all sorts of vegetable matters, as fragments of cab-
> bages and potatoes. . . . As these accumulated, they were scooped
> up and thrown upon the ground which was thus plentifully be-
> strewed with putrefying vegetable matters. With these were
> mingled no small proportion of substances still more loathsome.
> . . . The rear of the houses was separated from the stone wall
> which supported the side of the hill by a space of a few feet and

---

[1] City of Boston, Doc. no. 66, Report of the Committee on Internal
Health.

here the contents of drains from above found a receptacle, creating a perpetual humidity. . . .

The Committee on Internal Health reported, on the basis of Dr. Clark's disclosures, "This whole district is a perfect hive of human beings without comforts and mostly without common necessaries: in many cases huddled together like brutes without regard to sex or age or sense of decency, grown men and women sleeping together in the same apartment, and sometimes wife and husband, brothers and sisters, in the same bed." It was stated that the average length of life of the Irish in Boston was not over fourteen years.[1]

The rapid increase of the city population and the passion for speculative profits led to the building of homes on new ground before it had become solid, and with insufficient elevation. Dr. C. E. Buckingham declared that he had seen the tide "pouring into the back yard from all four sides, to the depth of a foot," and had known "men to sail around their kitchens in pursuit of their dinners and to coast along the shores of their cellars in tubs for their winter's wood!" [2] The numbers of families in these houses reached inconceivable proportions. "I have known," said Dr. Buckingham, "from six to forty or more in one house of two stories, eleven and more in one room constantly, and eight in one bed, men and women!" [3]

Lowell, the Manchester of New England, the 'City of Spindles,' the admiration of foreign visitors, had grown from a wilderness to a city of 20,000 inhabitants in a quarter of a century. But in spite of its youth it was no exception to the rule of congestion and misery of the poor. "One week ago I entered a house in a central location," said a resident in the Lowell "Courier" in 1847, "and found it occupied by one store and twenty-five different families embracing 120 persons, more than half of whom were adults. In one of the

---

[1] Boston, Doc. no. 66, p. 16.
[2] Curtis, *Hygiene in Massachusetts*, p. 5, note.   [3] *Ibid.*, p. 16.

rooms, which was inhabited by two families, I found one of
the families to consist of a man, his wife, and eight children
— four of whom were over fifteen years of age — and four
adult boarders. . . . This by no means furnishes the worst
case. . . ." [1] The same investigator visited a home in the
night which contained 537 cubic feet of air space with no
means of ventilation, and housed six individuals, three of
whom were adults.[2]

In a letter to Dr. Curtis, in 1849, the Reverend Henry
Wood, minister-at-large to Lowell, said that he knew of
numerous cases of from six to ten persons in a single room
and sometimes in one bed. Frequently every room in the
house had from four to twelve occupants. "The numerous
outhouses were of necessity near the windows, sometimes
filling the whole neighborhood with noxious exhalations."
In one cellar of two rooms lived four families of twenty-two
persons.[3]

In New York in 1850 an investigation was made of the
cellar population by the Chief of Police at the instance of
the health officer. The findings were published in the
"Tribune" under the title "Dens of Death." [4] One in
twenty of the population of New York at that time was
said to live underground. The census covered 18,456 persons inhabiting 8141 cellars. The average number living
permanently in one room among the very poor of the city
was six, the maximum number twenty. The average per
house was about sixty, and in addition to this permanent
population there were large numbers of transients that increased congestion to an incredible extent. The Old Brew-
ery at Five Points had often held as many as three hundred.
There were known to have been from two to four families
in one room and most of these took in lodgers.[5]

In the boarding and lodging cellars were found the lowest

[1] Curtis, *Hygiene in Massachusetts*, p. 36.   [2] *Ibid.*, p. 37.
[3] Curtis, p. 38.   [4] New York *Daily Tribune*, June 5, 13, 19, 1850.
[5] *Ibid.*, June 19, 1850.

standards of living and the most degraded industrial population America had known up to that time. In some of these there were three classes of boarders. The first class paid thirty-seven and one half cents a week for board and lodging, sleeping on straw thrown loose over the floor and eating at what was called the 'first table.' The second class paid eighteen and three fourths cents a week, slept on the bare floor, and ate at the 'second table.' The third class paid nine cents a week, slept on the floor on sufferance, being turned out when second-class lodgers were available, and ate at the 'third table.' These cellars were generally bare of furniture with the exception of one or two benches and a long table. The marketing was done by children who were sent out to beg food, or by professional beggar women with whom the boarding-house keeper made contracts. All the baskets were brought in at a certain hour, the boarders assembled, and the whole mass was thrown upon the table. The first-class boarders had the first picking, the rest took what was left as unceremoniously as could be imagined.

The Society for the Improvement of the Condition of the Poor pointed out in some detail in 1853 that these slums were not unprofitable, that a return of one hundred per cent interest on their value was not at all uncommon.[1]

The above is of course only one side — the worst side — of the picture. Most of the native workers were better housed, but it was this with which they were being brought into competition, and which serves in part to explain their own tendency to lower levels of living. The women factory operatives in Lowell in the corporation houses were better housed and much cleaner, though they too often slept six in a room. The skilled mechanics were well above this level. "On entering the house of a respectable mechanic in any of the large cities of the United States," said Grund, "one cannot but be astonished at the apparent neatness and

[1] New York *Daily Tribune*, November 2, 1853.

comfort of the apartments, the large, airy parlors, the nice carpets and mahogany furniture, and the tolerably good library, showing that the inmates are acquainted with the standard works of English literature." [1]

[1] Grund, *The Americans*, vol. 1, p. 47.

CHAPTER III

"THE SPIRIT OF THE AGE"

I⊤ is customary for later and perhaps more sophisticated generations to regard with complacency the vagaries of the forties, the 'hot-air' period of American history. And certainly there were enough freaks abroad to warrant some derision. Phrenology flourished alongside the 'Water Cure.' The Millerites waited on God. The Grahamites had a vision that was later to make famous Bernard Shaw, Upton Sinclair, and whole-wheat bread. The 'Disciples of the Newness' left Boston for a played-out farm. Robert Owen flitted back and forth across the Atlantic and about the cities of the New World catechizing prince and pauper in the true laws of life. The Land Reformers saw New York as a desert but for a few storage warehouses and docks, and every man under his own vine and fig tree on a ten-acre lot or a quarter-section farm. There was the ever-recurrent 'new woman' — at that time in bloomers — to worry the prurient. Temperance reform, the wrongs of Hungarian liberals, Association, capital punishment, and slavery, all gave birth to 'movements.' It was an era of lost causes.

It were well, however, in the midst of their hilarity, if later generations should pause to remember that this period nourished alongside of these Lincoln, Whitman, Emerson, and Poe and a host of lesser men. These too were a part of a fruition, the fine flowers of a long summer that had had some regard for things of the spirit. When another generation shall arise that can show a like splendor, it will be ready less for laughter than for understanding. The forties represented the last struggle of the liberal spirit of the eighteenth century in conflict with the exploitative spirit of the nineteenth.

The point of view which regards the reformers of the forties as amiable, even lovable, but utterly mistaken idealists, is obscurantist. They were in fact not very amiable and not at all lovable, but, so far as their diagnosis was concerned, quite truthful interpreters of the tendencies of their times. Their 'idealism' was a part of their common heritage, the heritage of most social philosophers who preceded Darwin and Spencer. They regarded society as malleable, as capable of being made over with little regard for tendencies that were implicit in the total social and economic *milieu*.

They were 'transcendental,' in that they proposed an appeal from objective experience to some inner standard, an escape from reality, a withdrawal into a specially created environment where their ideas of perfection might be achieved; rather than acceptance of the limitations always placed upon perfection by reality.

The new industrialism was repugnant to the liberal tradition of the eighteenth century. Workers and reformers alike considered that they were being enslaved, not only by the new power, but by their own acquiescence. The reformers proposed that men escape from this spoliation back into the past, a past either real or imaginary. This was their greatest limitation. They found, as did Henry Adams in his lifelong 'education,' that the past could not be re-created. Escape into a future of individual freedom was, as some of the workers discovered, the only avenue open to them.

Against the pessimism of the dominant economic theory the optimism of the reformers stands out in strong relief, and yet the latter seem not to have questioned the determinism of 'supply and demand.' They accepted, along with their generation, the theory that the price of labor and the price of goods were determined by natural law in a completely competitive market. No one seems to have imagined that wages could be affected artificially in the same way that the prices of cotton goods had been affected from the beginning of the industry.[1] If there were a labor surplus, they argued, wages would inevitably fall. Strikes and trade unions were useless, their achievements quite transitory. But a new world could be created devoid of acquisitiveness and exploitation, a new world simple and local like the old world that was being wiped out.

The generation that grew up in the forties was expectant of great and immediate changes for the better. They were always on tiptoe for 'signs of the times.' The titles of many of their papers show the attitude they readily assumed: "The Spirit of the Age"; "The Harbinger"; "Young America"; "Die Reform"; "The Herald of the New Moral Order."

Men generally were questioning the trend of their age. They were ill-attuned to the song of the machine — or it was ill-attuned to them. They saw the powers of the air, steam, and water, performing work that would have required the labor of thousands; labor-saving devices so-called that had not lightened labor, but had succeeded only in adding to the profits of the owners of the machine, "while those who labor are not only required to toil longer than before, but, compared with their employers, are as a class sinking day by day to a still deeper degradation." [2]

The source of the dissatisfaction with the achievements of the Industrial Revolution lay in the fact that they were accompanied by the degradation of the industrial population. Orestes Brownson wrote in 1840, "You know, Sir, if you know anything, that, notwithstanding the multiplication of necessities and conveniences of life, it is altogether more difficult for the common laborer to maintain the same social position now than it was fifty years ago." [3]

Brownson was of course not a typical representative of

---

[1] By corporate organization, agreement, and the tariff.
[2] *Operatives and Corporations*, p. 71.
[3] *Boston Quarterly Review*, July, 1840, p. 368.

his age, but he expressed as accurately as any one what most of the reformers and dissatisfied workers were trying to say. William Henry Channing spoke a language the people understood and held the attention of the workers better than any of the clergy of his time. To his religious egalitarianism, the whole course of modern civilization with its divisions and prosperity was distasteful:

> The victorious world, so confident and easy and jocular, so beautiful in its own right, so wrapped about in kingly purple — how strangely it is metamorphosed to the eyes of a child of God! Its factories change into brothels; its rents to distress warrants; its railroads to mighty fetters binding industry in an inextricable net of feudalism; from under the showy robes of its success flutter the unseemly rags of ever-growing beggary; from garret and cellar of its luxurious habitations stare out the gaunt forms of haggard want; the lash of the jailer, the gleam of swords, the glitter of bayonets are its garters and stars of nobility.[1]

Much of the language of these protests is hackneyed enough to-day. The ever-recurring contrast between the rich and poor leaves moderns cold. But even clever men in the forties were not deterred by the danger of platitudes. To them the poverty of the growing cities was new, alien, and wrong — a thing to be extirpated before it fastened itself irrevocably upon American civilization. Horace Greeley for instance is not usually accused of excessive bromidity, but he too revolted, as at an innovation, against the increasing disparity of fortune based on no discoverable principles of right and justice, that was to be found in the civilization that grew up with the Industrial Revolution.

The place of Greeley in the labor movement of the period is easily overestimated. He is of more value to the historian of labor than he was to the worker himself. While he and his paper did show a continuous interest in the workers during the forties and early fifties, he had other and more profound allegiances that often ran counter to and canceled

[1] Codman, *Brook Farm*, Appendix, p. 321.

his efforts on the workers' behalf. Horace Greeley was an editor first, a Whig second, and a friend of labor third. His Whiggism gave the workers the theory of a tariff to protect them against the pauper labor of Europe. His employer function led him to insist, long after it had ceased to be true, that there existed a basic community of interest between labor and capital. He had no faith and no interest in the workers' realistic methods of revolt, and failed to appreciate the validity and significance of organization for its own sake. His sympathy for the worker was unquestionably real, but it was sympathy for a downtrodden not an upstanding worker. His revelations of the conditions existing in the cities served in part to offset the criticisms that were being made of the conditions of labor in the factories, the creatures of the Whigs. Unlike Channing and Brownson, Greeley believed firmly in the beneficence of the Industrial Revolution if only it could be managed and made to serve all instead of a part of the community.

This humanitarianism of Greeley's and the rest of the Associationists is not however the authentic voice of the worker of the period. It has been regarded as such probably because the worker had difficulty in making himself heard among so many orators and editors.[1] But to find the

---

[1] Professor Commons calls Horace Greeley "the Tribune of the People, the spokesman of their discontent, the champion of their nostrums. He drew the line only at spirit rappings and free love." Commons, "Horace Greeley and the Working Class Origins of the Republican Party," *Political Science Quarterly*, vol. 24, no. 23; reprint, p. 469.

It is difficult to say who are intended by "the people" in this characterization. Not the industrial worker surely. He had no "nostrums," had never heard of free love, and had no interest in spirit rappings. Greeley was the spokesman of the industrial workers to the extent that he told of their condition — though even in this he usually avoided the subject of factory labor — gave them good advice and interested himself in philanthropic schemes for their deliverance. Much of his advice to the worker could be briefly summed up: "Don't strike. Don't drink. Save your money and start in business for yourself." This was good advice no doubt but it hardly entitled the giver to the resounding title "Tribune of the People."

real voice and spirit of the workers it is necessary to go to the letters in the labor papers, the resolutions of newly formed workers' organizations, and the working-men editors like Fletcher and Young. The temper of these is not generally of the humanitarian stripe.

"There is at this very moment," wrote Fletcher in 1845, "a great strife between capital and labor and capital is fast gaining the mastery — the gradual abasement of the working men and women of this country abundantly sustains this position.... The combined, incorporated, and protected capital can starve out the workers." The immigration of foreign operatives was conceived of as adding to the difficulties of the situation. "No tariff on these! No, no, it won't do to protect the capital of American working men and women, their labor ... for this would be anti-republican. But the rich capitalist must be protected and he will take care of the laborer." The capitalists of Danville protected themselves against "disorderly strikes" by importing surplus help from England, "help whose abject condition in their own country has made them tame, submissive, 'peaceable and orderly citizens,' that is, ready to work fourteen and sixteen hours a day for what capital sees fit to give them." [1]

This idea of the antagonistic interests of workers and their employers was of slow growth, but it is one of the two characteristics that divided the workers and their point of view from most of the reformers. The exceptions among the reformers were G. H. Evans and O. A. Brownson.[2] Evans carried enough of his earlier agrarian radicalism into the forties to align him in this regard with the emerging attitude of the workers, and Brownson was temperamentally extremist in all his ways. He was the only intellectual

[1] *Voice of Industry,* October 9, 1845.
[2] There were exceptions also among the later German socialists, but their radicalism was of alien origin to a much greater degree than that of Evans and Brownson, and their activities never made the impression on the industrial worker that was made by Evans.

of the period who had the temerity to contemplate the use
of force. In this respect he was quite out of sympathy with
the workers themselves who, though they frequently attempted in their strikes to gain their ends by its use, did so
only on impulse and never conceived of it as a method.
Brownson 'hoped' the matter would be settled peaceably,
but 'feared not.' "If a general war should break out," he
wrote, "it will resolve itself into a social war . . . between
the aristocracy and the democracy, between the people and
their masters. . . . Already does it lower on the horizon. . . .
But the war if it comes will not be brought about by the reformers, but by the conservatives in order to keep the people out of their rights." [1]

As the decade advanced there was a marked rise of expectation of some sort of release, which culminated with the
news of the European revolutions of 1848. According to
the "American Statesman," the new era had already begun,
and the most influential part of the press throughout
Christendom was more radical than the most advanced reformers of twenty-five years back.[2] Liberal sentiment was
said to be everywhere on the move; 'the times auspicious
for the cause of human rights.' The Free-Soil movement,
the Ten-Hour System, and all other measures of interest to
the workers were strengthening their hold. "We firmly
believe," declared Fletcher in 1847, "that speculative republicanism is near at an end and a brighter day is dawning
that shall free every son and daughter of toil — black or
white, native or foreign. Look, friends, at the signs of the
times and rejoice!" [3] "This is to me a prophetic age — it is
big with promise of a glorious future . . . almost every ship
that crosses the Atlantic brings tidings of its manifestation
throughout all Europe . . . [here] . . . in the railroad car, the
steamboat, the stage-coach, or wherever you go, the theme

---

[1] *Boston Quarterly Review*, October, 1840, p. 508.
[2] *Voice of Industry*, May 28, 1847.
[3] *Voice of Industry*, January 22, 1847.

merges into 'Reform,' 'Labor' and its rights, 'Slavery' and the 'Gallows.'" [1]

Much of this was of course self-stimulation, whistling in the dark, but much too was real. In spite of failures, working class and reform, hope grew that something was sure to emerge out of the fermentations of the forties of permanent value to the worker and to those who had espoused his cause.

By 1850 the bubble had burst — the Prophetic Age of American history had ceased to be. The spiritual energies generated in the decade passed into the slavery struggle and the conquest of a continent. Perhaps no single factor did more to disperse the movements of the forties than the discovery of gold in California. It served to set the seal of approval upon the new spirit of acquisitiveness that had previously to contend with a strong conservative temper. The new spirit was not confined to any one class. Had it been solely the vice of the 'capitalists,' as much of the propaganda suggests, it could not have conquered as it did. It was in fact the more vital 'Spirit of the Age.' "The first lesson a boy is taught on leaving the parental roof," said a Fall River labor leader in 1846, "is to get gain . . . gain wealth . . . forgetting all but self. . . ." [2]

[1] *Voice of Industry*, May 29, 1846.   [2] *Ibid.*, April 3, 1846.

CHAPTER IV

THE DEGRADATION OF THE WORKER

THE problem of primary importance for the industrial worker of the forties and fifties is to be found in the changes in his status and standards of living. A rising money wage is no sign of improved standards. Increasing commodity wages constitute a better test, but if accompanied by losses in other respects of greater significance, conclusions drawn therefrom are of little value. Working conditions, hours, speed, or effort must all be taken into account before an approximation can be made to a true estimate of the workers' condition. But in the last analysis the status of the worker is not a physical but a mental one, and is affected as much by comparisons with past conditions and with the status of other groups in the community as by the facts in themselves. In other words, the problem of status is one of satisfactions, and satisfactions are relative.

The depressions of 1837–39 left one third of the working population of New York City unemployed. Greeley estimated that there were not less than ten thousand persons in the city "in utter and hopeless distress with no means of surviving the winter but those provided by charity." [1] The same was true, in a somewhat less pronounced degree, throughout the industrial districts. The New England mills were either closed down or running only part-time and undermanned. Between 1839 and 1843 wages generally fell from thirty to fifty per cent, and the improved business conditions of the latter year were not reflected in the wages of the workers. In 1844 the same amount of labor that had once produced for the mechanic and his family a comfortable subsistence was inadequate to maintain his standards,

[1] *The New Yorker*, January 20, 1838.

and his only alternative was increased effort or the reduction of his wants.[1]

Pauperism was increasing. "Thirty years ago," said Evans, "the number of paupers in the whole United States was estimated at 29,166, or one in three hundred. The pauperism of New York City now amounts to 51,600, or one in every seven of the population." [2] In New York State the proportion of the poor was said to be increasing and the wages of labor to be steadily declining.[3]

The labor papers that sprang up in these years constantly complained that the condition of the worker was growing worse; that he was becoming more and more dependent on capital; that his resources were being curtailed and a new uncertainty had entered his life as to wages and employment.[4]

In the iron industry, the wage per ton of ore produced was being constantly reduced. The following are the 'prices' for certain kinds of work in the Pittsburgh district from 1837 to 1858: [5]

Year	Boilers	Puddlers	Hammermen
1837	$7.00	$4.25	$1.25
1838	7.00	4.25	1.25
1839	6.50	4.00	..
1840	6.00	3.75	..
1841	5.50	3.75	..
1842	5.00	3.50	1.00
1845	6.00	4.00	..
1850	4.50	3.50	..
1858	3.00 to $4.00	1.90 to $2.50	..

After a steady decline of wages in the iron industry from 1837, a strike of the boilers occurred in February, 1842, as a result of notification of a further cut to five dollars a ton.

[1] *The Awl*, September 4, 1844.
[2] *The Working Man's Advocate*, July 6, 1844.
[3] *Young America*, July 11, 1845.   [4] *Voice of Industry*, July 31, 1845.
[5] Compiled from *Report of the Bureau of Industrial Statistics*, Pennsylvania, 1882, p. 262, "Labor Troubles in Pennsylvania."

The strike lasted until July, when the boilers resumed work at the reduced price. This price was continued until May, 1845, when a second strike occurred for the recovery of the one dollar a ton they had lost between 1840 and 1842. This lasted until August and resulted in the advance being granted.[1] The new price, identical with that of 1840, lasted until 1850 when reductions were again proposed:

Puddlers .... from $4.00 to $3.50 per ton
Boilers .... from $6.00 to $4.50 per ton
Refiners............. from $1.00 to $0.80 per ton
Scrappers........... from $3.75 to $2.50 per ton
Heaters............. from $1.37½ to $1.00 per ton

These 'prices' were computed in wages, as follows: [2]

1. *A puddler* could make in two weeks of 11 turns,
   11 tons, 11 cwt. at $4 per ton................. $46.20
   Deduct for helper at $1.25 per turn............. 13.75
   Two weeks' wages before reduction.............. $32.45
   Proposed reduction of 50 cents per ton........... 5.78
   Two weeks' wages at reduced rate............... $26.67

2. *A boiler* could make in two weeks of 11 turns, 9
   tons, 12 cwt. 2 qtrs. at $6.00 per ton.......... $57.75
   Deduct for helper at $1.50 per turn............. 16.50
   Two weeks' wages before reduction.............. $41.25
   Proposed reduction of $1.50 per ton............. 14.44
   Two weeks' wages at reduced rate............... $26.81

3. *A refiner* could make in two weeks, 70 tons at $1.00
   per ton..................................... $70.00
   Deduct for helper at $1.25 per turn............. 13.75
   Two weeks' wages before reduction.............. $56.25
   Proposed reduction of 20 cents per ton........... 14.00
   Two weeks' wages at reduced rate............... $42.25

---

[1] Pennsylvania Bureau of Industrial Statistics, 1882, *Report*, pp. 270–71.

[2] *Ibid.*, pp. 273–74.

4. *A scrapper* could produce 10 tons per week at $3.75
per ton...................................... $37.50
Deduct for helper, 6 turns at $1.50 per turn...... 9.00

One week's wages before reduction.............. $28.50
Proposed reduction of $1.25 per ton............ 12.50

Weekly wages at reduced rate.................. $16.00

5. *A heater* could make 24 tons per week at 1.37\frac{1}{2}$
per ton...................................... $33.00
Deduct for helper, 6 turns at $1.50 per turn...... 9.00

One week's wages before reduction $24.00
Proposed reduction of 37$\frac{1}{2}$ cents per ton.......... 9.00

Weekly wages at reduced rate.................. $15.00

The strike against these reductions had not been broken
by February when some of the mills were started with imported labor. Riots broke out in which the puddlers took
possession of one of the mills, in the face of the protest of
some of their fellows and the pistol of the mayor. The wives
of the workers were said to have been the most violent of
the rioters. Some slight damage was done and arrests were
made. But by the end of March the mills were fairly well
filled with imported help working at the reduced rates.
Many of the strikers left the city and those who remained
returned to the mills in the summer. Of those who were
arrested, three men were acquitted and two men and four
women found guilty. The men were sentenced to pay fines
of six and one fourth cents and costs and imprisonment for
eighteen months. The women were sentenced to pay fifty
dollars each and costs and imprisonment for thirty days.
On petition of the jury that convicted them and of a large
number of citizens, they were pardoned and the fines re-
mitted in August, 1850.[1]

In 1858 the prices for boiling had been further reduced to
$3.50 and $4 a ton, and later in the year to $3.25. Some of
the Eastern mills were paying at that date as low as $3.
Puddlers in 1858 were paid $2.20, and at Danville, Pennsyl-

[1] Pennsylvania Bureau of Industrial Statistics, 1882, *Report*, pp. 274-75.

vania, there was an instance of $1.90 per ton. In addition to this, wages were paid in 'store orders' instead of cash, a practice that was very common in the period and meant a loss to the worker of from twenty to thirty and even fifty per cent. The men were said to be "as completely subjugated to the will of the employers as was possible in a free country." [1]

It was in this situation that the Sons of Vulcan came into existence. In 1858 a few men in the boiling department of the Pittsburgh Iron Mills held a meeting at "Our House" and organized the "United Sons of Vulcan." The existence of the society was kept secret because of the hostility of the employers, and in the fall of that year the members, "impressed with the perils incident to an effort to extend the organization," concluded to suspend further operations. [2] The Sons of Vulcan was revived again in 1861. The experience of the iron-workers was fairly representative.

In 1847 "the laboring man's prospect ahead just now is most drear and disheartening. Provisions, such as flour, meat, potatoes, butter, meal, are nearly one hundred per cent higher than ordinary prices, fuel is extraordinarily high and rents have advanced. . . . The mechanic or laborer who has a family to support finds that to-day's wages only pay to-day's expenses; he can lay up nothing for the winter season when his expenses are greatly increased, and, in the laborers' case, work and wages are always diminished." [3]

"The laboring class as a class," said Greeley to the printers, "is just where it was when I came here eighteen years ago, or, if anything, in a worse condition." [4]

Mr. Abbott Lawrence stated in a letter, in 1846, that the wages of mill operatives had risen since 1842 from $1.75 to

[1] McNeill, *Labor Movement*, p. 271.
[2] *Ibid.*, pp. 271–72.
[3] *Voice of Industry*, June 4, 1847.
[4] McNeill, *Labor Movement*, p. 117.

$2 a week. This was probably true, but the mills had reduced wages in the depression period so that the increase was only a partial return of the earlier cut. In addition to this, the operatives were doing much more work and turning out a greater product than ever before. It was claimed that, for the increase of one eighth in the wage, they were doing one third more labor with the same facilities, and that the wage for weaving a yard of cloth and the wages of the operatives who worked by the week had never been lower.[1]

The cost of living, especially in the cities, began to rise in 1843. Greeley estimated that there had been an increase of nearly fifty per cent in the cost of provisions in New York during the seven years from 1843 to 1850.[2] Wholesale prices had been high in 1840, fell sharply to 1843, rose again to 1847, but did not reach the figure of 1840 until 1851–52, then rose rapidly to 1857–58, and fell sharply to 1860.[3]

[1] *Voice of Industry*, April 17, 1846.
[2] New York *Daily Tribune*, November 14, 1850.
[3] Retail prices of food from 1848 to 1854 were reported as follows:

	1848	1849	1850	1851	1852	1853	1854
Wheat Flour........	$6.25	$4.81	$5.25	$4.31	$4.18	$4.62	$8.81
Rye Flour..........	3.62	2.81	2.87	3.50	3.31	3.81	6.12
Corn Meal.........	2.37	2.75	2.81	3.12	3.25	3.00	4.50
Candles mold........	.12	.11½	.12	.12	.13	.12	.15
Coal (anthracite)....	5.75	5.50	5.50	5.00	5.50	5.00	7.00
Coffee, Brazil........	.7⅛	.6½	.8¾	.9¾	.9⅝	.9½	.11
Fish, Dry Cod.......	3.68	2.62	2.81	2.75	4.18	3.25	3.37
Mackerel No. 1......	8.81	9.87	11.62	10.25	11.00	12.50	15.50
Molasses N.O........	.26	.23½	.26	.31	.29	.28	.29
Pork Mess..........	10.18	10.06	10.25	15.00	18.75	15.75	15.75
Beef Mess..........	8.25	12.12	9.25	9.75	10.00	10.00	11.50
Lard..............	.6¾	.6¼	6⅜	.9¾	.10	.9¾	.10
Butter.............	.25	.17	.18	.16	.22	.20	.20
Cheese.............	.8	.6½	.7¾	.7	.8½	.9½	.11
Rice..............	3.35	3.12	3.50	2.87	3.62	4.37	4.75
Sugar.............	.4½	.4⅝	.4¾	.5⅛	.4¾	.4⅞	.5

(New York *Daily Tribune*, February 21, 1854.)

The following table is that of the Aldrich Report, showing an average

In the winter of 1853–54, the average increase of family expenses for food and fuel was thirty per cent over those of May, 1853, and rents had been rising for four years "with perfectly appalling strides." [1] It was in these years of rising prices that there were found the recurrent spring strikes for higher wages among the skilled workers. Talk of strikes began about the middle of March each spring, and demands for increases of fifteen to thirty per cent were continuous down to the end of April. In most cases the demands were granted, and in many, the spring gains were lost in the summer or fall. For this reason it was frequently the case that the strikes of one spring were attempts to win back what was won the preceding year and lost again. It is extremely doubtful if the industrial workers, as a whole, gained wage increases even in this period that were commensurate with their losses as a result of increasing costs of living. Some groups of highly skilled artisans did undoubtedly improve their position, but the factoryized and partially factoryized workers did not.

of all articles (wholesale prices) according to their importance in the family budget and comprising 68.60 per cent of the total expenditure:

1840	97.7	1850	89.2
1841	98.1	1851	98.6
1842	90.1	1852	97.9
1843	84.3	1853	105.0
1844	85.0	1854	105.0
1845	88.2	1855	109.2
1846	95.2	1856	112.3
1847	95.2	1857	114.0
1848	88.3	1858	113.2
1849	83.5	1859	102.9

Grouped in five-year periods, these figures show an increase of 19.3 over the twenty years, thus:

1840–44	91.0
1845–49	90.1
1850–54	99.1
1855–59	110.3

The wages of all occupations, according to the Aldrich Report, show an increase of 11.7 when arranged in the same five-year periods. (U.S. Senate Doc. 52: 2, no. 1394, vol. 1, p. 9.)

[1] New York *Daily Tribune*, February 21, 1854.

No class of workers was better paid than those in the building trades. Where shoemakers, printers, hatters, cabinet-makers, and so on were getting $4, $5, and $6 a week, the carpenters, plasterers, and bricklayers were getting $10. But even this latter wage was inadequate to maintain the worker's family at anything like a decent comfort standard. In 1851 the carpenters of Philadelphia struck for an advance of twenty-five cents a day which would give them a wage of $10.50 a week. The "Tribune" published a week's budget for a family of five, as follows:

Budget for Family of Five for One Week

Barrel of flour, $5.00, will last eight weeks........	$0.62½
Sugar, 4 lbs. at 8 cents a pound.................	.32
Butter, 2 lbs. at 31½ cents a pound.............	.62½ (sic)
Milk, two cents per day.......................	.14
Butcher's meat, 2 lbs. beef per day at 10c per lb...	$1.40
Potatoes, ½ bushel...........................	.50
Coffee and tea...............................	.25
Candle light.................................	.14
Fuel, 3 tons of coal per annum, $15.00; charcoal, chips, matches, etc., $5.00 per annum..........	.40
Salt, pepper, vinegar, starch, soap, soda, yeast, cheese, eggs.................................	.40
Furniture and utensils, wear and tear............	.25
Rent..	3.00
Bed clothes.................................	.20
Clothing....................................	2.00
Newspapers.................................	.12
Total..................................	$10.37

"I ask," said Greeley, "have I made the working-man's comforts too high? Where is the money to pay for amusements, for ice-creams, his puddings, his trips on Sunday up or down the river in order to get some fresh air, to pay the doctor or apothecary, to pay for pew rent in the church, to purchase books, musical instruments?" [1]

[1] New York *Daily Tribune*, May 27, 1851.
A yearly budget was published in the New York *Times* for 1853 that

Compiled statistics for this period are very unsatis-
factory. The Aldrich tables have been questioned and no
statistician has as yet worked up the material of the Aldrich Report so as to show the trend of real wages from 1840
to 1860. W. I. King gives the following table for the later
decade: [1]

Year	Index of Money Wages	Index of Commodity Prices	Index of Wages in Purchasing Power
1850.........	47	100	46
1851.........	47	111	42
1852.........	48	110	44
1853.........	49	118	41
1854.........	51	118	43
1855.........	52	123	42
1856.........	53	126	41
1857.........	54	128	42
1858.........	53	127	41
1859.........	53	116	46
1860.........	54	112	48

This shows a decline of commodity wages from 1850 to
1858, the recovery coming only in the last two years of the
decade when prices were falling and unemployment was
extremely severe as a result of the panic of 1857.

Quotations of money and even of commodity wages do
not represent the true state of affairs. It was a very common
practice to pay in truck or store orders. The first complaint
of the shoemakers at Lynn, in the early forties, was against

required fifty weeks' work at $12 a week. While many trades at this time
reached and passed that figure, the great mass of workers fell much below
it. In 1854 Secretary Walker, in the Treasury Report, said that the wages
of labor had not augmented since the tariff of 1842, and in some cases they
had diminished, while prices had greatly increased. (Taussig, *State
Papers on the Tariff*, pp. 226–27.)

[1] King, *Wealth and Income of the United States.*

this system which was said to reduce the nominal wage any-
where from twenty-five to fifty per cent. Cash prices were
much lower than order prices. The difference between the
wholesale cash price of flour in 1837 and the retail order
price was nearly six dollars a barrel and the difference was
even greater between cash prices and prices charged by
manufacturers who kept a store to supply their workers.[1]
With the store system in vogue it was a simple matter to
reduce wages by merely increasing prices, and it seems to
have aroused less opposition. A group of spinners in a
jeans factory in Ohio went on strike against a reduction of
wages and the truck system. They claimed that they lost
twenty-five per cent of their wages by being paid in shop
notes instead of cash, and that when they were paid in
jeans, as was sometimes the case, they lost as much as
fifty per cent.[2] One of the virtues of the Lowell factory
system was the payment of cash on the date specified in the
regulations and this was regarded as an unusual procedure.

The following is a copy of a printed notice given by Benjamin Cozzens, a manufacturer who had two large cotton
factories and a print works and employed from 1000 to
1500 hands at Crompton Mills in Rhode Island. Single
men at board, who could not take goods, had ten per cent
deducted from their wages:

Notice. Those employed at these mills and works will take
notice that a store is kept for their accommodation, where they
can purchase the best goods at fair prices, and it is expected that
all will draw their goods from said store. Those who do not are
informed that there are plenty of others who would be glad to
take their places at less wages.

Crompton Mills, Feb. 1843.   BENJ. COZZENS [3]

Builders often engaged men to work for trade claiming
they could not pay cash. They then made arrangements

---

[1] Johnson, *Sketches of Lynn*, p. 166.

[2] Commons, *Documentary History of American Industrial Society*, vol.
7, pp. 54–55.

[3] Commons, *Documentary History*, vol. 7, pp. 50–51.

with some merchant to 'order on him,' and, as the laborer
had no choice but to deal with this merchant, he was
charged what the traffic would bear, and both merchant
and employer made an extra profit out of the already low
wages of the workers.[1] At an iron and nail works in Cincinnati and at other cut-nail works, the men were sometimes paid in casks of cut nails charged at high prices, on
which they lost about twenty-five per cent. When one of
the masters was told by Finch that England had laws prohibiting this practice he replied, "Here we do as we like;
ours is a free country." [2]

The development in the Eastern cities of America, with
her vast open spaces ready for occupation, of a highly industrialized working population during the forties and
fifties was a source of continual surprise to visitors from the
older and more crowded countries. They could not understand, nor could Horace Greeley and many of the philanthropists of the period understand, why a new country
should show so many signs of congestion and pauperism
like that of England. The land was there in abundance, but
for some reason the population did not move westward
sufficiently freely to escape the consequences of the rising
immigration and industrial centralization of the time. The
price of Government land, $1.25 an acre, was some obstacle,
but more important than that was its location far from
even the outposts of civilization. It was only the pioneer by
choice who would enter a wilderness or who could subdue it
after he got there. Land near civilization was too expensive
for the industrial worker and the new immigrants had no
capital and little hope of gaining it in the East. Thus
thousands of Irish and other immigrants, who had been
reared and spent their lives on farms, settled on their arrival in the filthy cellars of the seaboard cities. Having
earned a little money they married and began to raise

---

[1] Commons, *Documentary History*, vol. 8, p. 222.
[2] *Ibid.*, vol. 7, p. 51.

families in their poverty. "Remember," wrote Thomas Mooney to his cousin Patrick in Ireland, "the American cities are not the homes you seek for. Get out of them as fast as you can either on foot or otherwise. Face toward the setting sun." [1]

The spinners in the jeans factory of Ohio referred to above, on strike against a reduction of wages and the truck system, were advised by a traveler to go farming. But they pointed out that the land in Ohio was dear, that they needed money to go West, and could not save money at fifty cents a day. But the want of money was not the only difficulty. These people were, or were rapidly becoming, what the reformers of the time regarded with so much fear and distrust, "a permanent factory population." "Suppose we had the means, we know nothing about the cultivation of the land — we have all our lives worked in a factory and we know no other employment. . . ." And in the last analysis they did not want to farm. They had developed the urban complex, that strange herd impulse that has so often thwarted the efforts of philanthropists and their 'simple life' and 'back to the land' propaganda. "Besides which, we have always been used to live in a town where we could get what little things we want if we have money, and it is only those who have lived in the wilderness who know what the horrors of wilderness life are." [2]

Just how these people who had always lived in towns and worked in factories knew so much about the horrors of wilderness life, it is difficult to say, but at least they did not like the idea of it.

The gold discoveries broke in upon the drab imaginations of the Eastern communities as a new and splendid revelation. The seaboard cities were thrown into a fever of speculation. The nation became a gambler overnight. America was converted to acquisitiveness. This spirit had

[1] Commons, *Documentary History*, vol. 7, pp. 54–55.
[2] *Ibid.*

been growing in the past, but it advanced against an older tradition of considerable strength. With the gold discoveries, the new spirit came into its own. California drained off, in addition to 'many vagabonds,' probably 50,000 skilled workers.[1] This helped to raise the wages of those who remained behind to meet the advancing prices caused in part by the same gold importations.[2]

THE SHOEMAKERS

The changes in the boot and shoe industry in the forties and fifties were of two sorts: those that were simply a continuation and accentuation of changes found in the preceding period, and those arising from the introduction of machinery. In the preceding decades the wholesale manufacture of shoes was increasingly supplanting the custom and retail shop work and the rewards of labor had fallen correspondingly. Custom work had paid from $1.40 to $2.75 per pair from 1800 to 1810. In 1835, wholesale work paid only $1.12½ per pair. The important changes in the position of the shoemaker in our period were effected by the displacement of the merchant capitalist by the factory owner as the chief organizer of production. This change was facilitated by the failure of many of the older New England firms in the depression of 1837–39.[3]

Thus we find three stages in the social revolution in the shoe trade up to 1860: the stage of the master workman and his journeymen, up to 1830; the merchant capitalist stage, to 1840; and the stage of the factory owner, with or without machinery, until 1860. The character of the merchant capitalist stage, from the standpoint of the master and journeyman, is seen in the protest of the journeymen cordwainers of Philadelphia in 1835:

If we take a retrospective view of our trade we will find that a

---

[1] Carey, *Gold from California*, p. 6.
[2] Exec. Doc. 49:1, no. 1, pt. 5, p. 57.
[3] Clark, *History of Manufactures*, p. 381.

few years ago the slowest of our profession could earn at least seven or eight dollars per week and that by no greater exertion than it now requires to make four or five.... From that time to the present the trade has been gradually sinking, at least so far as the interests of the journeymen are concerned. The cunning men from the East have come to our city, and having capital themselves, or joining with those who had, have embarked in our business and realized large fortunes by reduction of our wages....

The transition to the factory system was not far advanced in the beginning of our period. Lynn, Massachusetts, was the center of the women's shoe trade and was only emerging at this time from the domestic system. The domestic worker at Lynn had been part farmer, part artisan, part fisherman. If one of his three props failed him, he could fall back on another. He felt that he could work in the fields or in the shop as he chose, and when disinclined for either he could lock up his 'ten-footer' [1] and go fishing. When it was too cold for work indoors or out, he sat in his kitchen reading. Both the men and women who worked on shoes in the earlier days did so irregularly and at their own request.[2]

The change of status involved in the transfer to the factory system is best seen in the character of unemployment. In domestic production, unemployment meant leisure and a change of work — a change that was often pleasant and sometimes profitable. But as trade specialization and urban conditions developed, unemployment spelled increasingly want and discontent.

In 1830 nearly all the shoemakers of Lynn had owned their homes with some land about them. Even those who rented had usually large gardens where they were able to raise sufficient vegetables for their winter supply. Almost

[1] The 'ten-footer' was the small shoe shop beside the shoemaker's home. In size it varied from 10′ × 10′ to 14′ × 14′, and averaged about 12′ × 12′. The numbers working in these shops varied from four to eight. The shops contained benches and tools, fireplaces, and, later, stoves.

[2] Hazard, "The Boot and Shoe Industry in Massachusetts," *Quarterly Journal of Economics*, vol. 27, February, 1913.

every family kept a pig and many had their own cow. Discipline in the little shop was slack. When an apprentice left his work at night, "he might be expected back in the morning, but there were no special grounds for the expectation. He might drop in the next morning or the next week." [1]

The panic of 1837 was less distressing in its results for the Lynn shoemakers than it would have been at a later period because of the still primitive nature of the industrial situation. With a garden, a pig, and some fishing tackle the shoemaker "could bid defiance to financial tempests." In the winter he could go clam and eel hunting, and if he had two or three cords of wood split and piled in the shed he considered himself in easy circumstances.

When the spring opened, the horizon of his hopes expanded. Less clothing and fuel were needed. The clam banks discounted more readily; haddock could be got at Swampscott so cheap that the price wasn't worth quoting. The boys could dig dandelions. ... Then if the poor man had his little "spring pig" that he had kept through the winter, "pork and dandelions" were no small items in the bill of fare while "greens" lasted. [2]

It is well no doubt to be skeptical of a Golden Age either past or future, and well, too, to discount reminiscences, but the evidence is considerable of the reality of the freedom and security of these people.

The shoemaker had always been regarded as a thoughtful and intelligent artisan. Every shoeshop was a lyceum. It was a common thing for the journeymen to hire a boy to read the paper to them while they worked. [3] No villages stood higher than the shoe villages of New England, according to Amasa Walker, in the moral, social, and intellectual condition of their inhabitants. The shoemakers were distinguished for general intelligence. It was a social business, conversation was not drowned by the noise of machin-

---

[1] Johnson, *Sketches of Lynn*, p. 30.
[2] *Ibid.*, pp. 157–58.
[3] McNeill, *Labor Movement*, p. 195.

ery, and there were many opportunities for reading and mutual improvement.[1]

But the days of independence, culture, and security were fast passing for the shoemakers of Lynn at the beginning of the forties. Increasingly they were being drawn into the new order of things, their standards of living declining, and their dependence upon the masters increasing. The depression of 1837–39 had done much to reduce them, but seven lean years intervened before they gave voice to their discontent. From 1831 to 1837, cash had been substituted for store orders in the payment of wages. But in the years of the depression, the process was reversed and store orders were again substituted for cash. It was claimed by the manufacturers that they were forced to accept truck in payment for shoes and that during the bad years the journeymen were glad enough to get what payment they could.[2] But with the improvement of business conditions in 1843, the old wages and old methods of payment were continued, though prices were beginning to advance.

The store-order system of payment was the immediate cause of the protest of the shoemakers in 1844. At this date there was formed at Lynn a Journeyman Cordwainers' Society which began the publication of a workers' paper, "The Awl." The journeymen claimed that the shoe manufacturers, while pretending to pay a living wage, "did by other means reduce them to degradation and the loss of that self-respect which had made the mechanics and laborers the pride of the world";[3] that they had suffered much privation for several years because of the low price paid for their work; and that they were "cursed with the order system" which was known to rob the families of their support, their children of the benefit of "the higher branches of

---

[1] Convention of Manufacturers, Dealers and Operatives. . . . Boston, 1842, *Proceedings*, p. 30, President's address.

[2] Johnson, *Sketches of Lynn*, p. 168.

[3] *The Awl*, March 29, 1844.

education," and themselves of many of the comforts of life, while it enriched employers and tradesmen, created distinctions "anti-republican in character, which assimilate very nearly to those that exist between the aristocracy and the laboring classes of Europe." The system was characterized as a "willful and deliberate attempt by the moneyed aristocracy to degrade, freeze, and starve the poor. . . ."

The Lynn shoemakers, after they had completed their own organization, sent a circular to the shoemakers throughout New England asking their coöperation in an attempt to get better prices. "Let us prove," they wrote, "that we are not menials or the humble subjects of a foreign despot, but free, American citizens." [1] At the same time they admitted, "We are slaves in the strictest sense of the word. For do we not have to toil from the rising of the sun to the going down of the same for our masters — aye, masters, and for our daily bread?" Strangers, like Miss Martineau, said of them, "How happy these shoemakers must be! Look at the beautiful dwellings! How neat and comfortable they look!" But that was the bright side of the picture. "Who owns," they ask, "these neat and pretty houses which are a delight to look upon? Why, those who have grown fat upon the earnings of the toil-worn laborer. . . ." [2]

The shoemakers signed a 'declaration of independence':

Whereas, our employers have robbed us of certain rights which they will, in our opinion, never voluntarily restore . . . we feel bound to rise unitedly in our strength and burst asunder as freemen ought the shackles and fetters with which they have long been chaining and binding us, by an unjust and unchristian use of power and a host of advantages which the possession of capital and superior knowledge furnishes. . . . [3]

Alongside this language of agitation that tends frequently to class consciousness, there is found as well the older attitude of community of interest between journey-

[1] *The Awl*, July 17, 1844.   [2] *Ibid.*, July 24, 1844.
[3] *Ibid.*, August 14, 1844.

man and boss. The shoemakers were still far from having extricated themselves from the older tradition, and much of the language in which their protests are couched must be discounted. They frequently stop themselves in their tirades against the bosses to distinguish between 'good' bosses and those that were not so good. "The Awl" started out with a statement that its purpose was to benefit every one connected with the trade. "We do not advocate the claims of the jour in opposition to those of the employer, nor seek to benefit the one at the expense of the other." [1] But this did not involve the dependence upon the philanthropy of the employers that is to be found in the pitiful appeal of the needlewomen "To the Humane." It was as far removed from subservience as from ideas of class war. "This society," said the cordwainers, "intends . . . to respect our employers, but no more than any other man — ourselves likewise." [2] "We hold it our duty to maintain the value of labor that it may itself be respectable . . . and respected." [3]

As compared with other mechanics, the wages of the Lynn shoemakers were low. Some could earn from $8 to $10 a week at certain seasons of the year, and some might earn $300 to $400 a year. But as a class, they did not average more than $4 or $5 a week, while carpenters, painters and masons were receiving $1.25 to $2 a day.[4] Taking $5 a week as the average, a journeyman would earn $260 a year. This was not paid in cash except by special agreement, but in orders on the Lynn Mechanics' Union and other stores. The journeyman had to take these orders or nothing, and the goods at these stores were marked up at exorbitant prices. In dull times it was often impossible to get adequate quantities. The loss to the worker as a result of the order system was about 33 per cent, so that his income of $260 shrank to $175, supposing he received $5 a week. If he

[1] *The Awl*, July 17, 1844.   [2] *Ibid.*
[3] *Ibid.*   [4] *Ibid.*, September 25, 1844.

averaged only $4 a week, his annual wage was reduced to $139.[1]

A committee was sent out by the Lynn Society to help organize all the shoe towns in New England and arrange to have them send delegates to a New England Convention of Cordwainers to be held on August 1st. One object of this convention was to prepare for the New England Convention of Mechanics and Laborers that had been called by the Fall River mechanics and laborers. A further purpose was the fixing of a scale of prices for the shoe industry over the whole country as far south as Philadelphia, and setting a day when every journeyman should "march up to his boss and demand a just and fair compensation for his labor." They hoped, too, to do away with the practice of the employers of taking apprentices for a few weeks and "learning them to make one kind of shoe, or what is called a shoe, and thereby multiplying poor workmen and filling our market with miserable goods." Finally they proposed to raise the reputation of the town by doing their work more faithfully.[2]

A strike call was sent to all the shoemakers' societies of New England, New York and Philadelphia. Some of the outside societies signified their intention of taking the matter up, but nothing was done and no strike took place. Several "Associated Labor Societies" were formed to make shoes from their own stock and secure to themselves the profits of their labors. Twenty-five or fifty journeymen would invest fifty to one hundred dollars each, select one of their own number as agent, and go to work.[3]

A meeting of the New York cordwainers was held on June 26, 1844, at which the call for a New England convention was approved and it was decided to send delegates.[4] The New York meeting asserted that labor not only "does

[1] *The Awl*, September 25, 1844.
[2] *Ibid.*, July 17, 1844.
[3] *Ibid.*, September 18, 21, 24, 1844.
[4] *Ibid.*, July 17, 1844.

not receive its just reward in this Republic, but that its compensation is growing less . . ." and resolved to have a union of trades, "to render labor independent of, if not master over, machines, and get a fair average of fruits for a fair average of work." [1]

There is no class of mechanics in New York [it was claimed by the "Tribune"] who average so great an amount of work for so little money as the journeymen shoemakers. The number of journeymen out of employment is also large. . . . There are hundreds of them in the city constantly wandering from shop to shop in search of work, while many of them have families in a state of absolute want. . . . We have been in more than fifty cellars in different parts of the city, each inhabited by a shoemaker and his family. The floor is made of rough plank laid loosely down, the ceiling is not quite so high as a tall man. The walls are dark and damp, and a wide, desolate fireplace yawns in the center to the right of the entrance. There is no outlet back and of course no yard privileges of any kind. The miserable room is lighted only by a shallow sash, partly projecting above the surface of the ground and by the little light that struggles down the steep and rotting stairs. In this . . . often live the man with his work-bench, his wife and five or six children of all ages, and perhaps a palsied grandfather or grandmother and often both. In one corner is a squalid bed and the room elsewhere is occupied by the work-bench, a cradle made from a dry-goods box, two or three broken, seatless chairs, a stew-pan and a kettle.[2]

There were at this time 5000 to 6000 shoemakers in New York City and, as a result of recent immigration, "competition had been carried to such a degree as almost to drive the American mechanic from his work-bench." [3] The greater part of the new journeymen were Germans, Irish and French. The shoemakers in the 'men's branch' had had a society, "The United Benefit Society of Cordwainers in the Men's Branch of the City of New York," since the close of the Revolutionary War. This society had always been in a flourishing condition, and in 1845 had three hundred mem-

[1] *Working Man's Advocate*, June 29, 1844.
[2] New York *Daily Tribune*, September 9, 1845.
[3] *Ibid.*, September 5, 1845.

bers, most of whom were Irish. Its objects were the regulation of hours and prices and the maintenance of sickness and death benefits.[1]

A New York shoemaker at this time could make three pairs of bottoms a week, working ten hours a day, and was paid $1.75 to $2.25 a pair. His average wage was between $4 and $6 a week, but many could earn $7, $8, and even $9. Paid by the month, the journeyman would get from $4 to $12 and board, lodging, and washing. This was on the coarser sort of boots.[2]

The New York cordwainers in the ladies' branch had no permanent organization, but a meeting was called in April, 1846, to protest against reduced prices. They claimed that a reduction of 29 cents had been made in prices since the spring of 1843, and that the advance gained by the strike of 1845 was lost again in the winter of 1845–46.[3]   In 1853 it was said that the New York cordwainers could average $7 to $8 a week, an increase of about $1 a week over the wages of 1842–43, "yet in consequence of the much enhanced price of provisions and rent . . . it is certain that the condition of the boot and shoe makers in this city has retrograded." There were many shops where even money wages had declined.[4]

From 1855, or a little later, the workmen began to leave the little shops to work in the factories, and in a few years vacant 'ten-footers' were seen all over Lynn. These were transformed into hen-houses or coal-pens, and some of the larger ones were sold to the poor to be fitted up as dwellings, probably improved by an addition.[5]

Wage reductions in the shoe trade in 1858 and 1859 resulted in numerous and prolonged strikes. One of the largest of these was at Natick in 1859, when eight hundred men

[1] New York *Daily Tribune*, September 5, 1845.
[2] *Ibid.*
[3] *Young America*, April 26, 1846.
[4] New York *Daily Tribune*, May 27, 1853.
[5] Johnson, *Sketches of Lynn*, p. 342.

were successful after being out for fourteen weeks for an advance of wages to cover the reductions of the panic year. A compromise resulted from a similar strike at Marlboro, where one hundred men were out for three weeks. At Lynn, the journeymen struck against a reduction of wages in February, 1860. They had no organization at this time, but held processions and meetings and there was some rioting. Troops were called out and the Boston police were sent in. The strike spread through the shoe towns of Massachusetts and a general labor demonstration was projected for March 7th at Lynn. On March 5th, the women stitchers, binders, and machine operatives joined the strikers, and meetings were held at Liberty Hall where delegations were received from Salem, Beverly, Danvers, Woburn, Marblehead, etc. Over five thousand men and one thousand women marched in procession carrying one hundred banners and twenty-six American flags, and accompanied by five bands, and military and fire companies. It was said to have been the largest labor demonstration Massachusetts experienced up to 1880. But 'the vacant places in the shops were being filled' and by April 1st the strike was over, having been utterly lost.[1]

In 1862 the McKay machine completely revolutionized the work of the journeymen as the stitching machine had done that of the binders.[2]

Before 1852 the binding of the upper had been done by hand by women. The price was from seventeen to twenty-five cents a pair, and a clever woman could make four pairs or even more a day for which she would receive from sixty-eight cents to one dollar.[3] By competition and the introduction of the machine this remuneration was reduced by one half to two thirds. In 1853 binding children's shoes paid

---

[1] Massachusetts Bureau of Labor Statistics, *Eleventh Annual Report,* 1880, pp. 16–19.
[2] Johnson, *Sketches of Lynn,* pp. 342–43.
[3] *Ibid.,* p. 338.

three cents for two pairs or eighteen cents a dozen, and full-sized shoes brought five cents a pair, or sixty cents a dozen. A first-rate binder, by the closest application for fourteen to seventeen hours a day, "if uninterrupted by domestic cares," could make four dozen pairs a week, for which, "after delivery and approval," she was paid $2.40. This was a maximum and represented eighty hours of labor. If the cost of light and fire were deducted the average would be nearer $1.60 a week.[1]

THE NEEDLE TRADES

There was not in our period, or probably in any other, a more helpless and degraded class of workers than the needle-women of the cities. Their condition had earlier enlisted the efforts of Mathew Carey and others, without appreciable result. They were incapable of organizing themselves permanently because of the semi-industrial nature of their trade and the surplus of that sort of labor. What little organization was achieved among them depended rather on the spasmodic efforts of 'humane persons' who interested themselves in their behalf.

From 1840 to 1860 a complete revolution occurred in the tailoring industry as a result of the introduction of ready-made clothing in common use. Until 1835 the only clothing kept for sale was 'shop clothing' which was sold almost entirely to seamen. The wholesale manufacture of clothes began in New York in 1835, but went under in the panic of 1837. In 1840 the trade revived and offered employment, such as it was, to thousands of women.[2] At first, much of this work was sent into the country to be made up, but it was gradually being brought into the 'factories.'

The sewing machine made its appearance in the clothing trade in the early fifties. At first the tailor was required to buy his own machine and, as those who had sufficient sav-

[1] New York *Daily Tribune*, May 27, 1853.
[2] Freedley, *Philadelphia and Its Manufactures*, p. 223.

ings to do this were few, those who had not were compelled
to pay the machine tailor for straight stitching. The machine tailor soon discovered that his investment was not a
paying one. His earnings were no greater than before and
his savings were gone. The profit of the machine went to
the bosses; "they got their work quicker and it was done
better." [1]

The needle is sure soon to be consigned to the lumber-room
[wrote Greeley in 1853], wherein our grandmother's "great
wheel," "little wheel," loom and "swifts" are now silently mold-
ering. Twenty years more may elapse . . . before the revolution
will have been completed, but the sewing of a long straight seam
otherwise than by machinery is even now a mistake, an anachronism. And the finger-plied needle, though it may be retained a
few years longer for button-holes and such fancy work, has but a
short lease left. . . . [2]

There were at this time four groups of needlewomen corresponding to the classes of work and the stages of advance
toward the complete factory system of a later date. The
journeymen dressmakers, who were employed by the week,
often worked fourteen to sixteen hours a day, and were paid
from $1.25 to $2.50 per week. The dressmakers who went
into the homes of their customers were better paid, receiving 62½ cents, 75 cents, and $1 a day. Apprentices were
usually paid nothing for the first six months and boarded
themselves. They were frequently required to pay the employer $10 or $15 for the privilege of 'learning,' and, if they
were unable to pay, they worked for a year without wages
and boarded themselves. Instead of being taught the trade,
the apprentices were usually kept at plain sewing, and at
the end of the apprenticeship two thirds or three quarters
of them were not trained dressmakers at all. The last
group, and the lowest in the scale in every respect, were
those who worked in their own homes, calling for their work

[1] *Capital and Labor*, 1885, p. 414.
[2] New York *Daily Tribune*, June 18, 1853.

and returning to the shop with it when finished.[1] There were ten thousand of these women in New York City alone in 1854,[2] and their wages, hours, and conditions of work were inconceivably bad. Widows in Cincinnati were supporting children by making shirts for ten cents each and pants for fifteen and seventeen cents. It was estimated that they could make nine shirts in a week, or ninety cents for a long week's work.[3] In New York, in 1845, some of the needle-women were being paid ten to eighteen cents a day for twelve to fourteen hours' work, while others, who were more proficient, were paid twenty-five cents a day. Work which had brought 97½ cents in 1844 was paid only 37½ cents in 1845.[4] The average earnings of these women were $1.50 to $2 a week, though many of them could not earn more than $1.[5]

A great number of females are employed in making men's and boys' caps [said the "Tribune" reporter in 1845]. By constant labor, 15 to 18 hours a day, they can make from 14 to 25 cents. We are told by an old lady who has lived by this kind of work for a long time that when she begins at sunrise and works till midnight, she can earn 14 cents a day. . . .

The manner in which these women live, the squalidness and unhealthy location and nature of their habitations, the impossibility of providing for any of the slightest recreations or moral or intellectual culture or of educating their children, can be easily imagined; but we assure the public that it would require an extremely active imagination to conceive the reality.[6]

When the industrial worker and his friends protested that there was white slavery in the North as evil as the black slavery of the South, they were thinking of conditions of this sort. But the wages, hours, and homes of these women were not their only difficulties. It was a common

---

[1] New York *Daily Tribune*, September 3, 1845.
[2] *Ibid.*, August 14, 1845.
[3] Andrews, Senate Doc. no. 645, 61:2, vol. 10, p. 58.
[4] *Working Man's Advocate*, March 8, 1845.
[5] New York *Daily Tribune*, March 7, 1845.
[6] *Ibid.*, August 14, 1845.

occurrence for one of the seamstresses to carry back to her employer, after a week's work, a heavy bundle of clothing in her arms and find that it would not pass his examination.[1] Many of the cheap 'slop shops' required the women to pay a deposit of the full value of the material before it could be taken out. When work fell off and there was no more to be given out, this deposit was frequently retained by the employer.[2] Needlewomen receiving only five cents for shirts, on which they were required to deposit the full value of the material, were said to have been paid at the rate of ninety-six cents on the dollar. In some cases only a part of the money due was paid, the woman being told to allow the remainder to stand over for later settlement.[3] In this way many of the employers who professed to pay good wages reduced them to the level of the worst. Instances were known where fifty cents was paid on account and the remainder postponed week after week until the claimant became discouraged and gave up trying to collect. In the mean time she had to neglect her chances of getting other employment.[4] One woman after seeking work for two days managed to get something that paid her sixty cents for the first week. When she returned the goods, she was given credit on the books to be settled when the amount was worth while.[5] In another case, the girl delivering her work and asking for payment was kicked into the street and left without money to cross the ferry to her home.[6]

Another feature of the trade, and the most disheartening, was its utter hopelessness and constant tendency to grow worse. The needlewoman market was flooded. An advertisement from a Philadelphia journal was reproduced under the title "Buying a Seamstress":

[1] *The Awl*, September 4, 1844.
[2] New York *Daily Tribune*, June 8, 1853.
[3] *Ibid.*   [4] *Ibid.*
[5] *Ibid.*, October 14, 1845.
[6] *Ibid.*, June 8, 1853.

Wanted — by a young girl, a competent dressmaker, the loan of $100.00 for which she will give one year and a half of her time as a dressmaker and seamstress. Public Ledger, December 9.[1]

In July, 1844, the 'tailors and tailoresses' of New York and Boston went on strike against a reduction in their wages. The New York "Herald" was burned at a public meeting for its criticism of the strike. The "Herald" modified its original attitude sufficiently to declare:

On the whole, and after full investigation, it seems strange that the present improvement in business will not allow the employers to add $1.00 or $1.50 to their workmen's wages. As to the workmen themselves, if they continue orderly and permit no agitation to lead them into passionate courses, they will receive their due share of sympathy, but they should behave well.[2]

In Boston, Marlboro Chapel, the largest auditorium in the city, was filled for a meeting of the tailors to consider the proposed reduction. This was one of the greatest labor demonstrations Boston had experienced. "The body of the hall was crowded with ladies, while the rear of the desk and the galleries were occupied by sturdy mechanics and operatives of our city." [3] The tailors passed a resolution asking the assistance of the women in their attempt to secure a fair compensation for their work.[4] They met again in September at Faneuil Hall, when "the galleries were thronged from the lowest to the highest seats with a living panorama of the fair sex, who, to their praise be it said, obtain their living by honest industry." [5]

Again, in March, 1845, the needlewomen of New York met in the park in front of the City Hall. Among them were seamstresses, tailoresses, bookfolders and stitchers, shirt-makers, cap-makers, straw-workers, crimpers, dressmakers, and fringe and lace makers. The authorities invited the Women into the City Hall where they organized

---

[1] *Voice of Industry*, January 14, 1848.
[2] *Working Man's Advocate*, August 3, 1844.
[3] *Ibid.*   [4] *Ibid.*
[5] Boston *Times*, September 30, 1844.

the Female Industry Association.[1] The "Herald" was
more sympathetic toward the women. "Seldom or never,"
it reported, "did the Superior Court of the City Hall contain such an array of beauty and suffering." Seven hundred
women were present, and the President, Elizabeth Gray,
declared that they intended to get better wages, "by ap-
pealing to the public at large and showing the amount of
the sufferings under which they labored." Signor Palmo
offered to assist them by giving a benefit performance at
the Opera House.[2]

In the resolutions of the meeting and in the tone of the
addresses there was no sign of an aggressive spirit on the
part of the needlewomen. They were helpless and realized
it. All they could do was to appeal to the sense of justice of
the public, and there the matter rested.

In 1846 they met again, when it was stated that they
were making shirts at four cents apiece, "while agents of
debauchery circulated among them with offers of ease and
plenty." [3]

In 1850 the same helpless plea was repeated by the
sewing-women of Philadelphia, addressed:

To the Humane

The winter is upon us and distress and want stare us in the
face. By reason of the low prices for which we are obliged to work
many of us are found by the midnight lamp and until daybreak at
the needle laboring for a pittance which is scarcely sufficient for
the necessities of the summer season. . . . If we must become
beggars we would do so in a body and entreat our whole community to make one effort for us. . . .

They proposed to start an Association shop and "become
their own employers," but were too poor and needed the
assistance of the charitable. The prices they were receiving

[1] Later, a philanthropic society, the American Industrial Union, provided funds to employ seamstresses on a non-profit making basis. (New
York *Tribune*, July 1, 1850.)

[2] *Working Man's Advocate*, March 8, 1845.

[3] *Voice of Industry*, September 4, 1846.

were about the same as those quoted for New York and Boston in 1844 and 1845.[1]

In New York, in 1853, prices were as low as they had been in 1845: summer vests were eighteen cents; pantaloons, twenty cents; light coats, eighteen cents. A twelve-hour day gave a return of about twenty-four cents, "provided [the goods] were not returned upon the hands of the worker." Shirts were made for four, five, seven, and eight cents apiece; three of them were a hard day's labor and brought the worker from twelve to twenty-four cents a day. "The average yearly income of these women at the best of the above prices, all doing full work the year round, amounts to ninety-one dollars!" [2]

The beginnings of the 'sweating system' are to be found here. The "Tribune's" reporter described it in 1853 as a 'middle system.' Near one of the streets running from the Bowery to the East River an old Irish woman was found with four girls working for her. Their pay consisted solely of their food for six days a week. Another woman had hired four 'learners,' two of whom received only board and lodging, while the other two were paid one dollar a week without their food.[3]

The milliners of New York were better off than the sewing-women. As apprentices they received no pay or board for a year, and, in the better shops, had frequently to pay a bonus for the privilege of 'learning.' The hours were from ten to twelve, and at the end of the year they were turned out to find employment and a new batch of apprentices was taken on. All through the period and in very many trades the apprenticeship system had become little more than a cheap method of getting the greater part of the work done. There was no attempt made to teach the full trade. One or two journeymen were sufficient as overseers

[1] New York *Daily Tribune*, February 23, 1850.
[2] *Ibid.*, June 8, 1853.
[3] *Ibid.*

to supply all the craft knowledge and skill required for the shop and the routine work was done by so-called 'apprentices.' The journeymen milliners working from sunrise to 9 P.M. could earn from $2.50 to $3 a week. Their board and washing cost at least $2.[1]

THE PRINTERS

As was the case with most of the skilled trades in the period, the chief forces operating to undermine the status of the printers were: the passing of control from the 'profession' itself into the hands of outsiders, the introduction of machinery, and the employment of boys and 'two-thirders,'[2] or partially trained journeymen. At least as early as 1836 the transfer of control that reduced the printers from men with a profession to wage-earners was well advanced.[3]

Mechanically, the printing trade was revolutionized by the invention of the Napier press and the use of steam power. The Napier was first introduced in the newspaper offices, and by 1845 had entirely superseded the hand press in all but job and extra fine bookwork. Hand presses were general in the book offices as late as 1834. The average wage of pressmen had been $10 a week. This was higher than that of the compositors, because it was impossible to make 'two-thirders' pressmen. The introduction of the Napier and Adams presses threw nine tenths of these men out of employment, and in 1845 "only a solitary sort of forlorn hope are found in their places or near them gazing upon the Napiers and the foreign force which surrounds them."[4]

The new compositors who were rapidly displacing the old

[1] New York *Daily Tribune*, September 16, 1845.

[2] Boys were paid $1.50 to $2 per week and kept at type-setting for one or two years, and then became 'two-thirders,' and were paid 18¾ to 20 cents per 1000 ems. (New York *Daily Tribune*, September 11, 1845.)

[3] Stewart, *Documentary History of the Early Organizations of Printers*, Bulletin no. 59, U.S. Bureau of Labor, July, 1905, pp. 978–79.

[4] New York *Daily Tribune*, September 15, 1845.

fully trained journeymen were not considered printers at
all; "they are scarcely competent to make up the matter
they set and would be as much bothered as a hod carrier if
called upon to 'impose' and make ready a form for the
press!..." [1] Two thirds of them were boys with a few
good workmen to 'impose.'

"So far as the journeymen are concerned," Greeley
lamented, "the Golden Age of printing is passing away."
Those who were yet young were advised to go West "where
independence and plenty may be found." While they remain at their trade "they are always slaves ... despite
their proud boasts of freemen, living from hand to mouth
and seldom in possession of twenty dollars clear of the
world. Pride and poverty are miserable companions. Let
them leave the first with their fashionable garments behind
them, and betake themselves to the soil." [2]

The National Typographical Society had collapsed in
1838, and the local societies, falling back on their benefit
functions, maintained an existence of a sort. The New
York Society in 1844, attempted to increase wages, but the
employers were able it was said not only to resist the increase, but to force the printers to accept a reduction. [3]
The New York Typographical was a benefit society that
had been organized in 1809 and incorporated in 1818. [4] It
had 250 members, but was quite powerless to fix a uniform scale of 'prices.' It chiefly represented the newspaper
printers and failed to help the job printers to any extent. [5]

[1] New York *Daily Tribune*, September 15, 1845.
[2] *Ibid.*
[3] Stewart, Bulletin, Bureau of Labor, no. 59, pp. 332–33.
It is probable that the increase asked by the printers was granted by
some employers in the spring and withdrawn in the summer. (*The Awl,*
July 31, 1844.)
Evans said that the printers got an advance of wages by a strike in
April which did not nearly cover the increase in rents. (*Working Man's
Advocate,* April 20, 1844.)
[4] New York *Daily Tribune*, June 11, 1850.
[5] *Ibid.*, September 11, 1845.

In 1845 there were about 1600 printers in New York City, one third of whom were foreigners, British, German, and French. Wages for compositors on newspapers, when steadily employed, were $9, $12, and $15 per week. Jobbing offices paid $6, $7, $9, and $12 a week, a yearly average of about $6 a week. Boys who were usurping the places of the journeymen were paid $1.50 to $2 a week.[1] Ten per cent of all the printers in the city could earn $10, $12, $14, and $18 a week with continuous work. Ten per cent could earn $8, $9, $10, and $12 a week. These were unemployed one or two months in the year. Forty per cent were paid $6, $7, $8, $9, and $10 a week. Two thirds of these were unemployed from four to ten weeks, and the remainder, three months in the year. The last forty per cent were paid from $1 to $3, $4, and $5 a week, and had steady employment.[2] Wages were sometimes withheld by jobbers as a fund with which to do business. In that case, the journeymen to whom the employer was in debt would get the 'fat' work and those who were paid cash would get the work that was more difficult.[3]

The New York Society was resuscitated in 1850 under the title "The New York Printers' Union." The objects of the union, as laid down in the new constitution, were: "the maintenance of a fair rate of wages, the encouragement of good workmen, the support of members in sickness or distress, the relief of deserving printers who may visit our city in search of employment, the establishment of a library for the use and instruction of members, and to use every means which may tend to the elevation of printers in the scale of social life." The initiation fee was to be $1 and the dues $6.50 per annum, with the right of additional assessment up to $2 a year. Sick benefits were to be paid of $4 a week,

[1] New York *Daily Tribune*, September 11, 1845.
[2] *Ibid.*
[3] *Ibid.* In 1848, the Boston Typographical Society gave the wages of printers as: 156 journeymen working twelve hours a day would average $9.25 a week; 325 journeymen working ten hours a day, $6 a week.

and death benefits for members, or the wives of members, of $20. One year's membership was required before benefits would be paid. The Society had 150 members at the time of its reorganization.[1]

The new spirit of denial of the accepted doctrine of community of interest between employer and employed, was, as has been pointed out, first to be found among the factory operatives and perhaps the laborers, in the early part of the forties. Among the printers it emerged in 1850 in the address of the National Typographical Society to the printers throughout the United States:

It is useless for us to disguise from ourselves the fact that, under the present arrangement of things, there exists a perpetual antagonism between Labor and Capital . . . one striving to sell their labor for as much, and the other striving to buy it for as little, as they can. . . .

But the new radicalism went further than this. It is evident that the trade had become indoctrinated with the larger plans and outlook of the reformers. Neither benefits nor wage agreements were to be considered final. They would not stop short of the complete reorganization of the industrial system. This attitude was not uncommon in the general labor societies of the forties, but in an old benevolent craft union it was more remarkable:

To remedy the many disastrous grievances arising from this disparity of power [between employer and employed] combination for mutual agreement in determining rates of wages and for concert of action in maintaining them, has been resorted to in many trades and principally in our own. Its success has abundantly demonstrated its utility. Indeed, while the present wage system continues in operation, as an immediate protection from pressing calamities it is clearly the only effective means which labor can adopt. So far as it extends it destroys competition in the labor market, unites the working people and produces a sort of equilibrium in the power of the conflicting classes. . . . [We] re-

---

[1] New York *Daily Tribune*, May 6, 1850.

gard such an organization not only as an agent of immediate relief, but also as an essential to the ultimate destruction of those unnatural relations at present subsisting between the interests of the employing and the employed classes.[1]

Thus a combination

merely to fix and sustain a scale of prices is of minor importance compared with that combination which looks to an ultimate redemption of labor. Scales of prices to keep up the value of labor are only necessary under a system which, in its uninterrupted operation, gives to that value a continued downward tendency. But when labor determines to sell itself no longer to speculators, but to become its own employer, to own and enjoy itself and the fruit thereof, the necessity for scales of prices will have passed away and labor will be forever rescued from the control of the capitalist. It will then be flourishing, free, fruitful, honorable....[2]

In 1853 a second union among the printers was organized, "The New York Printers' Co-operative Union," to take care of the book and job printers who were not included in the Typographical Society. They were not received with much enthusiasm by the older organization and appealed to the National Society for recognition. They claimed that the old union did not include more than one tenth of the printers, while of these, nine tenths were in newspaper work, and that the society had no interest in job and book printers. The old society insisted that the members of the new organization could and should unite with the Typographical, but the new men objected to the benefit feature and the high fees which this feature involved. The fact was that the small benefit unions were the only ones that were able to weather the repeated depressions of the period from 1800 to 1837. The high fees made for stability and a restricted appeal. But when general conditions began to improve, as they did in 1853–54, and the craft as a whole found it necessary to organize to bargain collectively over wages, the old-line, high-fee, benefit organizations

[1] New York *Daily Tribune*, December 26, 1850.
[2] *Ibid.*

stood in the way of successful action. The high fees had kept most of the printers who were being paid from $6 to $10 a week out of the movement altogether.

The National Society was reluctant to recognize two printers' unions in New York, and it was proposed that a reorganization be effected and the benefit feature abolished "as being detrimental to an efficient trade organization." But the opposition of the old local society was so great as to prevent any satisfactory solution being achieved, and the National Society dropped the matter by advising the New York Typographical to improve its organization and expand.[1]

Recognition came, however, to the book and job printers' organization from another quarter. The employing printers, who had formed an employers' association for bargaining purposes, invited the new union to meet them to discuss the proposed wage scale. At the first meeting there were not sufficient delegates to do business and the matter was postponed,[2] but a conference was held a week later. The printers had demanded an increase of three cents per one thousand ems, to meet the advancing cost of living. At the conference held toward the end of April, the employers offered an advance of two cents per one thousand ems. The printers' representative asked for another meeting to which he might convey the reply of his union and was told that no further meeting could be held, and that the offer of two cents was final.[3] The printers' demands were then presented to the individual employers, the attempt at a collective agreement having fallen through, and a strike was called on the employers who refused to grant the three-cent advance. The strike fund was maintained by the payment of the increase, by those who had succeeded, into a fund for the maintenance of those who had failed.[4]

The following year a strike of the lithograph printers oc-

---

[1] New York *Daily Tribune*, May 5, 1853.   [2] *Ibid.*, April 22, 1853.
[3] *Ibid.*, April 30, 1853.   [4] *Ibid.*, May 3, 1853.

curred, because the employers had insisted on new rules that were regarded as arbitrary and "conflicting with the liberties of American working-men." One of these rules was that the workers were not to have visitors while at work, and another that they must supply their own black roller and pallet knife.[1]

THE HAND-LOOM WEAVERS

The competition of a cheaper labor force that was made possible by the introduction of machinery, with the consequent reduction of the standards and status of the skilled worker, was seen nowhere more clearly than in the case of weaving. The astonishing thing in this instance is not the decline of the weaver, but the remarkable tenacity with which he clung to his loom. There is no more striking illustration of the great conservatism of the industrial classes. Their one possession, their craft skill, had been, one would think, almost worthless since the beginning of the century, but this little group held out in some fashion down even to 1867.

It is a remarkable fact [said Freedley] that notwithstanding the rapid substitution of power for the production of textile fabrics and the growth of large establishments from the results of accumulated capital, there is no actual decline in the number of hand looms in operation. There are fewer looms devoted to certain classes of goods, and in certain localities, than formerly; but the aggregate of such looms now in operation is probably fully equal to that in any former period. Philadelphia is now [1867] the great seat of hand-loom manufacturing and weaving in America. There are now within our knowledge 4700 hand looms in operation . . . and it is probable that the true number approximates 6000.[2]

The material of the hand-loom weavers was supplied by the manufacturers and the weavers were paid by the yard. Ordinarily, the weaving was done in the houses of the operatives, but in some cases the manufacturer had ten or

---

[1] New York *Daily Tribune*, January 11, 1854.
[2] Freedley, *Philadelphia and Its Manufactures*, p. 282.

twelve looms in a building attached to his dwelling and employed journeymen. Occasionally the journeymen boarded and lodged in the house of the manufacturer. "Throughout parts of the city [Philadelphia], especially that formerly known as Kensington, the sound of these looms may be heard at all hours — in garrets, cellars, and out houses, as well as in the weavers' apartments." [1]

A resolution was passed at the National Trade Union meeting in New York, in 1836, "that the wages at present obtained by the hand-loom weavers is quite incompetent to secure the means of a comfortable sustenance and far below that which is generally obtained by other mechanics." It was decided to investigate the evils connected with the trade, to discover whether they resulted from foreign or home competition, the power loom, or all of these put together. [2] In 1842 the weavers of Moyamensing and Kensington, Philadelphia, struck against a reduction in their prices. There was some rioting, the strikers entering the homes of the 'scab' weavers and cutting the chains from the looms and burning them. An attempt was made to burn down Kemptons Mill at Manayunk, but it was defended by the Roxborough volunteers and a number of citizens. Hearing that the manufacturers were to hold a meeting in a certain house, the weavers threatened the tenant that they would tear the house down if the meeting were allowed to be held. Attempts to arrest the leaders only caused further disturbance and one prisoner was rescued from the constables. Again, in January, chains were cut from the looms and dragged through the streets and threats were made to destroy factories. One of the weavers was put in jail and a crowd of rioters, numbering 400 to 500, collected in the market-house intending to effect a rescue. The sheriff collected 200 to 300 deputies and attempted to dislodge the market-house garrison, but was driven off, leaving a num-

---

[1] Freedley, *Philadelphia and Its Manufacturers*, p. 282.
[2] Commons, *Documentary History*, vol. 6, p. 341.

ber of wounded behind. Nine of the rioters were arrested and three military companies called out to disperse the band. The matter was settled by a conference between the weavers and the employers, January 13, 1843. "God knows," said a contemporary, "some of the poor fellows have great cause to feel rebellious. Empty stomachs and empty purses are not the best advocates of good order." At the prices they were paid, in some cases, a man and his wife, with constant, close application sixteen hours a day, could not earn over $2.50 a week.[1]

By 1846 the weavers had been reduced to "a state of abject misery and suffering." Three years before they had been able to earn, by constant work, $4.25 to $4.75 a week, but that had rapidly fallen to $2.50. "The broken-down, haggard, and toil-worn appearance of these men, bears faithful witness to the severity and increasingness of their labors. While the squalid poverty which surrounds their miserable homes, their ragged, haggard-looking wives and children, are enough to move the stones themselves to raise their voices against the heartless oppression which produces such human suffering. . . ." [2]

Piece rates for hand-loom weaving, from 1836 to 1845, were as follows: [3]

	1836	1840	1845
Check fabrics...............$	.07	.05½	.03½
	.08	.06	.04
	.10	.06½	.05
	.11½	.09½	.06
White work................	.13½	.10	.07
	.11¼	.09	.06
	.09½	.07¼	.04½
	.07	.06	.04
	.06¾	.04½	.02½
	.05½	.04	.02

[1] Pennsylvania Bureau of Industrial Statistics, 1882, *Report*, pp. 266–68.

[2] *Young America*, January 3, 1846. It was, of course, not 'heartless oppression' that produced this suffering, but the competition of power looms. But that did not make the suffering less painful.

[3] *The True Sun*, quoted in *Young America*, January 3, 1846.

This was a decline of about fifty per cent in ten years. There was, of course, no improvement in the loom or any other way in which the output might be increased except by adding to the already long hours or effort of the work.

The carpet weavers were not so badly off as the rest of the hand-loom weavers until the Bigelow power loom was introduced in the forties and women began to supplant the men. In 1845 the carpet mills at Lowell were said to be the only ones in the world using power looms and a young woman could easily do the work which, with the hand looms, required the hard labor of three men.[1] There were, at this time, about five hundred rag-carpet weavers in New York City, of whom only three hundred were working at their trade. "The low wages and scarcity of work have caused a large number of them to turn their attention to other branches of industry."[2] Journeymen weavers worked ten hours in the summer, and in winter from 7 A.M. to 9 P.M. Six dollars a week was considered good wages and the average was four dollars a week.

The Thompsonville and Tariffville carpet weavers went on strike in 1846 against a reduction to sixty cents a day,[3] and a Carpet Weavers' Convention was held in the fall to attempt, by united action of some sort, to ward off impending reductions. The proposed reductions were said to be made necessary by the new tariff and involved a considerable cut in the weavers' average wages which were, at that time, about $4.50 a week. Much was said at this convention of the control exercised by the Thompson Carpet Mills at Thompsonville, Connecticut, over the rest of the manufacturers,[4] and it was claimed that the proposed reduction would make American wages eleven per cent lower than those of carpet weavers in England.[5] This reduction seems

[1] Miles, *Lowell as It Was and as It Is*, p. 100.
[2] New York *Daily Tribune*, September 26, 1845.
[3] *Voice of Industry*, November 6, 1846.
[4] *Ibid.*, September 8, 1846.
[5] *Ibid.*, November 6, 1846.

either to have been avoided, or regained at Thompsonville and Tariffville the following year.[1]

THE HATTERS

Formerly the journeyman hatters had been better paid than almost any other class of mechanics, receiving $16, $18, and $20 a week. But for many years the business of hat-making had been falling off. A hat that was made in 1845 for seventy-five or even fifty cents would have brought the journeyman $1 in 1840, $1.25 in 1836, and $1.25 to $1.50 in 1832. The prices for finishing were about the same.[2] Men who were getting $12 a week in 1835 could make only $8 a week in 1845, and while, at the earlier date, they could depend on constant employment, they later lost one third of their time.[3]

The hat finishers of New York had been organized in the "Hat Finishers Protective Society" since 1820. They had about three hundred members and maintained or tried to maintain strict apprenticeship regulations.[4] An apprentice was required to serve four full years, "and any one who binds himself for a short period after the age of twenty-one is considered an intruder upon the rights of journeymen, and any employer who engages such a 'foul' journeyman will not be held blameless for thus opposing the known rules of the trade with respect to the apprentice system."[5] A shop with more than three apprentices was to be considered 'foul' after April, 1849.

There was also among the hat finishers a benevolent

---

[1] *Voice of Industry*, April 28, 1847.

[2] New York *Daily Tribune*, November 7, 1845.

[3] *Young America*, November 29, 1844, and July 19, 1845.

[4] The Hatters' Union and the manufacturers had some trouble in Massachusetts in 1859 because a Boston dealer refused to obey the union regulations regarding apprentices and non-union men. The union struck and for three years this dealer ran a 'foul' shop, but finally met the union requirements and came again into the trade agreement. (Massachusetts Bureau of Labor Statistics, *Eleventh Annual Report*, 1880–81.)

[5] New York *Daily Tribune*, June 1, 1850.

society organized in 1843, with 130 members and $3000 in the treasury. It paid a sick benefit of $4 a week.

In 1844 a convention was called of the journeymen hatters of the United States, "to consider the cause of the decline of the trade for the last ten years, the inadequacy of the wages of the journeymen, and to suggest a remedy for both evils." [1] This convention met in New York in July and drew up a scale of prices which was accepted by many of the New York employers,[2] though in Philadelphia and Newark the work was said to have been done for less than half these prices.[3] At these rates the average worker, who could make from twelve to fifteen hats a week, could earn $8 to $12. Finishers could make from $9 to $10 a week. The sewing and trimming of the hats was done by women and girls.[4]

CABINET-MAKERS

During the same ten years a great falling-off in wages was experienced by the cabinet-makers. In 1836 the average journeyman could make, when paid by the piece, from $12 to $15 a week and those who were paid by the week averaged about the same. In 1840 wages had fallen to $8, and, in 1845, it was said that a majority of the journeymen could earn no more than $5 a week. The very best workmen at the later date, in the finest kind of work, were paid only $8. The reason given for this falling-off was the growth

---

[1] *Working Man's Advocate*, June 8, 1844.

[2] *Ibid.*, August 24 and September 21, 1844.

[3] New York *Daily Tribune*, November 7, 1845. This list was as follows:

Full brush hats	87½¢	No. 1 plain hats	31¢
Half brush hats	62½¢	No. 2 plain hats	34¢
Fine Nutrias	75¢	No. 3 plain hats	40¢
Napping sax	34¢	No. 4 plain hats	44¢
Napping half spun	31¢	No. 5 plain hats	50¢
Sizing sax and half sax		9 cents	
Sizing Spanish		7 cents	

[4] *Ibid.*

of wholesale work for the auction shops. This work was done chiefly by Germans who were said to "work rapidly, badly and for almost nothing." The manufacturers were said to go on the immigrant ships as they arrived in New York and engage these men for a year at $20 or $30 and their board.[1]

A journeyman cabinet-maker in Philadelphia, in 1843, complained that "already by the gradual reduction of the price of labor, the journeymen are reduced to the necessity of laboring twelve and fourteen hours a day to gain a mere subsistence." The employers admitted the facts, but contended in rebuttal that the fault lay with the journeymen.

We also feel sorry to confess that it is true that the wages are low. . . . Some years ago when the trade was brisk the journeymen made out and we agreed to a certain rule to govern the price of labor; it continued in force until, from the hardness of the time and the general scarcity of money, we were compelled to ask and, in fact, insist on a reduction in the prices of making all the articles sold by us. The offer was instantly rejected by the men, and they, with a view to compelling us to accede to their demands, commenced working for a set of individuals who manufactured a kind of furniture so miserably made and so poorly finished that an auction room was the only proper place to have it exhibited and sold. This small fry of employers, to enable them to sell their work cheap, actually gave the journeymen much lower wages than we offered. . . . In course of time the prices given by these men became in a great measure the standard price of labor; and now the consequences to the workmen are very plain.[2]

LABORERS

General statements about the conditions and wages of laborers are subject to so many exceptions, because of the wide diversity of conditions from place to place and from winter to summer, as to be almost useless. Because of the scarcity of manual labor in the early years in America,

---

[1] New York *Daily Tribune*, November 11, 1845.
[2] Commons, *Documentary History*, vol. 7, p. 107.

wages had been relatively high, but with the influx of the Irish and Germans in the forties there was a decline in the centers of population, at least. In the fifties laborers' wages increased somewhat with rising prices.

The normal wage for day labor in the thirties was one dollar a day, and in Philadelphia, in 1839, the laborers struck for an advance to $1.12½. This was allowed by some of the contractors, but most of them either refused it altogether or increased, in lieu of wages, the ration of whiskey. The whiskey allowance was one and a half pints a day, given out in nine doses.[1]

A schedule of wages of masons and masons' laborers published in 1846 showed no increase in either case for the preceding decade. In 1836 the wages of masons in New York were $1.75 a day and of laborers, $1. In 1840 masons' wages had fallen to $1.50 and those of laborers to 75 cents. By 1845 they had recovered and masons were again getting $1.75 and laborers, $1.[2] In 1843 the laborers' union in New York declared that $1 a day was a reasonable wage,[3] and objected to the employment of convicts on the roads, a method of using prison labor that was supported by the mechanics.[4]

The "Laborers' Union Benevolent Association" of New York was formed in 1843 and chartered in 1845. The initiation fee was $2 and the monthly dues 12½ cents. A sick benefit was paid of $2 a week and a death benefit of $15.[5]

In the spring of 1846 a large number of Irish laborers who had been at work during the winter for 65 cents a day went on strike for 87½ cents. As a result of the strike, the contractors hired

a cargo of freshly landed Germans to take their places and ordered the old laborers to quit the premises, which they refused to do

---

[1] Pennsylvania Bureau of Industrial Statistics, 1882, *Report*, p. 266, vol. 9.

[2] *Mechanics' Mirror*, June, 1846.

[3] New York *Daily Tribune*, September 16, 1843.

[4] *Ibid.*   [5] *Ibid.*, May 8, 1850.

and resorted to the lawless and unjustifiable step of endeavoring
to drive the Germans from the work by intimidation and vio-
lence. Of course the military were called out, the Irish overawed,
the Germans protected in their work, and thus the matter stands.
So far, the contractors may be said to have triumphed.[1]

Laborers' wages in the mills and elsewhere were no
higher. Laborers with families to support were receiving as
low as $250 a year at Lowell and were said to work harder
than any other class of men.[2] The Essex Corporation in
the "new city" of Methuen became involved in a strike
at this time as a result of an attempt to reduce the wages
of the Irish laborers to eighty-four cents a day.[3] In 1848
the Irish laborers, on an extension of the Connecticut River
Railroad, were being paid seventy cents a day and struck
for eighty-five cents.[4] In 1850 Mooney reported that laborers' wages in the United States were eighty cents a day,[5]
and in New York they varied from $1 to $1.25. The same
year the Laborers' Union decided to strike for a general rate
of $1.12½.[6] The "Tribune" pointed out that the laborer
could work on an average only 200 days in the year,
which would give him $200 a year at the common rate and
$225 at the rate demanded by the laborers, and that this
was not equal to 62½ cents a day in a farming community.[7]

Wages of laborers began to increase after 1850 with the
general rise in prices that followed the gold discoveries. In
1852 the New York laborers demanded $1.25 a day, an ad-
vance of 12½ cents over their demand of 1850,[8] and the
following year laborers in leather stores demanded $1.50 a
day and passed a resolution that "as all mechanics and
laboring men have justly asked and obtained an advance in
wages, we feel that we are justly entitled to do the same so

---

[1] New York *Weekly Tribune*, May 2, 1846.
[2] *Voice of Industry*, July 3, 1846.
[3] *Ibid.*, October 16, 1846.   [4] *Ibid.*, March 10, 1848.
[5] Commons, *Documentary History*, vol. 7, pp. 75–77.
[6] New York *Daily Tribune*, May 13, 1850.
[7] *Ibid.*, May 14, 1850.   [8] *Ibid.*, May 1, 1852.

as to enable us to supply our families with the necessaries of life, which we cannot do at present, rents and provisions being so enormously high." [1]

[1] New York *Daily Tribune*, May 2, 1853.

The following table, compiled by Miss Edith Abbott, shows a slight increase of general laborers' wages over the two decades:

Wages: Unskilled laborer.

	Gen. Lab.	Team- ster	Watch- man	Yard hands	Coal- wheelers	Quarry- men	Fact. Op. unskilled	Help- ers	Sum- mary
1840..	101.5	137.6	108.9	64.6	68.3		80.0	89.2	95.9
1842..						85.1			
1860..	103.0	103.6	101.9	105.1	90.3	106.9	98.7	105.8	104.0
									Plus 8.1

(Abbott, "Unskilled Laborer," *Journal of Political Economy*, vol. 13, p. 366.)

CHAPTER V

THE NEW POWER: THE FACTORY CONTROVERSY

THE new industrialism found its completest expression in the textile mills of New England, New York, and Pennsylvania. Here the New Power was most firmly established and the new discipline most intense. In the barracks-like mills by the swift rivers of the northern seaboard the Industrial Revolution reached completion, and the lesser status of the industrial worker was revealed. And there developed in the forties a remarkable controversy over the Factory System, originating, in part, in the political field and involving the tariff question, and, in part, in the feeling that the new industrialism was alien to and destructive of American ideals and standards.

The introduction of the cotton industry in Massachusetts at the beginning of the century was achieved under difficulties that arose, on the one hand, from the want of a labor force and, on the other, from the English control of the new machines and the technical knowledge required to set them in operation. A new labor force was available in the women and girls of New England, once their initial aversion to the factory discipline could be broken down.[1] The degraded condition of the operatives of the English mill towns was notorious, and Americans, including the

[1] When General Humphrey built a paper-mill and cotton and woolen factories at Humphreysville, 1804, he "entertained the project, among others, of improving the lot of the poor by providing them with work. In carrying out his paternalistic scheme he built cottages for his workmen, each of which had a small garden. He also provided teachers for the apprentices. Every act of immorality was punished by instant dismissal. But the prevailing opinion was so unfavorable to the factory system, the horrors of which were fully described in the English newspapers, that many parents refused to allow their children to accept employment in his works." (*Old World Questions and New World Answers*, 1887.)

Boston capitalists intent on cotton manufacture, had no desire to reproduce those conditions here.

"The question . . . arose and was deeply considered," said Nathan Appleton, "whether this degradation was the result of the peculiar occupation or of other and distinct causes. . . ." [1] The matter was decided in favor of the latter hypothesis, and the Boston capitalists who had interested themselves in cotton manufacture proceeded to make such arrangements as seemed good to them to attract the New England women into the mills and guard them from immoral influences as best they could.

This protection involved what is known as the "Waltham System" which was copied in the foundation of Lowell and came to be regarded as the perfection of what an industrial community should be. The basis of the Waltham system was the company boarding-house, where the girls were required to be in at 10 P.M. and generally to live under the somewhat fictitious supervision of the boarding-house keeper. Upon this basis was erected a puritanical paternalism originally intended for the welfare of the girls, but capable — in the hands of agents less high-principled than the early mill-owners — of being turned into a very effective and harmful despotism. In addition to the boarding-houses, the Waltham system involved the payment of wages in cash, the 'moral police' or community censorship of morals, the requirement that the girls should attend church, discharge for immoral conduct, and a thorough understanding among the corporations as to wages, hours, and the 'blacklist.'

I visited the corporate factory establishment of Waltham within a few miles of Boston [said Harriet Martineau in 1834]. The establishment is for spinning and weaving of cotton alone and the construction of the requisite machinery. Five hundred girls were employed at the time of my visit. The girls can earn two and sometimes three dollars a week besides their board. The little

---

[1] Appleton, *Introduction of the Power Loom*, pp. 15–16.

children earn one dollar a week. Most of the girls live in houses provided by the corporation. . . . When sisters come to the mill it is a common practice for them to bring their mother to keep house for them and some other companions, in a dwelling built by their own earnings. In this case they save enough out of their board to clothe themselves and have two or three dollars to spare. Some have thus cleared off mortgages from their fathers' farms; others have educated the hope of the family at college; and many are rapidly accumulating an independence. I saw a whole street of houses built with the earnings of the girls; some with piazzas and green venetian blinds, and all neat and sufficiently spacious.

The factory people built the church which stands conspicuous on the green in the midst of the place. The minister's salary, eight hundred dollars last year, is raised by a tax on the pews. The corporation gave them a building for a Lyceum which they have furnished with a good library and where they have lectures every winter, the best that money can procure. The girls have, in many instances, private libraries of some value.

The managers of the various factory establishments keep the wages as nearly equal as possible and then let the girls freely shift from one to another. . . . The people work about seventy hours a week on an average. . . . All look like well-dressed young ladies. The health is good, or rather it is no worse than elsewhere.[1]

This picture is somewhat *couleur de rose* and naïve in its treatment of the compulsory tax for the upkeep of the church and the uniform wage and freedom of movement of the operatives. The only fault Miss Martineau found with the mills was the overcrowding of the boarding-houses where girls sometimes slept three in a bed and six or more in a room. She must have been misinformed as to the hours of labor which were nearer seventy-five than seventy a week.

But making all allowances for the enchantment of distance, the laudatory intentions and propagandist purposes of those who celebrated the ideality of the early mills, the fact remains that the same broader basis of security and well-being is found there that was found in the earlier conditions in the shoe trade and other occupations. Before the

[1] Martineau, *Society in America*, vol. 2, pp. 57–58.

appearance of the greatly dreaded "permanent factory population," bad times had few terrors for the mill operatives. They simply returned to the farms from which they came, welcoming the holiday, and suffering no ill effects from unemployment or low wages. But the progress of the Industrial Revolution destroyed, not only the semi-agricultural factory population, but the New England farm that made its independence real. "So long," said Professor Clark, "as every neighborhood had its small water-driven factory, rural workers might obtain industrial employment without leaving home. . . . But when the manufactures were gathered into large establishments remote from the farm household the latter were no longer self-sufficing. . . ." [1] As the New England farms disappeared, the freedom of the mill operatives contracted. They could no longer escape. Unemployment ceased to be a vacation in the country and a permanent factory population became a reality.

In sharp contrast with the Waltham system there was found in the Middle States, and especially in Rhode Island, what can be called the English system of *laissez-faire*. This was the original method of cotton manufacture in New England, having been established by Samuel Slater at Pawtucket before the beginning of the century. The Rhode Island system, to be found also at Fall River, Massachusetts, was not a conscious method at all, but simply a growth along English lines with the material at hand. Instead of employing adults almost exclusively, as in Massachusetts, whole families were employed, and it is in this district that child labor was chiefly found. There was no attempt made by Slater and those who followed him to guard the morals of the operatives or to do anything for them within or without the mills. There were no company boarding-houses, the operatives being allowed to find what homes they could, and instead of cash wages being paid,

[1] Clark, *History of Manufactures*, pp. 392, 393.

factory stores were established and store orders issued.[1] The first mill opened by Slater was operated by seven boys and two girls between the ages of seven and eleven, and some of the early mills recruited children from the almshouses and overseers of the poor.[2]

The contrast of the two systems is interesting because the scarcity of factory labor was probably as great in Rhode Island as in Massachusetts, which suggests that the Waltham system was the result of the Puritan traditions of the Boston capitalists, rather than the real necessities of the case, while the presence of the company store in Rhode Island reveals it as less a convenience for the operatives than a means of exploitation by the companies. For if the company store had been a real convenience to the operatives, as is often assumed, it would probably have been found in Lowell rather than Pawtucket, though the large percentage of single women at Lowell would have reduced its trade.

"In collecting our help," said one of the Connecticut mill-owners, "we are obliged to employ poor families and generally those having the greatest number of children . . . where their only means of livelihood has been the labor of the father and mother, while the children spent their time mostly at play."[3] In 1853, in the Rhode Island mills, "little, half-clothed children" were found "seeking their way to the factory in the very darkness of a winter's

[1] Batchelder, *Introduction and Early Progress of Cotton Manufacture in the United States*, pp. 74–75. The Rhode Island system was described by the mayor of Fall River: "If there happened to be, in a given family of eight or ten or twelve persons, two or three who were old enough and strong enough to work in a mill, the whole family came with them without preliminary arrangement for tenement or food. He had known as many as three generations in one house, and the united earnings of the workers therein were not adequate to the maintenance of the whole, especially in times of low wages." (Mass. Senate Doc. No. 21, 1868, p. 25.)

[2] Josiah Quincy, "Journey . . . " Mass. Hist. Soc., 2d Series, *Proceedings*, vol. IV, p. 124.

[3] White, *Memoir of Samuel Slater*, letter from Smith Wilkinson, Pomfret, Connecticut, p. 127.

night." [1] And their numbers, until checked by effective legislation, were increasing. [2]

In 1831 "Pitkins Statistics" showed Rhode Island as the only state with a large child labor force in the mills. [3] In 1853 there were, in the mills of Rhode Island, 59 children under nine years of age; 621 between nine and twelve years; and 1177 between twelve and fifteen years, a total of 1857 under fifteen and 680 under twelve. It was claimed that a great reduction had been made in the employment of young children in the previous four years as a result of improvements of machinery which rendered their employment less desirable. [4] But in 1857 it was said, "the number of our children are annually increasing; while those of them which we are educating are actually decreasing." [5] In 1872 the school commissioner recommended "the enforcement of a law which shall not allow a child to be employed in a manufacturing establishment under twelve years of age." [6] And, in 1875 there were 80 children in the state under nine years employed in the factories and 1178 between nine and eleven years, making a total of 1258 under twelve, as against 680 in 1851. [7]

But the essential difference between Lowell and Rhode Island or Fall River was the psychological one between paternalism and *laissez-faire*. General Oliver, who had been an agent at Lowell, visited Fall River in 1855 and was

[1] Rhode Island Committee on Child Labor, 1853, p. 5.

[2] Towles, "Factory Legislation in Rhode Island," *American Economic Association Quarterly*, 3d series, vol. 9, no. 3, p. 63.

[3] *Pitkins Statistics:* Children under twelve in the mills: New Hampshire, 60; Massachusetts, none; Connecticut, 439; and Rhode Island, 3472; but the Committee on Education of the New England Association of Farmers, Mechanics and Other Workingmen, in 1832, gave the number of children of both sexes as 1600 between seven and sixteen years in New Hampshire, Massachusetts, and Rhode Island. (Commons, *Documentary History*, vol. 5, pp. 196–98.)

[4] Rhode Island Committee on Child Labor, *Report*, pp. 4–7.

[5] Committee of Public Schools, 1857, *Report*, p. 13.

[6] *Ibid.*, 1872.

[7] Commissioner of Industrial Statistics, 1887, *Report*, vol. I, p. 18.

greatly shocked by the attitude of the agents at the latter place.

I inquired of the agent of a principal factory whether it was the custom of the manufacturers to do anything for the physical, intellectual, and moral welfare of their work-people. . . . "We never do," he said. "As for myself, I regard my work-people just as I regard my machinery. So 'long as they can do my work for what I choose to pay them, I keep them, getting out of them all I can. What they do or how they fare outside my walls I don't know, nor do I consider it my business to know. They must look out for themselves as I do for myself. When my machines get old and useless, I reject them and get new, and these people are part of my machinery." [1]

A Holyoke manager found his hands 'languorous' in the early morning because they had breakfasted. He tried working them without breakfast and got three thousand more yards of cloth a week made. [2]

It would appear at first glance that there could be no comparison, from the standpoint of the operatives, between the two systems; that the puritanical paternalism of Lowell was infinitely superior to the callous indifference of Fall River. Nevertheless, two rather unexpected facts emerge to modify this opinion: the attack on the factory system by the intellectuals centered not on the evil conditions of Fall River, but on the relatively admirable conditions of Lowell; and the operatives' revolt began at the former rather than at the latter place. This would suggest, at least, that there were elements in the Lowell situation that were regarded as even more harmful than bad conditions, and that the Fall River system left the operatives greater initiative. It would be unwise to press these deductions too far because it is equally possible to say that the Fall River revolt was the result of exceptionally bad conditions and the attack on Lowell, the result of its proximity to Boston.

The Lowell factory system was being attacked in our period from two directions. The Battle of Books repre-

[1] Mass. Senate Doc. no. 21, 1868, p. 23.   [2] Ibid.

sented the opposition of the intellectuals and was directed
chiefly against the alleged tendency to degrade the morals
and health of the operative, while the attack of the operatives themselves was chiefly against the 'tyranny' and
'despotism' of the system, its increasing discipline and anti-
republican nature.

That the factory system contains in itself the elements of slavery, we think no sound reasoning can deny, and every day continues to add power to its incorporate sovereignty, while the sovereignty of the working people decreases in the same ratio.[1]

Like other workers of the period, the factory operatives
— men and women — felt that they were losing something
of their dignity and independence, so that, from the point
of view of the workers, much of the heated argument over
factory conditions missed the point. The worker objected
to his cage, whether it was gilded as in Lowell, or rusty and
unkempt as in Fall River.

In the matter of discipline the Fall River system had
advantages over that of Lowell. Once out of the Fall River
mills, the worker was free, while in Lowell there was hardly
an hour of the day or a relationship of any sort that was not
covered by the regulations, written or understood, of the
corporations.

The manufacturing interest of New England is a new world
[said a eulogist of the Lowell corporations], in its police it is *impe-
rium in imperio*. It has been said than an absolute despotism,
justly administered . . . would be a perfect government. But the
police of Lowell adds a trait which would not be found in such a
government, though administered with perfect justice. For at the
same time that it is an absolute despotism, it is a most perfect democracy. Any of its subjects can depart from it at pleasure without the least restraint. . . . Thus all the philosophy of mind which
enters vitally into government by the people . . . is combined with
a set of rules which the operatives have no voice in forming or administering, yet of a nature not merely perfectly just, but human,
benevolent, patriarchal in a high degree. . . .[2]

---

[1] *Voice of Industry*, October 9, 1846.
[2] *New Bedford Mercury*, quoted in the *Voice of Industry*, January 14,
1848.

This sort of casuistry was bound to emerge in a situation that wanted explaining, as that created in a republican society by the development of a despotic industrial power undoubtedly did. It was not a theory of democracy that would have satisfied Lincoln and it did not satisfy those who were actually involved. It was against despotism, whether benevolent or malicious, that the industrial worker was in revolt. "It is the monopoly feature that we have opposed. . . . It is the divorce of labor and capital in the repartition of dividends — the fact that labor is not represented in these companies. . . . They who work in the mills ought to own them." [1] "This gathering is to be held in Lowell," said the "New England Operative" of one of the working-men's conventions. "Here in this famed 'Manchester of America' amidst thousands of living — perhaps we should say dying — witnesses of the blasting influence of monarchical principles on democratic soil." [2]

In dealing with the conditions of the mill operatives in New England, and especially in Lowell, it is important to understand the nature of the source material. The usual sources for this information are the works of Miles, Scoresby, Green, Bartlett; the descriptions of Chevalier, Dickens, and Harriet Martineau; and the "Lowell" and "New England Offering." The descriptions of prominent travelers are liable at all times to be superficial, and are especially misleading in this instance because of the contrast they had always in mind with the darker conditions of the English mill towns. The rest of this material is — though this has not been generally recognized — a part of a rather elaborate defense of the factory system, propagandist in its nature, and elicited by attacks from various quarters upon the corporations. It is necessary, then, if this material is to be given its proper weight, to place it in the controversy over the factory system, of which it was a part.

[1] *Voice of Industry*, March 28, 1848.
[2] Quoted in *The Awl*, March 8, 1845.

The factory controversy began with an editorial in the
Boston "Daily Times" (Democrat) for Saturday, July 13,
1839, entitled "A Manufacturing Population." The interest of the "Times" in the matter was partly political. The
Whigs had always contended that the factories gave easy,
pleasurable, and remunerative employment to women
and girls who would otherwise have been idle, and that
the fears of the opponents of the system were unfounded.
The "Times" undertook to show that

the young girls are compelled to work in unhealthy confinement
for too many hours every day; that their food is both unhealthy
and scanty; that they are not allowed sufficient time to eat: . . .
that they are crowded together in ill-ventilated apartments in the
boarding-houses of the corporations, and that in consequence
they become pale, feeble, and finally broken in constitution . . .
and that hundreds of the vilest of the female sex throng to the
manufactories with corruption in their manners and upon their
tongues to breathe out the pestilence of the brothel in the
boarding-places.[1]

The "Times" objected to the fact that the girls were
made to board at the company houses except when they
had friends or relatives in Lowell; that they had to be in
their rooms at ten o'clock; and that the price of their board
was fixed by the corporations at $1.50 a week [2] and de-
ducted from their wages. It was claimed that the price of
board was too low, that a decent table could not be maintained at the price when potatoes were selling for 75 cents
to $1 a peck, flour was $9 to $12 a barrel, and beef 10 to 16
cents a pound. The girls were underfed and unhealthy-
looking except the newcomers from the country.

In the early days, the "Times" contended, conditions
had been better. When the Merrimack Mill was started, besides the workmen employed from Europe the proprietors
had to rely on such girls as they could obtain to attend the
looms and spindles. These girls came in gradually from the

[1] Boston *Daily Times*, July 13, 1839.
[2] It was $1.25 at this time.

surrounding country — daughters of farmers and mechanics, "generally poor, but of unblemished reputation." Provisions were cheap, the food sufficient, and the girls seemed happy and healthy. They dressed well and preferred the mills as their own mistresses to being servants. Many of them saved money and went home, but others squandered their earnings and found themselves tied to the mills. But the supply was still inadequate and the corporations had to send men out to scour the country through New Hampshire, Vermont, and Canada. Thus the permanent mill population increased and their dependence upon the corporations. The labor turnover was tremendous, one hundred girls arriving and leaving every day for several weeks in the spring and fall, but always some remained behind to swell the factory population, unfitted to be wives and mothers, in slavish dependence on the mills.

When the corporations began to realize, said the "Times," that this permanent factory population was increasing, they reduced wages by agreement. On the first occasion the girls 'turned out,' but new hands were found, and "there has been created and there is now growing up in Lowell a manufacturing population whose tendency in the scale of civilization, health, morals, and intellectuality, is manifestly downwards." [1]

As to the morals of the girls, the "Times" quoted a Lowell physician to the effect that

there used to be in Lowell an association of young men called "The Old Line" who had an understanding with a great many of the factory girls and who used to introduce young men of their acquaintance, visitors to the place, to the girls for immoral purposes. Balls were held at various places attended mostly by these young men and girls, with some others who did not know the object of the association, and after the dancing was over the girls were taken to infamous places of resort in Lowell and the vicinity and were not returned to their homes until daylight.[2]

---

[1] Boston *Daily Times*, July 16, 1839.   [2] *Ibid.*, July 17, 1839.

Another medical practitioner in Lowell stated that, in one week, he had more than seventy persons apply to him for remedies for venereal diseases, most of whom were girls. Occupants of brothels in New York and Boston who had become diseased were also said to have entered the mills. The late deputy sheriff of Lowell had stated that he had found three houses to which these professional prostitutes were in the habit of bringing factory girls.[1]

Dr. Elisha Bartlett of Lowell replied to the "Times" articles in the Lowell "Courier,"[2] and this was later published as a pamphlet under the title "A Vindication of the Character and Condition of the Females Employed in the Lowell Mills against the charges contained in the Boston Times and Boston Quarterly Review."[3] The editor of the "Courier" also replied, as did Harriet Farley, editor of the "Lowell Offering."

As is frequently the case in controversies of this sort, the opponents were not talking about the same thing and never really came to grips. Bartlett insisted that the morals and health of the factory operatives were good, while the "Times" claimed that their morals and health were getting bad. Bartlett was thinking of a condition, often of a past condition, and the "Times" of a tendency. Neither was concerned with the problem that bothered the worker, the problem of social status and freedom. The mill girls had been, and the majority perhaps still were, what Bartlett claimed, but at the same time they were becoming more or less what the "Times" insisted they were: "a permanent factory population" of a more degraded sort than the New England mill girls of the twenties and thirties.

Dr. Bartlett dealt chiefly with health, morals, chances of marriage and wages, and his argument was followed

---

[1] Boston *Daily Times*, July 18, 1839. "Not a year has passed in the last six lustrums that has not witnessed the slaughter of more innocents in Lowell than Herod slew in Bethlehem." (Cowley, *History of Lowell*, pp. 121–22.)

[2] July 20, 23, 25, 27 and 30, 1839.

[3] The *Review* criticisms were similar to those of the *Times*.

quite closely by Miles and Scoresby in 1845. He made a statistical comparison between Lowell and Portsmouth, New Hampshire, that will be treated later, and declared that "the manufacturing population of this city is the healthiest portion of the population." [1] He defended the morals of the factory girls, claiming that the mill overseers, the 'moral police' of the corporations, and the censorship of the girls themselves kept the tone of the community high.[2] He insisted even that the morals of the girls improved on coming from the country where all was not as pure as it looked.

As to wages, the average, clear of board, amounted to about two dollars per week. The number of depositors in the Lowell Savings Institution was 1976 and the amount of deposits $305,796.75. Of these depositors, 978 were factory girls. The amount of their deposits is not given, but it is estimated at not less than $100,000, while it was a common thing for a girl to have $500 in the bank. Bartlett claimed that the girls' chances of marriage were good and the boarding-house keepers quite able to make a living and supply satisfactory food if they managed properly.[3]

The controversy was continued by a reply to Dr. Bartlett which appeared in the "Vox Populi" of Lowell in 1841. This was written by "A Citizen of Lowell" and was later published under the title "Corporations and Operatives: Being an exposition of the condition of factory operatives and a review of the 'Vindication' by Elisha Bartlett, M.D." The reply was an able discussion that left nothing of Bartlett's mortality and marriage statistics, but began in a demagogic vein that tended to obscure the value of the later argument. The Lowell "Citizen" charged the defenders of the factories with being paid "servants of in-

[1] Bartlett, *Vindication*, p. 13.

[2] *Ibid.*, p. 19. The corporations maintained a rigid blacklist and no operative who was not given an 'honorable discharge' could get work in any corporation in Lowell or the vicinity.

[3] *Ibid.*, pp. 21-22.

terested aristocracies," a "pensioned press" and "bought
priesthood." The question of the hours of employment,
that later supplanted all others, was here first emphasized.
It was claimed that the operatives had only fifteen minutes in which to eat their meals when time was deducted
for going to and from the boarding-houses. The price allowed for board had been $1.25 until 1836, when it had
been raised to $1.37½ because the boarding-house keepers
had been unable to live. There it remained until 1841,
when it was again reduced to $1.25.[1] The boarding-houses
were overrun with vermin. The hours in the mills were
nearly thirteen a day and not less then twelve and one-half
of actual toil. But this was to reckon only the time actually
in the mills, and even this was not correct because some
corporations cheated the operatives by starting before the
ringing of the bell. Reckoning the time stolen and the time
occupied in preparing for meals, eating, and going to and
fro, the operatives were engaged fifteen hours out of the
twenty-four.

Not only were the hours long, but they were getting
longer. The corporations were adding to them "year after
year, week after week, minute by minute," until they ran
fifteen minutes a day longer in 1841 than twelve years before. "I do not believe," said the "Citizen of Lowell,"
"that there is upon the face of the earth any large class
of persons who labor incessantly for so many hours each
day as do the factory operatives of New England." [2]

In the matter of health, no class of persons in the country
were so unfavorably situated. The slaves were infinitely
better off than the factory operatives, and if the moral and
intellectual condition of the latter was better no thanks
were due to the factory system, "for that allows less time
for the improvement of the intellect and morals than the
slaves enjoy."

[1] This was paid by the corporations out of the operatives' wages.
[2] *Corporations and Operatives*, p. 43.

Wages, too, had been cut, by organized combination among the corporations, three times in the last eight years (1832–40) and a further reduction was made in 1841. The corporations were short of help and had to send agents into Maine, New Hampshire, and Vermont, and these were paid so much per head for getting girls for the factories. In addition to this, they circulated propaganda to the effect that Lowell was a paradise — such as "A Sketch of Lowell" by a former postmaster, which was circulated throughout New England, and "The Lowell Offering," the operatives' magazine. No criticism was made of the "Offering" itself, but only of the use made of it by the corporations who were said to have been active in circulating and maintaining it as propaganda. The "Citizen" claimed that there would be no scarcity of female labor for the factories if it were not for their evil reputation and that the "Offering" was being used by the corporations to eradicate this. The character of the articles in the "Offering" were such as

to quiet all discontent among the operatives so that they may remain and submit without murmur to all the evils of their condition. There is no breath of complaint to be found in any of the productions of these female writers; they speak of nothing but their enjoyment. . . . Like poor, caged birds while singing of the roses . . . they forget the bars of their prison. . . .[1]

The publication of this magazine had been transferred to William Schouler, editor of the Lowell "Courier," "well known as the pensioned press and political organ of the corporations in this city." [2]

The Lowell "Citizen" then considered the defense of Dr. Bartlett. As to the health of the operatives and the low mortality of Lowell as compared with Portsmouth, he

[1] *Corporations and Operatives*, p. 25.
[2] *Ibid.*, p. 27, note. William Schouler was made Chairman of the Committee of the Massachusetts Legislature which reported against the Ten-Hour petitions in 1845, and this report was used as a basis for later rejections.

says, in the first place, that the girls go back to the country when they are sick; second, that the employment affects the health "by gradually encroaching ... by slow and imperceptible advances"; and, third, that Dr. Bartlett's comparison with Portsmouth is entirely misleading.

Lowell, said the "Citizen," was a young and vigorous city that had sprung up within a few years and had a population of 22,000, most of whom were young persons who had not been born there, but had come in from the country in the prime of life and did not stay long enough to grow old. When their health became frail they left the city and their places were taken by other young and vigorous persons. In 1830 the population of Lowell was only 6474, and, in 1840, it had grown to 20,816, an increase of 14,000, mostly young and marriageable persons. In 1840, 10,717 of Lowell's 20,816 were between the ages of fifteen and thirty years, and 13,573 between fifteen and forty years. The number over sixty was only 275 and those under ten, 3681.

Portsmouth, New Hampshire, on the other hand, was an old and decaying community, only one third the size of Lowell, and there was no good reason why Dr. Bartlett should go outside of Massachusetts for his comparison, except to find one to his liking. The population of Portsmouth instead of growing was declining, from 8083 in 1830 to 7834 in 1840. Of these, 2345 were between the ages of fifteen and forty years, 452 were over sixty, and 1949 under ten.

But, our statistician points out, "by far the greatest mortality to which mankind is subjected occurs under the age of ten and over the age of sixty." The number in Lowell under ten years of age was one in six, while the number in Portsmouth was one in four. The number over sixty in Lowell, with three times the population of Portsmouth, was 275 as against 452 in Portsmouth. There was then an obvious reason why Lowell should show a lower mortality rate in relation to the total population than was shown for Portsmouth.

As to the chances of marriage, the disingenuousness of Dr. Bartlett's choice for comparison was again revealed. The marriage rate of a young city might be quite small and yet be greater than that of a city inhabited mostly by old people and children. Dr. Bartlett had shown that there was one marriage to eighty-nine persons in Portsmouth, as against one to eighty persons in Lowell. But the proper comparison was between populations of marriageable age. Thus Portsmouth, with one marriage per eighty-nine persons and a population of 7834, must have had eighty-eight marriages. The number of women between fifteen and forty was 1768, which would give one marriage per twenty marriageable women. Lowell had one marriage in eighty of the population and a population of 20,816, or 260 marriages. The number of women in Lowell between fifteen and forty was 9513, or one marriage per thirty-six and a fraction marriageable women, "notwithstanding that Portsmouth is a place more unfavorable to marriage than any other, not a manufacturing center, in New England." [1]

The fact was, as the "Citizen" pointed out, that "there could not be found in the United States two considerable places more completely opposite." Bartlett had committed the statistical crime of comparing "the chances of marriageable young persons of Lowell with the chances of the unmarriageable old persons and children of Portsmouth." And his comparisons were "completely demolished" when the simple fact was recollected that "in Portsmouth there is an unusual proportion of the population at that age at which persons by the course of nature are most liable to die, while in Lowell there is quite an unusual number at that age in life when persons most usually marry." [2]

The factory controversy waxed warmer, but not more

[1] *Corporations and Operatives*, p. 62.   [2] *Ibid.*, p. 63.

enlightening when the Lowell "Courier" replied to the
"Times," and the latter retorted with the charge that the
"Courier" was owned by one of the corporations of Lowell
and "managed, so far as there is any management about it,
by one of th⌄se miserable, pettifogging young lawyers who
cringe and crawl beneath the nod of wealth and power."
And if said young lawyers wished a gutter argument "let
them come on. The art of blackguarding is easily learned
and we can cull vituperative epithets from a dictionary as
fast perhaps as any man." [1] The "Courier" denied that it
was owned by any corporation and the "Times" asserted
that it was owned by the Locks and Canals Company[2] "not
long since" and would be again if it didn't keep 'right
side up.'

The place of the "Lowell Offering" in this Battle of
Books is worth considering. In 1839 the Reverend Abel C.
Thomas and the Reverend Thomas B. Thayer, pastors of
the First and Second Universalist Churches in Lowell,
organized 'improvement circles' among the young people
of their parishes, the majority of whom were operatives in
the mills. At these meetings there were presented articles,
stories, and so on, written by the members and read without revealing the names of the authors. Some of these were
published by Mr. Thomas under the title "The Lowell
Offering." The first series of four numbers appeared from
October, 1840, to March, 1841, and their reception was so
enthusiastic that a monthly magazine of thirty-two pages
was launched. This was issued regularly by Mr. Thomas
until October, 1842,[3] when it was sold to William Schouler,
proprietor of the Lowell "Courier." [4] "The Operatives'

---

[1] Boston *Daily Times*, July 19, 1839.
[2] This was the original Lowell Company which held the power rights,
manufactured mill machinery, and owned the land on which Lowell was
built.
[3] Robinson, *Loom and Spindle*, pp. 103–04.
[4] The *Lowell Offering*, vol. 3, p. 48.

Magazine" was a similar venture published by "an association of females," edited by Lydia S. Hall and Abby A. Goddard, and issued in 1841–42.[1] It was merged with the "Offering," under the editorship of Harriet Farley and Harriot Curtis.[2] Thus both publications came into the hands of William Schouler. In 1844 this connection was broken and the Misses Farley and Curtis carried on as publishers and editors.

The facts seem to be that these papers, which attracted very wide notice at home and abroad and were advertised as written entirely by the girls in the Lowell mills, came into existence in a quite natural manner under the wing of the church; that their propagandist value was readily seen by the corporations, and they were saved from an early grave, the usual destiny of much of the press of the period, by the intervention of the unofficial representative of the corporations, the Lowell "Courier." In 1845 Miss Curtis retired and the "Offering" ceased publication. It was revived again by Miss Farley in September, 1847, under the title "The New England Offering." It appeared again in 1848 from April to December in 1849, and to March, 1850, when it was finally discontinued.

The "Lowell Offering" was advertised as written entirely by mill operatives and was highly praised by many important people, including Dickens and Whittier. The "New England Offering," which succeeded it, did not pretend to be written by the operatives, but an invitation to contribute was extended to all "who were or had been" such.[3] Mrs. Robinson said that there were in all about fifty-seven contributors [4] and Miss Farley claimed seventy.

Miss Farley started her editorial duties with the explicit refusal to be drawn into any controversies over the con-

---

[1] Robinson, *Loom and Spindle*, pp. 107–08.   [2] *Ibid.*, pp. 103–04.
[3] *Ibid.*
[4] *Ibid.*, p. 118. There was, of course, nothing to astonish in the fact that out of seven thousand New England girls of that time, fifty or seventy should be able to write.

ditions in the mills. "With wages and board, etc., we have nothing to do. These depend on circumstances over which we have no control."[1] But she did not retain this attitude and was increasingly drawn into the defense of the corporations, replying to attacks she interpreted as being made upon the operatives. She, in fact, began by defending the operatives against attacks that were leveled at the corporations and finished by defending the corporations at the expense of the operatives. She herself had left the mills in 1840.

Sarah Bagley, a Lowell mill operative, who led the Ten-Hour movement among the women, declared at Woburn, in 1845, that the "Lowell Offering" was not the voice of the operatives, but was controlled by the manufacturing interests "to give a gloss to their inhumanity," and that any article calling in question the factory system or any vindication of the operatives' rights was sure to be rejected by the editors.[2] The "Voice of Industry" claimed that the "Offering" "is and always has been under the fostering care of the Lowell corporations as a literary repository for the mental gems of those operatives who have ability, time, and inclination to write, and the tendency of it ever has been to gloss over the evils, wrongs, and privations of factory life."[3] Amelia Sargent charged that Miss Farley and the "Offering" were maintained by the corporations and that they refused to publish any reference to abuses in the factories; that one mill agent subscribed for twenty-five copies, another for twenty copies, "while the number of female operatives who support it are but fifty-two, twelve of whom only reside in the city."[4] An obituary notice of the "Offering," which appeared in the "Voice of Industry," stated that on the whole it had hurt rather than helped the operatives. It had started out to show that

[1] *Lowell Offering*, vol. 3, p. 48.   [2] *Voice of Industry*, July 10, 1845.
[3] *Ibid.*, July 17, 1845. This was probably Sarah Bagley again.
[4] *Ibid.*, September 25, 1845.

there was "mind among the spindles," but "this does not show that mind was made among the spindles, or that factory life under the present system is conducive to the expression and cultivation of the intellectual powers of the operatives." All that it proved was, that "out of six or eight thousand girls employed in the Lowell factories, a sufficient number could be found who had enjoyed privileges before entering the mills or during subsequent vacations which had qualified them for conducting a monthly magazine." [1]

In taking over the editorship of the "Offering" in 1843, Harriet Farley had in a general way discussed the conditions in the mills. The confinement, she said, was no greater than in other occupations; cotton dust was hurtful 'to some'; the mill life was regular and the work light; when the girls were in bad health it was often their own fault; and if the mills were unhealthy the operatives should try to counteract their influence by sensible precautions outside the mills. If the agents could improve the mills "we would earnestly request them to do so." The companies should provide bathing facilities, but "we do not ask a reduction of hours — the operatives do not want it." [2]

The following year she quoted Bartlett's statistics of mortality, wages, savings, and his statements about the religious influences that were thrown about the operatives: this in reply to a letter from Madame Dumas, who had seen the "Offering" and was interested in the intellectual mill girls. [3] In 1845 Miss Farley seems to have changed her mind about the hour question and suggested that the Legislature should have reduced the hours perhaps by increasing the time for meals. [4] This was actually done by the Lowell corporations in 1847.

[1] *Voice of Industry*, January 2, 1846; September 25, 1846; March 27, 1846.
[2] *Lowell Offering*, vol. 3, pp. 190–92.
[3] *Ibid.*, vol. 4, pp. 45–48.   [4] *Ibid.*, vol. 5, p. 36.

The articles and stories in the "Offering" were probably not directly intended as propaganda, but they were certainly not critical of the factories, and the corporations would have been very stupid not to have seen their value for propagandist purposes.

When Miss Farley returned to edit the "New England Offering" in 1848, her attitude had changed. She then wrote, not as a factory operative, but as one who had been in the mills.

There can be no greater mistake among the operatives than to imagine that those who have left the factories cease to remember and care for those who are left to labor there. They do think of them, sympathize with them, and are willing still to labor for their good.[1]

The first article in the new issue was on "The Duties and Rights of Mill Girls," in which Miss Farley replied to the critics and defined her attitude toward the corporations:

Let me not be misunderstood. I dislike heartily the long-hour system in families and in corporations, but I have a joyful faith in the corporations. . . . I have no doubt that, in their own good time, they will introduce the ten-hour system; and will not this be a noble deed? — a noble deed?

But until this 'noble deed' materialized — which it never did — "it is a pity" that the critics of the "Offering"

cannot understand that all the diseases and inconveniences of factory communities do not spring from the inherent corruptions of the factory system, but that, on the contrary, the greater part of them proceed directly and indirectly from a neglect on the part of the operatives themselves . . .[2]

In this way Miss Farley advanced from her original intention of defending the character of the operatives and proving that there was "mind among the spindles" to her final position of defending the corporations at the expense of the operatives. If the "Lowell Offering" was only incidentally corporation propaganda, the "New England

[1] *New England Offering*, vol. 1, p. 1.   [2] *Ibid.*, pp. 2–4.

Offering" was directly so. It was no longer written by the operatives, by "females actively employed in the mills," but "by those who are or have been factory operatives," and, in 1849, was extended further to include "fellow operatives of every occupation." [1]

In 1848 a letter signed "Mechanic" appeared in the Boston "Chronotype" charging that "the 'Lowell Offering' was the especial pet and favorite of the factory authorities" who had given the editors at one time one thousand dollars for their back numbers, which was equivalent to a bonus of that amount, and that when the "Offering" succumbed, its affairs were administered by the factory authorities. The "New England Offering," the "Mechanic" claimed, was the "Lowell Offering" revived, with the same editor and the same corporation guardianship, and, contrary to the strict rules of the corporations with regard to other papers, it was being circulated in the mills by the agents and overseers and subscriptions were being obtained in this way among the girls. [2]

Miss Farley replied to this letter, not in the "Offering," but in the Lowell "Journal," and the reply appeared also in the "Chronotype." [3]

Why [said the editor of the "New Era" [4]] does she so studiously avoid making a reply in her own organ? Does she know that the suspicions with which the "Offering" is regarded are but too well founded and that the discussion of the subject in its columns would naturally lead its readers to feel the weakness of her defenses? [5]

Like everything else in the period, the factory controversy worked itself out into the slavery issue. The Southern members of Congress, realizing that attack is the best sort of defense, took up the occasional scraps of the contro-

---

[1] *New England Offering*, p. 216.
[2] Boston *Chronotype*, May 13, 1848; also June 29, 1848.
[3] *Ibid.*, May 18, 1848.
[4] The *New Era of Industry* succeeded the *Voice of Industry*.
[5] *New Era*, June 22, 1848.

versy that filtered into the general press and portrayed the
conditions of the New England mill operatives as a white
slavery of the North as degrading as the black slavery of
the South. This had been frequently asserted by the workers themselves and by their friends, the Associationists,
including Horace Greeley. It had been vigorously denied by
the Whigs and by Garrison in the "Liberator." In 1850
Senator Clemens repeated these charges and Harriet Farley replied.[1] In her reply she quoted a letter from Whittier
describing the idyllic conditions at Amesbury, Massachusetts, under the first agent. But the Amesbury strike of
1851 changed all this. The home-owning American workers
left the mills under the severer discipline of the new agent.
Both Miss Farley and Whittier were thinking of conditions
that were passing away, while their opponents were concerned with tendencies that were implicit in the mill situation.

There can be no question of Miss Farley's sincerity. She
was living in the enchanted past of her mill experience under
a mild paternalism tinctured by the strong religious con-
victions and puritanical morals of the older capitalists and
their agents. She had left the mills in 1840, and failed to
realize that the old order was passing; that a change had
come over both the mill-owners and the mill operatives;
that 'community of interest' was no longer self-evident,
and that reliance upon the good-will of the owners, when the
mills had passed out of the control of men of good-will, was
hopeless. The critics of the factory system and the critics
of Miss Farley were, on the contrary, thinking, not of a
past condition, but a present tendency, the changes that
were going on in the purposes and methods of the mill-
owners and the dangers to the operatives of the old absolut-
ism joined to the new purposes and methods.

At the present time [said the organized factory women in the
first Factory Tract published in the interests of the Ten-Hour

---

[1] Farley, *Reply to Hon. Jere. Clemens*, 1850.

movement], when the manufacturing system is making such rapid strides in the country, it should become a matter of serious consideration with the people, as regards its ultimate effects upon society in general; especially when we have the destructive effects produced in other countries by an unlimited operation of its powers before our eyes.[1]

In 1845 there were published three works that portrayed the factory system in an exceedingly favorable light. Dr. Scoresby, an English clergyman, wrote "American Factories and Their Female Operatives"; the Reverend Henry Miles of Lowell, "Lowell As It Was and As It Is"; and an article appeared in the New York "Tribune," August 16, "A Visit to Lowell."[2] Scoresby's enthusiasm for the Lowell factories, especially for the 'moral police' and boarding-house system, was the result of their contrast with the conditions in the mill towns of England. He described the New England girls as "altogether very orderly in their manner and very respectable in their appearance." This was, of course, just what the English mill girls were not, and the roughness, profanity, and general looseness of the latter were the more pronounced in contrast with the intellectuality and company manners of the Lowell operatives. The Lowell girls were neatly dressed and clean,

many with their hair nicely arranged and not a few with it flowing in carefully curled ringlets. All wore a light calico-covered bonnet . . . large enough to screen the face and with a dependent curtain shielding the neck and shoulders. Many wore veils and some carried silk parasols. By no means a few were exceedingly well-looking — more pallid than the factory girls with us, and generally slighter in the figure. There was not the slightest appearance of boldness or vulgarity; on the contrary, a very becoming propriety and respectability of manner approaching with some to genteel.[3]

---

[1] *Voice of Industry*, June 19, 1846.

[2] Greeley never showed the sympathy for the factory operatives that he did for the workers of the cities, and it is difficult to escape the impression that his portrayal of the conditions among the needlewomen was intended in part to offset the criticism of the mills.

[3] Scoresby, p. 14.

Most of the girls were from the country from fifty to one hundred miles around, and preference was given in employment to those from a distance "as affording a safe supply under the contingency of slack times ... by being able to return to their homes where they can be sufficiently provided for as before, without any suffering to the community." [1] They were usually farm girls, "many being the daughters of able and independent yeomen." [2] The average time of working in the mills was said to be four and a half years and the girls usually returned home with their savings. Scoresby was enthusiastic about the boarding-house system and would have liked to see it introduced in England, but he was afraid the English mill girls were too rough and independent to put up with this discipline.

Dr. Scoresby [said Aiken], seeing the immense superiority of our system, and discovering the value of our boarding-houses as a means of sustaining character as well as of promoting comfort, attempted to introduce the same system at Bradford. But the experiment failed. The English girls, accustomed to regulate their own hours, amusements, and company, refused to place themselves under the supervision and guardianship of a matron, or the regulations of a boarding-house. [3]

Miles's picture was rose-colored. [4] He reproduced un-

[1] Scoresby, pp. 48–49. This explanation of the corporations' preference for girls from a distance is somewhat naïve. The real reason was the scarcity of help near by, and the desire of the mill authorities that their help should serve out the full year at least of their engagement. With homes near at hand the temptation was too great for the girls to return, when they found conditions in the mills not to their liking.

[2] The *Voice of Industry* said that most of the "yeomen" did not possess a foot of land, but worked by the day and many of them were foreigners. (*Voice of Industry*, July 10, 1845.)

[3] Aiken, *Labor and Wages*, p. 9.

[4] John Allen, in a letter to Abbott Lawrence, said: "It matters not what your suborned witnesses, whether clerical or medical, have testified relative to the health of Lowell ... your factory system is worse by far than that of Europe. You furnish your operatives with no more healthy sleeping-apartments than the cellars and garrets of the English poor ... the keepers are compelled to allow ... but one room for six persons and

critically most of Dr. Bartlett's figures and waxed eloquent over the beneficence of the corporations, because, in 1839, they "purchased the spacious and elegant mansion-house erected by Kirk Boott, Esq. . . ." at the cost of $20,000 and set it apart for sick operatives, charging the men four dollars a week and the women, three dollars. If the operatives were unable to pay, the corporation in which they worked was responsible for the charge and took it out of their future earnings.[1] "The Harbinger" admitted the general truthfulness of Miles's description, but challenged the validity of his assumptions. Miles stated that the "great questions relating to Lowell are those which concern the health and character of the laboring classes." But "The Harbinger" contended that the opposition to the corporations was not primarily concerned with these, but with their feudal and monopoly character and their "soul-destroying ownership of the workers."[2]

Various newspaper items that went out from Lowell further added to the mystification of the country as to the real conditions in the factories. Bartlett had estimated the savings of the operatives at $100,000. This appeared in the press in the form of a story that the operatives had each $1250 in the bank. As there were from 6300 to 7000 women operatives in Lowell, this would mean a total savings ac-

generally crowd twelve and sometimes sixteen females into the same hot, ill-ventilated attic. . . . You shut up the operatives two or three hours longer a day in your factory prisons than is done in Europe. . . . You allow them but half an hour to eat their meals. . . . You compel them to stand so long at the machinery . . . that varicose veins, dropsical swelling of the feet and limbs, and prolapsus uter, diseases that end only with life, are not rare but common occurrences." (*Voice of Industry*, September 18, 1846.)

[1] Miles, pp. 207–08. Dr. Curtis said that only a small number of the operatives used the hospital, and that the authorities had to send a circular to the boarding-house keepers threatening their discharge if they neglected or refused to "use all proper means" to induce the sick operatives to avail themselves of the privileges of the institution. (Curtis, *Hygiene in Massachusetts*, p. 43, and note.)

[2] *Voice of Industry*, September 18, 1845.

count of $8,750,000, or nearly the equal of the capital of all the Lowell corporations.[1]

Another story was told of a woman who had laid by $3000 by factory labor and bought a farm for herself and boy. "Vox Populi" declared that she had only half that sum, and half of that, "it was strongly suspected, was obtained as hush money of a prominent factory man who had been intimate with her and was the father of the boy now living in the country." [2]

The first scientific attempt to discover the effect of the factories upon the health of the operatives was made by Dr. Josiah Curtis and his findings were presented in an address before the American Medical Association. This was published in 1849 under the title "Hygiene in Massachusetts." Dr. Curtis was given access to the Merrimack Mill and took it as typical of the best the factory system had produced. The Merrimack Company was the oldest and best of the Lowell cotton corporations. It employed 1300 to 1400 women and girls and 350 men and boys. Its daily payroll was $1000 and had been $1200 previous to the reductions of 1848. It had five mills, each of which had five rooms, 151 feet long by 40 feet wide and 10 feet high, making 64,670 cubic feet to a room. The company owned 178 boarding-houses, 35 of which were devoted to the use of the women operatives, the remainder being tenements for the families of the married men. The average term of the operatives in the mills, from 1840 to 1849, was only nine months, and in other corporations it was frequently less than that.

It had been claimed by Miles and Green [3] that the rooms in which the operatives worked "are kept at a uniform temperature and are lofty and well ventilated."

We will make a liberal deduction [said Dr. Curtis], and assume 1350 operatives (out of the total of 1650) as actually in the mills. . . . This gives 270 for each mill and 55 for each room con-

---

[1] Quoted in the *Voice of Industry*, September 11, 1845.
[2] *Ibid.*   [3] *The Factory System in its Hygienic Relations.*

taining 64,670 cubic feet, inclusive of the space occupied by machinery. ... Here then we find a certain number for a definite time in a limited space without any ventilation whatever, except that of an accidental nature at the doors of entrance in winter and the same with open windows in summer, and this, too, with the thermometer ranging from sixty-five to eighty-five degrees throughout the winter months.[1]

If we assume ten cubic feet of air per minute to each person as the proper standard, and this is the minimum of the most recent investigations, we find the 55 operatives in a room requiring 550 cubic feet per minute, 33,000 per hour, and not less than 450,000 during each day's period of labor. Whereas we have shown that they have about 60,000 cubic feet. ... In winter, moreover, for four months when the windows are closed and generally double, each room has fifty solar lamps burning morning and evening, which assist not only in impuring the confined air, but also in raising the temperature frequently to ninety degrees before closing work at night. In all kinds of weather the operatives, with hastily adjusted dress, emerge from this atmosphere, to their boarding-places, partake of a plain but substantial dinner, and return to resume their labor in the space of forty-five minutes.

The air in these rooms, which ought to undergo an entire change hourly, remains day after day and even month after month with only the precarious change which open doors occasionally give! There being no ventilation at night, the imprisoned condition of many of the rooms in the morning is stifling, and almost intolerable to unaccustomed lungs. After the day's work is ended, two hours' release is enjoyed, a part of which is frequently spent in a crowded lecture room, and then they retire to dormitories scarcely better ventilated than the mills. From four to six, and sometimes even eight, are confined during the night in a single room of moderate dimensions.[2]

Dr. Curtis made the same criticism of the death-rates quoted by Miles that the "Citizen of Lowell" had made of those quoted by Bartlett.[3] He pointed out that a larger proportion of the population of Lowell than of almost any other city was between the ages of ten and thirty years.

The dwelling-houses of the masses [he said] and the factories of the few are less cared for than our prisons.[4]

---

[1] Curtis, *Hygiene in Massachusetts*, p. 30.   [2] *Ibid.*, p. 33.
[3] *Ibid.*, p. 17. Miles had used Bartlett's statistics.   [4] *Ibid.*, p. 47.

There is not a state's prison or house of correction in New Eng-land where the hours of labor are so long, the hours for meals so short, and the ventilation so much neglected as in the cotton mills with which I am acquainted.[1]

Of the typhoid patients at the Lowell Hospital from 1840 to 1849, 827 out of 1627 were operatives. The phy-sician of the hospital attributed their greater susceptibility to the disease to the imperfect ventilation of the mills.

Air thus confined for the space of several months in rooms occu-pied by some fifty persons for twelve hours each day except Sun-day must sooner or later make an impression upon the constitu-tion and thus indirectly at least become the means of inducing the disease.[2]

---

[1] Curtis, *Hygiene in Massachusetts*, p. 47, note.

[2] *Ibid.*, p. 45. There were about 7000 women operatives in Lowell in a population of 20,000, or 1 to 3, while the typhoid ratio was about 1 to 2.

CHAPTER VI

THE NEW POWER : THE DANGERS OF PATERNALISM

LOWELL was the creation of the corporations. It was a wilderness when the Boston capitalists purchased the land and water power, and began the manufacture of cotton. It grew in a quarter of a century to be the chief center of cotton manufacture on the continent, with a population of over 20,000, but it remained — its administration, churches, newspapers — very largely under corporation control. Many overseers in the mills were also aldermen of the city. The Lowell "Courier," the chief newspaper of the community, was under corporation control, and its editor, Colonel William Schouler, frequently represented Lowell in the State legislature. The churches of Lowell and their clergy were not immune from the all-pervading influence of the mills. And Pierce of Fall River said, when he visited Lowell in 1846, that his speeches on Reform so offended the agents of the corporations that people who were friendly to him dared not make it known and could not invite him to their homes lest they offend the corporations.[1]

This influence was not actively harmful politically so long as the Whig Party retained power and there was no local issue in which the corporations were greatly interested.

[1] *Voice of Industry*, April 3, 1846. Lowell was not the only mill town in the control of the corporations and perhaps not the worst case. The Labor Reform Association was refused the use of the city hall in Manchester, New Hampshire "... because forsooth certain corporation agents and clerks say they must be denied! Such an outrage could not be committed in Boston ... nor in Lowell, ridden to soreness as it is by corporations." (*Voice of Industry*, October 16, 1846.)

The hall was refused because the discussions of the reformers were "regardless of the regulations of society and the commandments of Heaven." (*Voice of Industry*, October 30, 1846.)

But in the fifties the Ten-Hour question got into politics, and, with the break-up of the parties, and the danger to the Whig cause, the unrecognized possibilities of paternal control began to appear. In 1851 a Coalition ticket (Democrat and Free Soil) captured the State from the Whigs. In Lowell this ticket was headed by the notorious Benjamin F. Butler, who, largely for political reasons, included a Ten-Hour plank in his platform. The City of Lowell elected nine out of ten Coalitionists, enough to give the party control of the State legislature. But a clerk in one of the wards made a mistake in his returns, reporting 8000 instead of 800 votes. The Mayor of the city and the Board of Aldermen were all Whigs and half of them overseers in the mills, and, though the ward officer offered to amend the return, they insisted on another election. Between the two elections the corporations, their agents and overseers, busied themselves to defeat the Coalition ticket and the Ten-Hour proposition. On the Monday before the second election a notice appeared outside the gate of the Hamilton Company:

Whoever, employed by this corporation, votes the Ben Butler, Ten-Hour ticket on Monday next will be discharged.[1]

The astonishing temerity of this threat in the face of a presumably self-governing electorate can be explained only by the assumption that the corporation had so long exercised undisputed control that it saw nothing out of the ordinary in openly dictating how its employees should vote. The Coalition politicians were said to have deserted Butler who called a meeting in the City Hall to protest against the notice. Here he made a rabid speech, in the course of which he threatened:

As God lives and I live, by the living Jehovah! if one man is driven from his employment because of his vote, I will lead you to make Lowell what it was twenty-five years ago — a sheep pas-

---

[1] Butler's *Autobiography*, p. 95.

ture and a fishing-place; and I will commence by applying the
torch to my own house. Let them come on. As we are not the ag-
gressors, we seek not the awful contest.[1]

The second election took place and five Coalitionists and
one Whig were returned, giving the Coalition a working
majority in the State legislature. The new legislature appointed a committee to investigate charges of coercion on
the part of the corporation agents and overseers between
the first and second election.[2] It was charged that the
agent of the Boott Corporation, the Honorable Linus Child,
had threatened to discharge men in his employ if they
should vote contrary to the interests of the corporation;
that the Lawrence Manufacturing Company, through its
agent, threatened one of the representatives-elect from
Lowell that if he took his seat in the legislature his connection with the company must cease; that men had been refused employment because of their political opinions; and
that Whig clubs had been formed in the mills with the intention of coercing the votes of the employees.

From 1840 to 1860 the Lowell corporations passed
through a series of internal changes that deprived them of
all that had been commendable in the early paternal administration. The companies were originally formed and
owned by a few sincere and religiously minded men who, if
despotic, were at least interested in the welfare of their
employees. But as the corporations grew and their stock
was put upon the market, control increasingly passed out
of the hands of the shareholders, and into the hands of
officers and selling agencies owning little stock in the corporations. The result of this, and the bleeding of the corporations by those in control was a considerable agitation toward the end of the fifties among the shareholders themselves. The corporations suffered severely in the fifties
from the depredation of inner rings, irresponsible in char-

---

[1] Butler's *Autobiography*, p. 104.
[2] Mass. House Doc. 1852, no. 230.

acter and with no interest in the welfare of the corporations or their operatives.

> It is the general belief [wrote Dr. Ayer in the interests of the
> shareholders in 1863] that the treasurers and directors in corpora-
> tions are large owners in them and consequently interested to pre-
> serve and foster their own prosperity. This was true formerly, but
> is not now. It has been asserted, and, so far as we are able to ver-
> ify it, justly, that there are individuals without the slightest voice
> in the management who own more stock than all the treasurers in
> both Lowell and Lawrence, excepting one who runs mills that are
> mainly his own. With few exceptions they [the treasurers] have
> but little interest in these properties. One of the treasurers who
> has been most prominent in the management of corporations and
> who has, at the present time, as much control of them as any other
> man, was lately found to own just one share in several of them.[1]

The result of these conditions was that only the selling
agencies and the officers of the corporations thrived upon
the cotton manufacturing industry. While these grew rich,
the owners, mechanics, and operatives remained poor.[2] In
1859 Governor Banks in his annual message called the attention of the legislature to this situation and a bill was
passed stipulating that not more than twenty votes should
be carried by an officer of a corporation and requiring
treasurers to divide their stocks into $100 shares and issue
new certificates. Only two or three treasurers complied,
the rest resisting until they could get the bill repealed. It
was claimed that in getting this repeal, money was spent
lavishly from corporation funds, the ablest lawyers of the
State retained, and an army of lobbyists supported throughout the session. Petitions for the repeal, made up and
printed in Boston, were sent to agents of the mills to be
signed by the operatives. These signatures were secured
under various threats of displeasure, loss of their places, reduction
of pay, etc. The Speaker's table was soon piled with these petitions signed by the operatives and others praying that the law for

---

[1] Ayer, *Usages and Abuses . . . of Manufacturing Corporations*, p. 15.
[2] *Ibid.*, pp. 17–18.

the division of stock into $100 shares (which brought it within their means of purchase) might be repealed!

After the first hearing of the matter before the Committee on Manufactures, Mr. Plunkett, the Chairman, said the new law was so wise and democratic that the legislature would not repeal it even if the committee so recommended. Later the Chairman reported for the repeal and the report was accepted by the legislature. The regulation that no more than twenty proxy votes might be carried by the treasurer of a corporation remained, but it was useless so long as a few of the friends of the treasurers and the selling agencies could carry large blocks of stock.[1]

Nepotism, the invariable offspring of autocracy, appeared. Instead of promoting the technicians in the mills, "the son, son-in-law, nephew or relative of some director, who in turn allows other directors to put their dependents in good positions also," [2] was given advancement. And the operatives under the new dispensation fared no better.

How [asked Cowley] would the great men who founded the factory system of Lowell regard this ruthless dismissal of hundreds and thousands of operatives [in the early years of the Civil War] dependent on their day's wages for their day's bread? The founders of Lowell were far in advance of their times. . . . To them, the condition of the operatives was a matter of the highest interest. Not so to their successors. The impartial historian cannot ignore the fact, painful as it is, that nine of the great corporations of Lowell, under the mistaken belief that they could not run their mills to a profit during the war, unanimously, in cold blood, dismissed ten thousand operatives penniless into the streets! [3]

---

[1] Ayer, pp. 19–20.   [2] *Ibid.*, pp. 21–22.   [3] Cowley, p. 60.

CHAPTER VII

THE DEGRADATION OF THE OPERATIVE

THE tendency of the factory system was to increase the strain and discipline under which the work was carried on. Both the management and the workers had, in the earlier years, been unaccustomed to thinking in terms of machine discipline and were ignorant of the possibilities that lay in water and steam power. They worked into the new methods almost unconsciously and often a very great change would come about before the worker, at least, realized its significance. Every one involved in the Industrial Revolution was being acclimatized to noise and speed as the process advanced.

> The din and clatter of these five hundred looms, under full operation, struck us, on first entering, as something frightful and infernal, for it seemed such an atrocious violation of the faculties. . . . After a while we became somewhat inured to it, and, speaking quite close to the ear of an operative and quite loud, we could make the inquiries we wished.[1]

This increasing tension was the result of both social and mechanical changes, the development of a policy of speeding up and of improvements in the machinery that permitted greater efficiency. As the control of the corporations passed out of the hands of the original owners, and a chiefly exploitive purpose came to dominate their policy, wages were cut, hours were not appreciably reduced, and the number of looms per worker or the speed of the looms, the noise and the dust, constantly increased. The New England girls found the old factories and their laxity not unpleasant and quite remunerative. They continued so to regard them while they played at mill work for a year or so. But in

---

[1] *The Harbinger*, November 14, 1846.

proportion as they came to regard the work of the mills as their permanent occupation and found themselves involved, year after year, in a severer discipline, the whole matter took on a new complexion.[1]

The factory and boarding-house regulations were innumerable, and covered every smallest corner of the operatives' lives. Aside from the printed rules, which were copious enough, it was said by one of the agents, in 1852, that not one tenth of the regulations were printed.[2] The operatives were told when, where, how, and for how much they must work; when and where they were to eat and sleep. They were ordered to attend church, for which they had to pay pew rent. They were discharged for immoral conduct, for bad language, for disrespect, for attending dancing classes,[3] or for any cause that the agents or overseers thought sufficient. When thus discharged, they were blacklisted and could obtain no employment in any corporation in Lowell or near-by towns. They were required to work one full year before receiving an 'honorable discharge' and to give two weeks' notice of intention to leave. The contract was entirely one-sided, however. The corporations accepted no responsibility as to length of employment and reserved the right to change the conditions as to wages, hours, speed and effort as they saw fit. Thus a girl employed at two dollars a week might be reduced to one dollar a week and still she must serve her full twelve months before she was entitled to an 'honorable discharge.'

The Lowell and other corporations were bound together by close agreements as to wages, hours, blacklists, etc. This combination and the requirement that an operative should work one year, and the blacklist that it involved, formed the basis of one of the major criticisms by the operatives in the Ten-Hour agitation. In 1842 the Middlesex

[1] *The Harbinger*, November 14, 1846.
[2] Mass. House Doc. no. 230, p. 134.
[3] *Voice of Industry*, January 30, 1846.

Corporation began operations in a new mill and transferred some of its weavers. The latter claimed that this meant increased work with no more pay, "that the company required them to tend four of the new looms in place of three," and some seventy girls left. For this they were blacklisted and informed by other corporations to whom they applied for work "that they wanted none of the turnouts from the Middlesex." The result was a petition to the legislature. Other similar petitions stated that "the effects of this regulation are becoming every day more grievous, giving the manufacturers great power over the operatives and leading to oppression and wrong; forming a combination which destroys the independence of the operatives and places them almost absolutely within the control of the manufacturer." [1] This matter was taken up in the Minority Report on the Ten-Hour petition in 1850.

To Miles and others, the blacklist was a part of the 'moral police' and a commendable method of maintaining the character of the mills and the operatives. To the workers it was an instrument of oppression capable of wide and effective use. In the investigation of 1851, the Honorable Linus Child gave evidence: *that*

If a man is discharged by us for any improper conduct, we send the other corporations notice. They cannot get work from one to another without a regular line. If they work a year, they have a right to ask for this, on giving fourteen days' notice. If they have not worked a year, they have no right. We do not bind ourselves to keep them a year. [2]

The power of discharge for the most trivial causes [said the Minority Report of 1850], and also, by an extensive system of combination with other corporations, to prevent the person so discharged from obtaining employment and the means of livelihood elsewhere, is a very dangerous power and liable to be abused to the oppression of the operatives and particularly those who are poor and friendless. [3]

---

[1] Mass. House Doc. no. 153, 1850, p. 5.
[2] *Ibid.*, no. 230, 1852, p. 44.   [3] *Ibid.*, no. 153, 1850.

The possibilities of the blacklist were very great. They explain, in part, the difficulty experienced by the operatives in making headway with their Ten-Hour movement and in maintaining their organizations. In the call of the Nashua Convention, to which the operatives were supposed to send delegates, Lowell operatives were advised to "play the hypocrite and go into the country sick, that you may attend the convention without having your name sent to the counting-room 'blacklists.'" [1] Much leeway was necessarily allowed agents and overseers in the determination of what should be a just cause for summary discharge. With so many regulations, written and unwritten, and many of them of a very general nature, it was a simple matter to discharge and blacklist the workers for any reason under the sun. Miles said, in his enthusiasm for the 'moral police,' that girls were discharged "for a suspicion of criminal conduct, association with suspected persons, and general and habitual light behavior and conversation." [2] To a moralist who had great faith in the judgment and intentions of the mill overseers and agents, this system had undoubted merits. It protected innocent girls from the communications of those who were at least notorious. But it also protected the corporations from 'agitators' and others who were attempting to organize the operatives in the interests of the Ten-Hour legislation. In the opinion of the workers, "these regulations conflict with our rights as rational human beings and we are regarded as living machines and all the rules are made subservient to the interest of the employer." [3]

The combination among the corporations extended

---

[1] *Voice of Industry*, September 11, 1846.   [2] Miles, p. 132.
[3] *Voice of Industry*, September 11, 1846. An agent of one of the mills was said to have told an operative to cease her activities in the interests of the ten-hour legislation or leave the company. "We will make the name of him who dares the act," said the vigorous Sarah Bagley in the *Voice of Industry*, "stink with every wind from all parts of the compass." (*Voice of Industry*, May 15, 1846.)

beyond Lowell to Newburyport, Nashua, Manchester, Cabotsville, and other places, and it is probable that the companies took greater liberties outside of Lowell, where the watchful eye and sharp tongue of Miss Bagley could not reach them. After the strike at Nashua, in 1846, one of the overseers was said to have threatened with discharge any one subscribing to a labor paper. A Mrs. Cummings and her two daughters were turned out of their tenement because the daughters were involved in the strike and their names were sent to Lowell and Manchester. A Miss Adams was also discharged for union activity and had visited "the great City of Spindles where they want 5000 more girls," but "the slandered girl could get no one to allow her the poor privilege of being enslaved again." [1] In connection with the treatment of one of the strikers at Fall River, it was said

that every person with intelligence and independence is marked. He is a suspected individual and must be either got rid of or broken in. Hundreds of honest laborers have been dismissed from employment in the manufactories of New England because they have been suspected of knowing their rights and daring to assert them.[2]

In the early days of the textile industry in America, the scarcity of labor and the experimental nature of the undertaking had resulted in wages that were relatively high. Scoresby drew attention to what he called an 'experimental price' for carpet weaving with the new machines in the forties. The result of the invention of the power loom was to reduce the cost of weaving from twenty-four cents to seven cents a yard. At first the women weavers were paid seven cents a yard, and, as they could weave fifteen yards a day, they received $1.05 or over $6 a week. "This was, however, only what might be called an experimental price." [3] The mill-owners could hardly be expected to con-

---

[1] *Voice of Industry*, October 16, 1846.   [2] *Ibid.*, April 7, 1848.
[3] Scoresby, *American Factories*, p. 24.

tinue to pay at this rate, when women could be got by the week for twice what these weavers were receiving per day. The result was a constant adjustment of the price until the correct figure was reached — the correct figure being the lowest figure possible.

In the mills there were three sorts of workers. The most important, so far as numbers were concerned, were the 'female operatives' or 'girls' — doffers, weavers, spinners, drawers, speeders, and so on — some of whom were paid a 'price' and some a weekly wage. The mechanics numbered about one third the female operatives and were paid wages commensurate with those of mechanics elsewhere. The overseers, in the earlier days, had been imported and were reasonably well paid. It is with the female operatives, nearly seventy-five per cent of the mill force, that we are here chiefly concerned.

The reductions in the operatives' wages in our period — reductions that occurred generally and at frequent intervals — were reductions of piece rates and did not necessarily mean reduced earnings. There were, however, only two ways in which earnings could be maintained and the piece rates reduced: by improvements in machinery that involved no extra effort on the part of the operatives, or by increasing their work and the amount of their product. As a rule, the changes that occurred in our period were of the latter sort. Over the whole twenty years the actual money earnings of the girls were maintained or even slightly increased, but only by a very great increase in the speed and amount of work done. Price reductions without corresponding reductions in earnings ordinarily meant speeding up.

Another caution is necessary, in considering different wage standards in different localities. Massachusetts and New Hampshire paid, on the whole, higher wages than any other of the factory communities. Connecticut, Rhode Island, and Pennsylvania were lower, and the Southern cotton mills were, of course, much lower still. Our information as to wages is most complete with regard to Massachusetts, so that it represents the best conditions the factory system achieved.[1]

Between 1828 and 1836 the weekly earnings of women weavers rose from $2.61 to $4.33 per week. By 1840 they had declined to $2.75.[2] The general average of women's wages in the factories had been about $2 per week and board in the thirties, and, in 1840, had declined to $1.50.[3] The depression of 1837–39 had resulted in a very general reduction of wages, and a competent witness declared, in 1840, that they could not be reduced much lower.[4] The lowest wage paid to any girl in the card rooms of Massachusetts was said to be $1 a week and board. The lowest figure for board was $1.20 per week, which would make her money wage $2.20.[5]

In 1842 a strike occurred in the Middlesex Corporation against a reduction of twenty per cent, though the mill was in full operation and "had never done so profitable a busi-

[1] Comparative wages in Massachusetts and Pennsylvania were as follows in 1840:

Wages per week:

		Phila.	Mass.
Carders.......10 years of age.......		$ .72	None
12 years of age.......		.96	None
Drawers......14 years of age.......		1.20	1.80
16 years of age.......		1.44	2.00 to 2.20
Rovers.......18 years of age.......		1.92	2.20 to 2.50
Spinners...........................		1.20 to 1.92	2.50 to 2.75

Wages per day:

	Phila.	Mass.
Machine makers...................	$1.20	$1.20 to 1.50
Overseers........................	1.20 to 1.44	1.75 to 2.25
Assistant overseers...............	.72 to .96	.84 to 1.25

(Montgomery, *Cotton Manufacture*, p. 133.)

[2] Clark, *History of Manufactures*, pp. 396–97.

[3] Aiken, *Labor and Wages*, p. 29, note. At Lowell wages were reduced 12½ per cent in 1836. (Mass. Bureau of Labor Statistics, *Eleventh Annual Report*, p. 5.)

[4] Montgomery, *Cotton Manufacture*, pp. 137–38.

[5] *Ibid.*

ness." [1] The reduction was explained as a reduction of the piece rate, made possible by improved machinery, and it was said that the girls could make nearly as much as before, at the reduced price. The girls, however, refused to be satisfied with 'nearly as much,' and their places were taken by others. In 1843 a strike occurred at the Chicopee Mills because of increased work without increased pay, [2] and in the same year the Lowell operatives, petitioning for a Ten-Hour law, referred to the "compensation as illy proportioned already to the task of the operatives and being reduced at a fearful ratio." [3] In 1845 the wages of woolen operatives were greatly reduced [4] and many of the girls left the mills as a result.[5] But the investigations of the Ten-Hour Committee of that date found wages running from $1.62 to $6 per week, and board.[6] In the same year Miles said that spare hands were paid 55 cents a week and board, and in a few months they could earn 62 cents, $1, and $1.50. The average for all females was $1.93 per week and board. The board cost the companies $1.25 per week for women and $1.75 for men.[7] A wage of $1.75 a week without board was quoted as common at the time.[8] Scoresby gave the wages of men as 70 cents a day clear of board, and the average wages of women as $1.75 a week and board, which would make the average money wage of the women $3 a week.[9]

In 1846 the wages of weavers in Newburyport were re-

[1] New York *Daily Tribune*, January 3, 1843.
[2] New York *State Mechanic*, May 18, 1843.
[3] Persons, *Labor Legislation in Massachusetts*, pp. 27–28.
[4] *Voice of Industry*, July 17, 1845.   [5] *Ibid.*, August 14, 1845.
[6] Mass. House Doc. no. 50, 1845, pp. 140–42. Sarah Bagley claimed that this committee suppressed evidence in favor of the ten-hour law and produced only the evidence most favorable to the corporations.
[7] Miles, pp. 112–13. Miles quoted average wages as follows: Drawers, $1.62½; warpers, $2.75; dressers, $2.50–$3.50; speeders, $2.00; spinners, $1.75; drawers-in, $2.00–$3.00; weavers, $2.00–$2.25; all exclusive of board. (Miles, pp. 79–83.)
[8] *Voice of Industry*, June 19, 1845.   [9] Scoresby, p. 30.

duced ten per cent,[1] and in Lowell it was said that never since the beginning of the industry had the operatives received lower wages, though "they are compelled to do all of one third more work and, in some cases, double." Whereas in 1840 weekly time wages were from 75 cents to $2 per week and board, in 1846 they ran from 55 cents to $1.50, making a 25 per cent reduction in spite of the fact that they were doing 33 per cent more work. "This is about a fair average as far as about one half of the girls in the factories here come into the account." [2] The remaining half of the 7000 or 8000 girls in Lowell were 'piece' or 'job' hands. They were receiving, "for the same amount of work, the lowest wage they had ever been paid." In one corporation the price for weaving a certain common cotton, which was $11\frac{1}{2}$ cents before the cuts of 1841–42, had fallen to $9\frac{3}{4}$ cents in 1846. In another, the same goods that were woven in 1840 for 16 cents a piece were, in 1846, being done for 11 cents. The reductions would average 25 to 33 per cent. But, in spite of this, the piece workers

make more per week than they did a portion of the time in 1841 and 1842, but they are obliged to do much more work than in 1840 as the "week" hands are. We may say that the average wages of between 7000 and 8000 girls here in the mills are less than $1.50 per week exclusive of board, for regular work.[3]

---

[1] *Voice of Industry*, February 6, 1846.

[2] Quoted from the Lowell *Advertiser*, in *Young America*, March 7, 1846.

[3] *Young America*, March 7, 1846. Sarah Bagley, who had been in the mills for eighteen years, said that the proprietors did not calculate the average wages of women to exceed $1.50 per week, exclusive of board. (*Voice of Industry*, March 26, 1847.) And it was said that the average pay of the operatives of Lowell, including overseers and 'second hands,' was not over $75 a year and board. (*Voice of Industry*, March 5, 1847.) But Harriet Farley was paid more than $1 a day, and she had known of one girl who had averaged $7 per week and her board through the year, before the reductions of 1848. (*New England Offering*, vol. 1, p. 72, 1849.)

Aiken made the following wage analysis for the Lowell Manufacturing Company. for fourteen weeks, in 1849:

Number of days' work, $100,976\frac{1}{2}$; number done by men and boys, $22,871\frac{1}{4}$; number done by females, $78,105\frac{1}{4}$; amount paid men, $23,059.71

The operatives do more work than formerly [said Sarah Bagley]. A few years ago, no girl was required to tend more than two looms. Now they tend four and sometimes five, and, because they make a few cents more than they did on two, it is trumpeted all over the country that their wages have been raised.[1]

There were general wage reductions in 1848,[2] in part due to slackening demand and in part, perhaps, "to create political capital for a tariff President in 1849." [3] The corporations had made dividends from twenty-five to thirty-five per cent for five or six years. During this time the wages of the operatives had not increased and, on the first sign of a weakened market, wage cuts were made that involved an actual decrease in the operatives' earnings.

In 1848 the Boston Manufacturing Company of Waltham reduced the wages of piece hands and gave notice that, the next pay day, the wages of day hands would be reduced.

a week, or $6.49 per week each (includes overseers, mechanics and watchmen); amount paid women, $44,773.31, or $3.44 per week each; men's board, $1.75 per week; men's clothing, $1.00 per week; men's expenses, $2.75 per week, leaving the men an average net weekly income of $3.30 [should be $3.74]; women's board, $1.25 per week; women's clothing, .66 per week; women's expenses, $1.91 per week, leaving a net income of $1.53. [This estimate for clothing is very low and unnecessary. If the board is deducted from $3.44, it leaves an average weekly wage of $2.19.] (Aiken, *Labor and Wages*, pp. 12–13.)

[1] *Voice of Industry*, April 24, 1846. A plausible explanation is given by the *Voice of Industry*, of the method by which the increased speed was achieved. In 1842, when work was scarce, the agents had reduced the speed of the machinery from 130 to 70 strokes per minute and the girls were given double the number of looms to mind. When business revived, the looms were speeded up again, unknown to the operatives, to 130 strokes per minute. This meant, of course, that the operatives were making too much money and a cut ensued. Then the pieces of cloth, called 'cuts,' that were the basis of the wage were lengthened from 28 to 35 yards, while the price per 'cut' was reduced from 15 to 11 cents. In 1840 a day's work was 120 yards of cloth for 75 cents. In 1848 a day's work was 140 yards of cloth for 44 cents. (*Voice of Industry*, February 11, 1848.)

[2] *Voice of Industry*, February 24, 1848.

[3] *Ibid.*, February 11, 1848. "The wages of the Lowell operatives, under the low tariff of 1840, were double what they were under the high tariff of 1842, double what they have been at any time since."

"Many of the girls," it was reported, "are quitting work and going home." [1] The wages of the Fall River operatives were cut four or five dollars a month.[2] A notice of the reduction was given to the operatives on February 1st, to date from the previous Monday. It involved a reduction of four cents per 'cut' (a 'cut' brought the operative twenty-three cents). "The overseers told the help that all who dissented could get a settlement and clear out." The operatives in the Metacomet, Anawan, Troy, and Quequechan mills struck,[3] and 800 of them stayed out for three weeks. They tried to hold meetings, but the town hall was closed to them and they had to organize in the open. Two leaders were arrested. One of them, a man named Norris, was told by the president of the company that if he would cease agitating, all would be right, if not, he was a marked man, and would most undoubtedly suffer, and the manufacturers of the States would combine against him and refuse him employment.[4]

The strike failed and the operatives returned to work at the end of three weeks at the reduced rates.[5] It was said that they organized for a reduction of hours and recognized that 'turn-outs' were no longer helpful.[6] A strike of the operatives at Millbury the following year, for increased wages, also failed,[7] as did a strike at Cohoes, New York, against a reduction.[8]

Another great strike occurred at Fall River in 1850. In

---

[1] *Voice of Industry*, February 18, 1848.

[2] *Ibid.*, April 7, 1848: or 15–17 per cent, according to the *Eleventh Annual Report*, Massachusetts Bureau of Labor Statistics, pp. 5–6.

[3] *Eleventh Annual Report*, Massachusetts Bureau of Labor Statistics, pp. 5–6.

[4] *Voice of Industry*, April 7, 1848.

[5] *Eleventh Annual Report*, Massachusetts Bureau of Labor Statistics, pp. 5–6.

[6] *Voice of Industry*, March 10, 1848.

[7] *Eleventh Annual Report*, Massachusetts Bureau of Labor Statistics, pp. 5–6.

[8] New York *Daily Tribune*, September 3, 1849.

that year, out of 2,485,700 spindles in New England, 800,-000 were idle. On Wednesday, November 20th, all the Fall River corporations, except the Watuppa, posted notices of intended reductions, and the spinners struck, without notice or consultation among themselves. They complained of petty tyrannies, and said they would be treated, if they gave notice, like the spinners of New Bedford. The New Bedford spinners had told the companies that they would leave on a certain day rather than accept a reduction. The agent quietly sent to other towns for new men and as fast as they came the old ones were discharged.

At Fall River a union was formed and mass meetings were held by both spinners and weavers at which resolutions were passed asserting that the manufacturers were getting a fair return on their capital; that the reductions were made in the fall so that other work could not be had and winter expenses were coming on; and the alterations recently made in the work had increased their labor, in one mill the men being compelled to clean the machinery on Sunday.

The winter of 1850–51 was a severe one, but the strikers held out. A delegation from the Spinners' Union visited other cities and secured subscriptions to the amount of $20,000. In March, "The Trades Union and Fall River Weavers' Journal" was started, and the strikers seemed to be holding their own. But in May the Watuppa Corporation, which had continued to pay the old wages, fell in line with the reductions. By that time, the White, Quequechan, and Metacomet mills were running part time and others were gradually being filled up. "Few of the former employees had returned; many of the best operatives had left the town and the corporations were engaging newcomers." After June 1, 1851, the strike was broken. It had lasted six months and there were 1300 operatives idle for nearly the whole period.[1]

[1] *Eleventh Annual Report*, Massachusetts Bureau of Labor Statistics, pp. 6–9.

The wages at Fall River were generally lower than those at other places. During the strike of 1850–51 the Fall River spinners made the following comparison tending to show that their wages were not only lower than those of other American mills, but lower than the English mills also: [1]

> The cost of spinning 10,500 pounds of No. 29½ yarn:
>
> At Fall River (Metacomet, Pocasset and Massasoit Steam Mill) — 100 skeins at 2 cents, 8 mills.................................. $92.50
>
> At Lowell (Lawrence, Boott, Hamilton Mills) and at Great Falls...................... 162.05
>
> At Slatersville, Woonsocket, Hamlet, Mansville, Ashton, Quecanack, Phenix, Jackson, Hope, Blackstone, and Providence — 100 skeins at an average of 5 cents, 5 mills.
>
> In England, an average of 3 cents, 8 mills.

The weavers reported to the New York Industrial Congress that they could earn only $9 a month of 26 days, at 14½ hours a day, less 1¼ hours for meals, or a working day of 13¼ hours. "The fate of the operatives of New England," said the "Tribune," with a good deal of truth, "depends on the struggle." [2]

After this setback, matters in the mills continued without much change until the end of the fifties. Again, in 1857, depression hit the cotton industry and factories were closed and wage reductions common. The Chicopee Mills ran half time during the winter of 1857–58 and, in April, opened up at full time, with a wage reduction of twenty per cent. The women weavers struck and others followed, but there were many operatives out of work at the time and new help was engaged. Crowds gathered at the mills and there was some rioting. Extra police were put on, the village priest advised the operatives to return to work on the corporation terms, and the mills managed to get going again.

---

[1] New York *Daily Tribune*, February 3, 1851.
[2] *Ibid.*, February 3, 1851.

As business improved, after the reductions of 1857, there were a number of strikes for the old prices. Most of them failed, including those at Salem, Newburyport, and West Springfield. The operatives at the Blackinton Mills at Adams succeeded, as did those at Blackstone and Uxbridge.[1] In Philadelphia there had been similar wage reductions and similar strikes to force them back to their old level, but only a few of them were successful.[2] In 1863 "the labor employed in them [the corporations] has been pressed from low even lower, and down to the last *per diem* that will support life." [3]

The only weighted averages of wages in the mills over the period 1840–60 are those prepared by Miss Edith Abbott from the figures of the Aldrich Report. They are meager enough, representing only three establishments and covering the whole period for one establishment only. They show, in one establishment, in the case of the weavers and spinners — the two largest groups of mill operatives — a wage decline from 1842 to 1855 for the spinners which was a little more than recovered from 1855 to 1860, and, in the case of the weavers, a very considerable decline over the whole period:

Establishment No. 39 — Weekly Wages

Year	Spinners	Weavers
1842	$2.73	$3.66
1845	2.64	2.67
1850	2.61	2.58
1855	2.55	2.76
1860	2.85	2.76

The wages of the spoolers in another establishment (No. 38) fell from $3.60 in 1851–55 to $3 in 1860.[4] In a

---

[1] *Eleventh Annual Report*, Massachusetts Bureau of Labor Statistics, pp. 16–17.

[2] Pennsylvania Bureau of Industrial Statistics, 1882, *Report*, pp. 276–77.

[3] Ayer, *Usages and Abuses*, p. 22.

[4] Abbott, "Wages of Unskilled Labor," *Journal of Political Economy*, vol. 13, and "Women in Industry," Appendix, pp. 366–67.

third establishment (No. 43), the wages of spinners fell from $4.32 in 1850 to $3.36 in 1860, those of weavers from $5.28 in 1850 to $4.32 in 1860, and those of warpers from $5.40 in 1850 to $4.38 in 1860.[1]

Closely related to the problems of both hours and wages were those of the speed and effort required of the operatives in the mills. Wage reductions without corresponding losses of income were made possible to a considerable degree by the extra output and effort or speed required of the worker, as well as by improvements in the machinery itself.

In the thirties the operatives had tended but two looms.[2] Even in the early forties, according to Mrs. Robinson, "the girls were obliged to tend no more looms and frames than they could easily take care of and they had plenty of time to sit and rest. I have known a girl to sit idle twenty or thirty minutes at a time." [3] But at that, the speed of the American machines was greater than that of the British. A British manufacturer, in 1840, who was familiar with American cotton mills, said that mule spinning was cheaper in New England than in Glasgow, and throstle spinning was nearly as cheap because of the high speed at which the American frames were driven and the greater quantity produced in a given time.[4]

The cotton mills had been introduced into an industrially slack world. Men worked long hours, but they did not get the utmost possible out of themselves or others. It was necessary to acclimatize the rustic to machine production and the early mills were more or less leisurely run. It was thus possible for the New England women who lived isolated lives in farming communities to feel, when they went to Lowell, as if they were going to boarding-school, in spite of the long hours, the noise, dust, and heat of the mills. But

[1] Abbott, "Women in Industry," pp. 292–93.
[2] *Working Man's Advocate*, June 9, 1830.
[3] Robinson, *Loom and Spindle*, p. 71.
[4] Montgomery, *Cotton Manufacture*, pp. 136–37.

this did not last. The older amenities had to go, and they went with no equivalent compensation to the operatives in other directions. With the passing of the old school of manufacturers and agents, and the coming of the new, the boarding-school dream faded. The girls were no longer able to relieve one another at their work, to snatch a rest of fifteen minutes, to read a book propped up on the frame. They ceased the cultivation of window flowers — in fact, they left the mills altogether and were replaced by new workers.

By 1846 there was observed a considerable increase in the speed of the machines and the effort and attention required of the operatives. The editor of the "Voice of Industry" said:

It is a subject of comment and general complaint among the operatives that while they tend three or four looms, where they used to tend but two, making nearly twice the number of yards of cloth, the pay is not increased to them, while the increase to the owners is very great.[1]

It is an ingenious scheme which a few capitalists and politicians have invented to blind the eyes of the people — that, because the operatives receive one eighth more pay in the aggregate for accomplishing one third more labor with the same facilities than they did a few years ago, the price of labor has advanced. The price of weaving a yard of cloth never was lower in this country than at this time. The price for tending, spinning, carding, never was lower, nor the wages of those operatives who work by the week.[2]

In 1835, according to the statement of the treasurer of the Atlantic Mills, made in 1873, the girls tended two or three looms. This was equivalent to 216 or 324 picks per minute. In 1849 they tended four looms, making 480 picks per minute; and in 1873 four or five looms, making 620 or

[1] *Voice of Industry*, March 13, 1846.
[2] *Ibid.*, April 17, 1846. In 1847 the Washington Manufacturing Company, New Jersey, advertised for "thirty good female weavers who can make $1 a day on four looms, board at rate of $1.42 a week." (*Voice of Industry*, June 25, 1847.)

775 picks per minute. In spinning, the girls tended nearly double the number of warp spindles in 1873 they had tended in 1849.[1]

The average number of spindles per operative in the cotton mills in 1831 was 25.2. In 1885 it had increased to 72 — an increase of 185 per cent. The weavers in the old days wove 42 to 48 yards of common shirting per week. In 1885 a weaver tending six power looms would produce 1500 yards a week.[2] This tremendous increase was of course due to a considerable extent to improvements in the machinery. But it meant, too, much closer attention and greater effort and strain on the part of the operative. A Lowell factory girl said that in 1842 before the reduction of wages, she tended two looms running 140 beats per minute and earned $14.52 in 24 days. In June, 1842, when the speed of the machines and the prices were both reduced, she tended four looms running 100 beats and earned $13.52 a month. This girl was able to increase her earnings "by the gradual increase of the speed." In January, 1843, the speed of the looms was raised to 118 and the price still further reduced. She was then able to earn $14.60 per month. In June, 1843, the speed was evidently too great to keep on with four looms and one was dropped. The girl's earnings were $15.40. In June, 1844, "feeling able to tend four looms at a speed of about 120," she made $16.92.

This operative increased from two looms running at 140, and paying $14.52, to four looms at 120, paying $16.92. The reduction made in the speed of the looms was 14 per cent and the increase in their number was 100 per cent, making a net increase of 86 per cent. The wage increase was about 15 per cent. The girl claimed that she had not overworked herself.[3]

In 1843 the operatives of the Chicopee Mills struck

---

[1] Grey, *Argument on the Ten-Hour Petition*, p. 212.

[2] Exec. Doc. 46:1, no. 1, pt. 5, p. 83.

[3] Scoresby, *American Factories*, pp. 30–31.

against increased work without increased pay. They formed processions and marched to Springfield with bands and banners, but failed to get the other mills to follow them.[1] In 1846 the weavers of No. 2, Massachusetts Corporation, resolved "that we will not work under the proposed reduction embracing a fourth loom, and receive a cent less per piece. We will not tend a fourth loom unless we receive the same per piece as on three, and we shall use our influence to prevent others from pursuing a course that has always had a tendency to reduce our wages." [2] The girls pledged themselves not to accept the reduction, and any one violating the pledge was to have her name published in the "Voice of Industry" "as a traitor, and receive the scorn and reproach of her associates." This pledge was said to have been "kept inviolate." [3] The operatives of another company were warned against taking a third loom: "You will be obliged to work harder and perhaps take a fourth loom — as was tried by one corporation in this city — to make the same wages that you do now with two." [4]

"Be assured," somberly declared the "Voice of Industry," "that if you do not live to witness it, the time is not far distant when those who labor in the mills will (as is the case with many now) earn barely enough to purchase the necessities of life by working hard thirteen hours a day; recollect that those who worked here before you, did less work and were better paid for it than you are, and there are others to come after you. . . ." [5]

"If a worker," said Professor Clark, "is producing more and working harder at the end of a period than at the beginning, and is getting practically the same wage, he is then not participating in the prosperity of the industry." [6]

[1] *Eleventh Annual Report*, Massachusetts Bureau of Labor Statistics, pp. 5–6.
[2] *Voice of Industry*, May 15, 1846.
[3] *Ibid.*   [4] *Ibid.*, September 11, 1846.   [5] *Ibid.*
[6] Clark, *History of Manufactures*, pp. 389–90.

In addition to the increased effort required by the speeding-up of the machines and the addition of looms and spindles, the premium system began to develop in the forties, to stimulate production. Overseers and second hands were paid bonuses for getting out more work than was commonly required of the operatives, "or, in other words, for driving them up." [1]

This premium system is a curse to us [said a Manchester girl in 1846]; it ought not to be tolerated. I have worked under this plan and know it too well, the base treatment of the overseers, in many instances. Often girls have been so afraid of the "old man" they dare not ask to go out when sick, for they knew he would have a great deal to say. Some girls cannot get off as much cloth as others; such ones are apt to be treated unkindly and often reminded by the "old man" that "Sally and Dolly got off several cuts more the last four weeks. They come in long before the speed starts up and do their cleaning, and if you don't get off more next week, I will send you off." It is sometimes asked, "Why is it that the girls come to the gate before it is opened, if they are not willing to work so many long hours?" The premium is offered, the girls drove up, and they want to keep the "old man" good-natured if possible. I should like to see liberality and generosity from the directors extended to some subjects of misfortune crushed by their machinery. [2]

In 1847 the members of the Women's Union of Manchester complained that "money given to first and second hands to drive us factory girls is making a bad matter worse." [3]

[1] *Voice of Industry*, January 8, 1847.
[2] *Ibid.*, January 8, 1847.   [3] *Ibid.*, February 15, 1847.

CHAPTER VIII

THE TEN-HOUR MOVEMENT: INDUSTRIAL
1840-50

THE most obvious weakness in the armor of the textile corporations in this period, the outstanding abuse of the system, was the length of the working day. The ten-hour day had been achieved by the mechanics, especially the outdoor workers, except in New England, in the labor movement of the thirties. In Massachusetts the Ten-Hour movement had made no progress except among the carpenters, plasterers, and masons.[1] Everywhere the operatives of the textile mills were working from twelve to fourteen hours a day.

The agitation for the ten-hour day by legislative enactment in the forties was most energetic and best organized in Massachusetts and was there carried on almost entirely by the workers themselves. The reformers gave the movement their sanction and moral support, but the burden of the organization, petitioning, and propaganda fell upon a small group of men and women operatives and mechanics, led by William F. Young, editor of the "Voice of Industry," and Sarah Bagley. As a result of the failure of this movement and the changing personnel of the factories, the ten-hour agitation on the part of the workers themselves died down about 1848. The revival of the fifties was of quite a different nature and under new auspices. The Ten-Hour movement of the fifties was political rather than industrial in its methods and had no root in the working population of the mills. The American operatives had made their fight, and failing, had left the field. With the coming of the immigrant the ten-hour agitation had to be carried on, if it were to be carried on at all, by middle-class philanthropists,

[1] Commons, *Documentary History*, vol. 6, pp. 253-55.

such as William Robinson, and politicians like Ben Butler.
Thus the movement for shorter hours was the reverse of the
general labor movement of the two decades. The latter began under reformist auspices and finished as a *bona-fide*
working-class movement among the skilled crafts; while the
former began as a working-class movement and finished as
reformist in the political field.

The Ten-Hour movement among the mechanics in the
thirties had taken the line of asking Congress, and later the
President, for laws regulating the hours of labor. This had
resulted in 1840 in an executive order of President Van
Buren establishing a ten-hour system for Government employees. But, in order to reach the employees of private
concerns, it was necessary to appeal to the legislatures of
the States. The corporations had been created by the
legislatures; their existence depended upon legislative
action; without their charters they would cease to exist;
and it seemed evident to the public and to the workers that
these corporations could be required by the legislatures
that had created them to close their establishments after
ten hours of operation per day. The right thus to regulate
the corporations was nowhere disputed. The only question
that arose was as to the desirability of so doing, in the interests of the trade, the operatives, the corporations, or the
community.

In Massachusetts the principle of intervention in the
interest of the workers and the community had been established by the child labor laws of 1824 and 1836–37, which
were amended in 1842 so that no child under twelve years
of age could be employed more than ten hours a day in any
manufacturing establishment. The amendment of 1842
was the result of the report of Horace Mann in 1840 showing that the law of 1837 was not being obeyed.[1] In spite of

---

[1] Mass. House Doc. no. 21, 1840, pp. 41–42. The law of 1836–37 required that children under fifteen years of age should receive three
months' schooling per year before being allowed to work in the factories.

this early beginning, no legislation was obtained to shorten the hours of labor of adults in Massachusetts until 1874, although some reductions were made by the corporations as a result of the ten-hour agitation.

The explanation of the failure in Massachusetts of the remarkable Ten-Hour movements, which were carried on almost continuously for over thirty years, is to be found in part, as Professors Commons and Andrews suggest,[1] in the insistence on the part of the Massachusetts leaders that legislation, when it came, should be effective, whereas in other States, laws were passed that were neither intended nor expected to result in a shortening of the working day. Persons claimed[2] that failure was due in part to the disorganization of the ten-hour forces and the presentation of conflicting plans. But there were other reasons and more important ones. In the first place, there was the traditional Puritan dislike of idleness and regard for other people's morals. "The morals of the operatives," said an opponent of the ten-hour system, "will necessarily suffer if longer absent from the wholesome discipline of factory life, and leaving them thus to their will and liberty, without a warrant that this spare time will be well employed. No limits can be ascribed to the abuse of these privileges conferred, or time misspent, should the legislature see fit to accede."[3]

But the chief reason for the failure of the Ten-Hour movement is more obvious than any of these. The simple fact is that the corporations were able to prevent the passing of ten-hour legislation because of their control over the Massachusetts Legislature and their political domination of the electorate. Colonel Schouler, editor of the Lowell "Courier" and a stanch upholder of the corporations, was chairman of the legislative committee of 1845 that made

[1] Commons and Andrews, *Principles of Labor Legislation*.
[2] Persons, *Labor Laws and Their Enforcement*.
[3] *Voice of Industry*, March 20, 1846.

the argument for the corporations and against the ten-hour law. This argument was the basis of all later refusals in our period. Schouler was not originally a member of that committee, but was added to it [1] for reasons best known to the Speaker of the House. This was the beginning, but by no means the end, of the machinations of the corporations in the Massachusetts Legislature.

A great deal of confusion regarding the hours of labor in factories can be avoided by remembering that "hours of labor" often meant one thing for the defenders of the corporations and another for their opponents. The defenders of the corporations generally spoke of the hours as those of actual labor or the hours during which the machinery was running and turning out cloth; while their opponents frequently referred to the total number of hours between the opening and closing of the mills, making no allowance for meal-time recesses. The term 'eight' or 'ten' hour day has come to mean eight or ten hours of working time, exclusive of meal-time, but there was no such definiteness about it in the forties in regard to the mills. The wide divergence in the statements of hours worked is due in part to this two-fold basis of computation. The addition or subtraction of the dinner hour would make a difference of thirty to forty-five minutes, and in some cases an hour, in the working day, and as — for eight months out of twelve — the operatives worked before breakfast, a further difference of half an hour would be found. An instance of this confusion is seen in the statement of the factory operatives of Philadelphia in 1833, "We are obliged by our employers to labor at this season of the year from five o'clock in the morning until sunset, being fourteen and a half hours." It is statements of this sort that have contributed to the persistence of the idea that fourteen or fifteen hours was the common length of the working day in the early mills. In this case the operatives went on to explain what was meant by this fourteen-

[1] Mass. Archives, no. 1587/9, 1845.

and-a-half-hour day. It involved an "intermission of half
an hour for breakfast and an hour for dinner, leaving thirteen hours of hard labor. . . ." [1] It is not contended that
the operatives never worked fourteen or fifteen hours per
day. It was sometimes longer than that.[2] But it is fairly
safe to assume that the long hour quotations refer to the
total hours from opening to closing, rather than to the
actual hours of labor in the mills.

This confusion has led, I think, to a false idea of the extent of the improvement made in the hours of labor in the
mills in the forties and fifties. Thus the Aldrich Report
gives the hours of labor in "cotton goods" as 14 per day
from 1840 to 1842, and 11.6 in 1860.[3] This is entirely too
optimistic and can have resulted only from the confusion
referred to above. The so-called fourteen-hour day in 1840
was in reality a twelve-and-one-half-hour day or less,
when meal-time is deducted. But the Aldrich Report is not
the only offender. The impression is a common one and
erroneous, that the fourteen-hour day was normal in 1840
and that a reduction of nearly three hours a day was made
during the two decades.

It may be, that in the circumstances under which the
factory operatives lived, with the boarding-houses almost
a part of the mills, the meal hour should be considered as
part of the operatives' day. But that of course does not
warrant the use of one basis of measurement at one time
and another later. It is necessary in all discussions of hours
to distinguish between the early idea of the day's labor ex-
tending from the hour of opening to the hour of closing of
the mills, and the later idea of the hours of actual
work.

The hours of labor in factories appear to have increased

---

[1] Commons, *Documentary History*, vol. 5, pp. 330–31.

[2] The Niagara Flour Mills, New York, reported their working day as
eighteen hours for eight months in the year. This was probably on the
old basis of reckoning. (Senate Doc. 62: 1, no. 72, pt. III, 1758.)

[3] Aldrich Report, vol. 1, 52d Cong., 2d Sess., Sen. Rep. 1394, p. 178.

from the twenties into the thirties [1] and they showed no signs of reduction until near the end of the forties. The most satisfactory statement of the hours of labor in cotton mills was made by James Montgomery in 1839.[2] This statement showed a considerable variation in hours throughout the year, from a minimum of 11 hours, 24 minutes, in December and January, to 13 hours, 31 minutes, in April.[3] The average working day throughout the year was said to be 12 hours, 13 minutes,[4] or 73 hours, 18 minutes, per week. This, said Montgomery, was common to the factories of the Eastern States. In the majority of the factories of the Middle and Southern States the hours were longer, being 13¾ per day or 82½ per week in the summer, and averaging 75½ hours per week throughout the year.[5]

[1] Sumner, Sen. Doc. 61:2, vol. 9, p. 63.
[2] Montgomery, *Cotton Manufacture*, pp. 173–74.
[3] All these figures are of working time and exclusive of meal hours.
[4] The following table makes an average of 12 hours, 18¼ minutes.
[5] Montgomery's table is as follows:

MONTH	WORKING TIME		MEAL TIME (minutes)	
	Hours	Minutes	Breakfast	Dinner
January	11	24	None	30
February	12	..	None	30
March	11	52	30	30
April	13	31	30	30
May	12	45	30	45
June	12	45	30	45
July	12	45	30	45
August	12	45	30	45
September	12	23	30	30
October	12	10	30	30
November	11	56	None	30
December	11	24	None	30

These hours involved the practice of "lighting up" from September 20th to March 20th. This was greatly objected to, and the operatives were accustomed to celebrate the blowing-out of the lamps for the sea-

These figures give then an average working day in the Eastern States of about 12¼ hours, and in the Middle and Southern States slightly more than 12½ hours, which would average for the whole country from 12 hours, 20 minutes, to 12 hours, 25 minutes, as compared with the fourteen-hour day of the Aldrich Report and common belief.

Montgomery's statement seems to have been the official one in New England. It was used by Miles in 1845,[1] and by the Ten-Hour Committee of the Massachusetts Legislature in the same year.[2] It is as correct as any, and certainly not exaggerated.[3] At Great Falls, New Hampshire, it was said that only fifteen minutes was allowed for breakfast and thirty minutes for dinner throughout the year, which would increase the average working day quoted by Montgomery by 20 minutes, to 12 hours, 33 minutes.[4] The working hours in the mills of the York Company, Saco, Maine, in 1846, were:

September 20 to March 20, from one quarter of an hour before sunrise to 7.30 P.M., minus one half hour for breakfast at 7.30 to 8.00 and one half hour for dinner at 12.30. Except for the months of November, December, January, and February when breakfast will be taken before going to work.

---

son by decorating them with garlands of flowers. (*Voice of Industry*, March 26, 1847.)

A convention at Peterboro, New Hampshire, passed a resolution, that "although the evening and morning is spoken of in the Scripture . . . no mention is made of an evening in the morning. We therefore conclude that the practice of lighting up our factories in the morning, and thereby making two evenings in every twenty-four hours, is not only oppressive but unscriptural." (McNeill, *Labor Movement*, p. 107.)

In one room in Lowell there were said to be 293 small and 61 large lamps kept burning in the evening. (*Voice of Industry*, June 26, 1845.)

[1] Miles, p. 101.   [2] Mass. House Doc. no. 50, 1845, p. 9.

[3] Dr. Curtis said the daily average for the year was 12 hours, 48 minutes, before the reduction of 1847, and 12 hours, 33 minutes, after. (Curtis, *Hygiene in Massachusetts*, p. 27.) The *Voice of Industry* said that at no season of the year were the hours of work less than 12 hours, 10 minutes (Dec. 26, 1845), and that the average was 12 hours, 30 minutes, throughout the year. (June 26, 1845.)

[4] *Voice of Industry*, December 26, 1845.

March 20 to September 20, one quarter of an hour before sunrise to sunset, allowing one half hour for breakfast and one half hour for dinner. Except from May 1 to August 15, when work will commence at 5 A.M. and the mills will stop at 7 P.M. and dinner time from 12.30 to 1.15.[1]

Where these hours are comparable to those given by Montgomery — that is, in May, June, and July — the working hours are 12.45 in both cases.

The first sign of the agitation for shorter hours in our period is found in the factory controversy discussed above. The Boston " Times " had just mentioned the length of the working day. Bartlett said that the hours were too long, but that changes should be left to the philanthropy of the employers. And the Lowell "Citizen" made a strong argument for the ten-hour day in the interest of the operatives and the community.[2] In 1841 Miles was faced with the issue, in discussing Baines's "Cotton Manufacture in Great Britain," by the contrast between the 73 hours, 18 minutes, per week in New England and the hours in the English mills which had been reduced to 69 per week in 1833.[3] Miles was able to find a number of advantages for the American system over the British to counteract the discrepancy in hours.

The first active movement in our period, for the attainment of the ten-hour day in manufacturing establishments by legislative enactment, is found in the petitions to the Massachusetts Legislature of 1842 from Fall River, Mansfield, New Bedford, Attleboro, Taunton, and Newburyport, containing 1300 names.[4] The petition from Fall River was very general in its nature and did not contemplate hour regulation alone. "In consequence of the influx of foreign laborers," it read, "whose habits of cheap living

---

[1] *Mechanics' Mirror*, November, 1846, p. 278.
[2] *Corporations and Operatives*, pp. 69–70.
[3] *North American Review*, January, 1841, pp. 31 ff.
[4] Persons, *Labor Laws and Their Enforcement*, pp. 24–25.

enable them to work at very low prices, the wages of the workmen in many of the departments of manufacturing establishments are reduced so low as to be wholly insufficient to enable them, with the exercise of the utmost frugality and prudence, to obtain for themselves and families the necessaries and conveniences of life, and to provide for their comfort and support in old age." [1] The petitioners claimed that the Act of 1836, protecting the children, was almost wholly disregarded, and asked for an act prohibiting the employment in manufacturing establishments of children under a certain age. Perhaps the most interesting suggestion, in view of later developments, was that a Board of Commissioners should be appointed to see that any legislation passed would be enforced, and to report on conditions in manufacturing establishments for further legislation. [2] This is of course what finally came about in most States by the establishment of Bureaus of Labor and more recently, in some States, of Industrial Commissions. But nothing more was heard of it in the ensuing ten-hour agitation.

Other petitions in 1842–43 prayed that a law should be passed constituting ten hours a day's labor "in all cases where a different provision is not made by the agreement of the parties." [3]

In 1843 Lowell sent a petition containing 1600 names praying for a prohibitory law without exceptions to apply only to corporations. Such a law, said the Lowell petitioners, would lengthen the operatives' lives, give them time for "mental and moral cultivation" and to attend to their personal affairs. [4]

In 1844 Lowell again sent petitions with 1000 signatures. [5] They claimed that wages were being reduced and asked that the employees might be protected as the corporations had been. These petitions were referred to the next session

---

[1] Mass. House Doc. no. 4, 1842.   [2] *Ibid.*
[3] Persons, p. 26.   [4] *Ibid.*   [5] *Ibid.*, p. 27.

of the legislature.[1] At this time there were indications that the hours of labor were being lengthened instead of reduced. The "Factory Girls' Garland," of Exeter, one of the many papers that sprang up in these years, was quoted as saying that ten years ago "the corporations would not have dared to propose to the girls to work by lamplight in the morning and evening, and we trust the girls in every mill in New England will rise up against this outrageous custom."[2] A former overseer in the Lowell mills said, in 1847, that work by lamplight was done at both ends of the day.[3]

Alongside these petitions was a very considerable movement among the workers, described in a later chapter, involving a widespread organization of both women and men, the issuance of a dozen labor papers, and the holding of innumerable conventions and mass meetings to promote, among others, the ten-hour cause. The movement reached a climax in 1845 and galvanized the General Court into action. In this year the legislature was flooded with petitions. There were two from Lowell — one signed by John Quincy Adams Thayer and 850 others, the other signed by James Carle and 300 others; one from Fall River signed by John Gregory and 488 others; one from Andover signed by Samuel Clark and 500 others; and so on.[4] The total number of petitioners was 2139, of whom 1151 were from Lowell. Nearly one half of the Andover petitioners and most of those in Lowell were women, while those of Fall River were all men.[5]

These petitions asked for different varieties of legislation. One Lowell petition asked that ten hours be made a legal day's work, and that no one, incorporated company, non-

---

[1] Mass. House Doc. no. 48, 1844.

[2] *Working Man's Advocate*, September 28, 1844. Sarah Bagley said at Woburn, in 1845, that the employers were trying to add two hours to the working day when the women organized. (*Voice of Industry*, July 10, 1845.)

[3] *Voice of Industry*, March 26, 1847.

[4] Mass. House Doc. no. 50, 1845, pp. 1-2.   [5] Persons, p. 43.

incorporated company, or individual, should employ any one more than ten hours a day. The second Lowell petition, and those of Andover, Fall River, and Lynn, asked that ten hours be made a legal day's work in the absence of special agreement, and the Andover petition asked that the regulation should refer to corporations only.[1]

Lowell was the center of the agitation, and it was from Lowell that the only demand for an effective law came. The formula, "in the absence of special agreement," found in other petitions, was probably intended to protect the operatives' freedom of contract, but it ignored the fact, which became sufficiently obvious later, that the special contract was the very basis of the corporation system of employment. Any one entering the employment of the corporations was required to sign a "regulation paper" that was, in itself, a special agreement. All that the corporations had to do to nullify an act such as that asked for by most of the petitioners, and later passed in other States, was to insert in this paper a clause specifying twelve or thirteen hours as a day's work, and the matter was settled. The major group of the Lowell petitioners realized this, and, being anxious for a real limitation of the working day, they insisted on a prohibitory law. They probably made a tactical blunder by including other employers than the corporations.

The result of this agitation was the appointment, in 1845, of a committee of the Massachusetts Legislature, with William Schouler as chairman. They made a lengthy report that showed a reasonably thorough consideration of the subject on the part of men who were convinced beforehand that the factories were beyond reproach. The document was, in fact, a defense of the corporations. In calling the petitioners to give evidence before the committee, a letter was sent to the leaders of the operatives stating: "I would inform you that as the greater part of the petitioners

[1] Persons, p. 44.

are females, it will be necessary for them to make the defense, or we shall be under the necessity of laying it aside." [1]

Much of the argument of Miles [2] and of Bartlett was made use of to prove that the work of the factories was not injurious to the health and morals of the operatives. A law referring to corporations alone was objected to, although one of the Lowell petitions had specifically asked for a general law. It was claimed that factory labor was no more injurious than other indoor occupations and that a reduction of hours would mean a reduction of wages, though it is doubtful if wages could have been reduced any further at that time. "Labor in Massachusetts," said the committee, "is on an equality with capital and indeed controls it. . . . Labor is intelligent enough to make its own bargains." [3]

The committee noted that the hours of labor in English mills were fewer than those in Massachusetts and that, in England, there were six holidays a year as against four in New England.

[But] it is hardly possible to draw a comparison between operations in Great Britain and those in Lowell. The one is a manufacturing population in the strictest sense of the word; the other is not. There the whole family go into the mills as soon as they have sufficient bodily strength to earn a penny. Very little attention is paid to their moral or physical culture, and few can read or write, and unless they have attended Sabbath schools, few obtain knowledge of the Bible or of the Christian religion.

In Lowell but very few (in some mills none at all) enter into the factories under the age of fifteen. None under that age can be admitted unless they bring a certificate from the school teacher that he or she has attended school at least three months during the preceding twelve. Nine tenths of the factory operatives of Lowell come from the country. They are farmers' daughters. Their education has been attended to in the district schools which are dotted like diamonds over every square mile of New England. Their moral and religious characters have been formed by pious parents

---

[1] *Voice of Industry*, September 18, 1846.
[2] *North American Review*, January, 1841.
[3] Mass. House Doc. no. 50, 1845.

under the parental roof. Their bodies have been developed and their constitutions made strong by pure air, wholesome food, and youthful exercise.[1]

All this was true enough, but it had little to do with the point at issue. The committee failed to see that the above were just the reasons why the New England operatives should not be overworked in the mills, why the corporations should not be allowed to live by the destruction of those moral and physical qualities that had been created by nature and the community.

The committee visited the Lowell and Middlesex Mills and found them in the best of order.

Grass plots have been laid out, trees have been planted and fine varieties of flowers in their season are cultivated within the factory grounds. In short, everything in and about the mills and boarding-houses appeared to have for its end, health and comfort. . . . Your committee returned fully satisfied that the order, decorum, and general appearance of things in and about the mills could not be improved by any suggestion of theirs or by any act of the legislature.[2]

The hours quoted by the committee were given them by Mr. Clark of the Merrimack Company and were those of Montgomery, already noted.[3]

Finally, the committee did not wish to convey the impression that there were no abuses, that it would not be better if the hours of labor were fewer, and more time were allowed for meals and more attention paid to ventilation, but "the remedy does not lie with us. We look for it in the progressive improvement in art and science, in a higher appreciation of man's destiny, in a less love for money, and

[1] Mass. House Doc. no. 50, 1845. Also Commons, *Documentary History*, vol. 8, p. 148.

[2] *Ibid.*

[3] Mr. Thayer, one of the petitioners, said that, in 1845, some parts of the machinery of the Lowell corporations were run to 9 and 9.30 at night by the same set of hands. (Thayer, *Review of the Report of the Special Committee on the Petition relating to the Hours of Labor*, pp. 1–6.)

a more ardent love for social happiness and intellectual superiority." [1]

After the appearance of the report of the committee of 1845, the Lowell Female Reform Association, the organization among the women operatives which was pushing the ten-hour agitation, passed a resolution, "deeply deploring the lack of independence, honesty, and humanity in the committee . . . especially in the chairman [William Schouler], and as he is merely a corporation machine or tool, we will use our best endeavors and influence to keep him in the 'City of Spindles' where he belongs and not trouble Boston folks with him." The Lowell women were "highly indignant at the cringing servility to corporate monopolies manifested by said committee in this report, as in that document the most important facts elicited from the witnesses relative to the abuses and evils of the factory system are withheld, truth violated, and the whole shaped to please

[1] Mass. House Doc. no. 50, 1845. Miles in the same year published his *Lowell As It Was and As It Is*, in which he attempted a mitigation of the long day. In the first place, he said, the work "is comparatively light," and, in the second, "we have given the hours per day of operating the mills. . . . It does not follow that all operatives work this number of hours. . . . By a system adjusted to secure this end, by keeping engaged a number of spare hands, by occasional permissions of absence, and by an allowed exchange of work among the girls, the average number of hours in which they are actually employed is not more than ten and a half." (Miles, p. 103.)

This figure seems to have been quoted with approval by the New York *Tribune*. "We are at a loss to discover," said the *Voice of Industry*, "the consistency of the *Tribune* in the position it takes relative to factory labor. It even endorses and reiterates the false statement in Mr. Miles' work, that the average hours the operatives work in the mills are only ten and a half. Are the people to understand by this that the operatives get pay in full for a week's work when they labor only 63 hours? Every person who knows anything about the factory system knows that this is not the case. The mills in Lowell, Manchester, and throughout nearly every manufacturing town in New England are in operation 12½ hours, and thousands of operatives are in attendance this same number of hours, week after week and month after month, and those who do not work in accordance with the running of the wheels will not be paid full price nor be long tolerated at that. . . ." (*Voice of Industry*, November 28, 1845.)

their aristocratic constituents. . . ." [1] Whether as a result of the women's activities or not, William Schouler was not returned to the legislature at the next election.

Sarah Bagley claimed that her own evidence had been distorted. She had appeared before the committee and told them that the work of the mills was destructive of the health of the operatives and that she had to leave the mills frequently to recuperate. She was asked what use the operatives would make of their leisure should the hours be reduced, and replied that they would use it to cultivate their minds; that she conducted evening classes for them in her own room with even the present long hours. In the report it was stated that "Miss Bagley said, in addition to her labor in the mills, she had kept evening school during the winter months for four years, and thought that this extra labor must have injured her health." [2]

It was claimed by the operatives that their petitions were not allowed to be circulated in the mills, but "were tyrannically forbidden, and the individual who attempts to offer anything of the kind is driven from the premises as a lawless intruder," while petitions against the annexation of Texas were freely circulated by the corporations. [3]

John C. Cluer, an Englishman, was active in the Ten-Hour movement at this time. He came to America in 1845 as a temperance orator. He spoke at Croton Hall in New York for the Land Reformers, drifted to Lowell and threw himself into the ten-hour agitation. He held large and successful meetings, notably one at Manchester where there were said to have been two thousand present. [4] Here

---

[1] *Voice of Industry*, January 9, 1846.

[2] *Ibid.*, and Mass. House Doc. no. 50. Sarah Bagley was the leader of the women operatives in the ten-hour fight. She had organized the Lowell Female Reform Association in 1845 that was later extended to other places and took an important part in the labor movement of the forties. This association published the *Voice of Industry* for some time and Miss Bagley acted as editor. (See Chapter XIV.)

[3] *Ibid.*, December 26, 1845. [4] *Ibid.*, December 5, 1845.

he proposed a three-stage plan: first, an attempt to arrange a conference over hours between the manufacturers and their employees; second, in the event of the failure of the conference, to petition the legislature again for a ten-hour law; and, finally, if all else failed, to call a general strike of the operatives. Cluer attacked William Schouler in the columns of the "Voice of Industry," and Schouler went to the trouble of having his record investigated. It was discovered that Cluer was a reformed drunkard who had been connected in England with the Chartist movement; that he had neglected to obtain a divorce from his first wife before marrying his second — no uncommon proceeding under the English divorce laws; that he was something of a liar; in the habit of living off his friends; and that he had been arrested in New York. Not only was Cluer's own reputation involved by Schouler's exposé, but that of his mother and first wife as well.[1]

William F. Young, editor of the "Voice of Industry," came to the defense of Cluer, pointing out in regard to the bigamy charge that the latter's first wife had deserted him and that, because of the cost of divorce in England, poor men were not able to regularize their domestic affairs. Young admitted that Cluer was technically a bigamist, but claimed that this involved no reflection of a moral nature upon himself or his second wife. G. W. Hatch, assistant editor of the "Voice of Industry," was then sent to New York to investigate the other Schouler charges. The report he made on his return raked up a great deal of mud, implicating Cluer's mother and first wife in adultery and himself in lying, obtaining money under false pretences, bigamy, and drunkenness. A poor English weaver with a clever tongue, he had got on as best he could, as actor, lecturer, and Chartist agitator. The circumstances of his birth and early training were such as the slums of the British industrial towns of the period made common enough,

[1] *Voice of Industry*, January 30, 1846.

and the "Voice of Industry," a highly respectable paper, considered him exculpated. The Lowell Association (men and women) added a touch of humor to a none too humorous story, by declaring that "the character of John Cluer, so far as the investigation has been made, has proved better than our most sanguine expectations could have anticipated."[1]

While the New England Ten-Hour movement was thus in progress, a similar agitation had flared up in Pittsburgh. The Pittsburgh struggle was much more violent and suffered from lack of leaders among the operatives themselves. In the fall of 1843 a strike occurred among the girls in the Pittsburgh cotton mills as a result of an increase of one hour per day without extra pay. Up to that time they had worked from 5 A.M. to 7.15 P.M., with the exception of Saturdays when they quit at 4 P.M. The strike failed to spread and nothing was gained.

On September 15, 1845, a mass meeting of operatives and their friends, said to have numbered five thousand, was held in the market square of Allegheny. A committee reported the reply of the employers to the operatives' request for a ten-hour day. The employers did not admit "the right of persons interfering between them and their operatives," and considered it "entirely impracticable" to adopt the ten-hour system while other places continued to work twelve hours. They claimed, too, that their mills ran only 68 hours a week as against 72 hours in the Eastern States. It was mistakenly announced at the meeting that Lowell had adopted the ten-hour day. The operatives decided to strike, and a committee was formed of three ladies and three gentlemen from each ward to solicit funds. A mass procession was arranged which was held the following Friday and created considerable interest.[2]

---

[1] *Voice of Industry*, February 20, 1846. The *True Workingman* criticized Cluer for attacking the church, January 24, 1846, and Young seems quietly to have dropped him.

[2] *Young America*, September 27, 1845.

But the strike failed. The manufacturers agreed to adopt the ten-hour system when the manufacturers of other States should do so.[1] "On Monday last at the ringing of the bells, the greater part of the poor girls went reluctantly back to their factories to work twelve full hours as before."[2] The employers were said to have increased the hours of labor, "in petty spite."[3]

The contention of the employers that they could not compete with the Eastern mills unless the latter adopted the ten-hour day led to a *rapprochement* of the two movements. A correspondence was opened up by the Pittsburgh operatives and their friends with the operatives of Lowell, and the latter seem to have sent to Pittsburgh one of the Factory Tracts.[4] The two movements reached a point of agreement in the resolution at Cluer's Manchester meeting in December, to concur in the plan of the Pittsburgh and Allegheny operatives "that the Fourth of July, 1846, shall be the day fixed upon by the operatives of America to declare their independence of the oppressive manufacturing power which has been imported from old monarchical England, and is now being ingrafted upon the business institutions of our country."[5] No such declaration of independence was ever made, though the New England operatives busied themselves with preparations and talked about it.

At Worcester, Cluer's first proposal was given a chance. The Workingmen's Association invited the employers to meet them and show cause why men ought to work more than ten hours a day. ". . . Wherever the ten-hour system has been adopted more labor is generally performed and to the better satisfaction of the employer than where the dragging all-day system is continued . . ." and if the em-

[1] *Young America*, October 18 and 25, 1845.
[2] *Ibid.*, November 15, 1845.
[3] *Voice of Industry*, October 2, 1845.
[4] *Young America*, November 15, 1845.
[5] *Voice of Industry*, December 19, 1845.

ployers should fail to show cause "let the ten-hour system be established April 1st and let them forever hold their peace in the matter." [1] There was a plan to hold a meeting in Boston in May of the two parties "on account of the increasing dissatisfaction and strikes in the different manufacturing towns and cities . . . to determine by mutual consent what number of hours shall constitute a day's work." [2]

But the employers showed no interest in these proposals, and Lowell had little faith in either strikes or agreements. In Lowell there was "some talk of a declaration of independence," [3] but, in 1846, the workers resumed their own line of attack upon the Massachusetts Legislature.

By this time the Lowell leaders had got control of the machinery of petitioning and there was no such confusion of counsel as was found in the earlier demands. Only one form of petition was used, and that was a clear and explicit demand to "prohibit all incorporated companies from employing one set of hands more than ten hours a day." An additional protest was made against the corporation regulation that required of the operatives one year's service before they could receive a 'regular discharge.' The Lowell petition was 130 feet long and contained 4500 names, while 10,000 signatures were said to have come from all parts of the State. Another legislative committee was appointed which made a perfunctory report to the effect that any regulation should be of general application and not confined to corporations; that the legislature could define the number of hours that should constitute a day's labor, but could not deprive the citizen of his freedom of contract.

This now historic defense raises the question of the wishes of the operatives in the matter of shortening the working day. The size of the petitions, which were circulated under difficulties, suggests that a very large proportion of the operatives were actively interested in the

---

[1] *Voice of Industry*, February 13, 1846.   [2] *Ibid.*, May 8, 1846.
[3] *Ibid.*, February 13, 1846.   [4] Mass. Senate Doc. no. 81, 1846.

matter. But petitions are notoriously easy to get signed and the machinery for petition-making was, by 1846, very well organized. Many of the operatives were afraid that a shorter day would mean a smaller wage.[1]

"I have met some who never heard of Labor Reform," said one of the Lowell organizers. "On asking one of them if she would not join the Association, 'Oh,' said she, 'I belong to no religious society.' Some would ridicule, censure, and oppose me and ask what necessity there could be in establishing the ten-hour system." [2]

Nevertheless, the persistence of the agitation and the later acceptance of the ten-hour principle by the politicians indicates that the movement was well grounded in the working-class purposes of the period. It is probable that at no later date was it so truly a working-class demand. With the coming of the immigrant it became very largely a philanthropic measure.

A strike occurred in the Nashua Corporation in September, 1846, as a result of the refusal of the girls to work by candle-light. The mill gates were locked and the girls forced to remain in the yard until the bell rang. The machinists and others joined a demonstration and one thousand people surrounded the gates to receive the girls as they left the mills. A constable tried to read the Riot Act, but was shouted down. "If there was any riot, it is the opinion of many citizens that it was by the officers of the police." [3] The Manchester "Democrat" was "pained on Wednesday evening to see a turn-out procession headed by a large number of ladies." [4]

In September, 1847, the Ten-Hour Law, passed July 3d, went into effect in New Hampshire. The legislature of this State had not been pestered as had the legislature of Mas-

---

[1] "They do not wish their wages cut down, because they have barely enough to live on as it is." (*Voice of Industry*, March 26, 1847.)

[2] *Ibid.*, November 13, 1846.

[3] *Ibid.*, October 2, 1846.   [4] *Ibid.*, October 9, 1846.

sachusetts by an active group of reformers who knew the difference between 'effective' legislation and camouflage. If the Massachusetts Legislature had been wise enough, it might have headed off the whole ten-hour agitation by seizing upon one of the early petitions for the setting of a legal working day subject to special contract exceptions, and making it law. But they lost their chance, and in 1846, when the Senate seemed to be ready for that sort of an arrangement, it was too late — the community had been educated to the point where it knew the difference between a law for shorter hours and a law to avoid trouble.

In New Hampshire there was no such active public opinion, and on September 15th a law went into effect making ten hours a legal day's work, in the absence of special contracts. The "Independent Democrat" declared: "The ten-hour law will not reduce the hours of labor.... Its authors did not intend any such result. It will also fail, we think, to humbug the working-men — the only object had in view by the demagogues who originated it." [1]

The intentions of the New Hampshire companies were known beforehand. "We understand," said the "Tribune," "that in anticipation of its [the law] taking effect, papers have been circulated through many of the mills and machine shops soliciting a contract to labor as many hours as the employers think proper ... some of the employers and their agents were beating up for signatures with the avowal that all who do not give in shall be discharged." [2]

A 'great demonstration' was held at Nashua, in August, of two thousand operatives, at which it was decided to unite in their refusal to sign the special contracts. It was resolved

That, on and after the 15th of September next, we will not work more than the legal number of hours each day;

---

[1] Quoted in *Voice of Industry*, August 27, 1847.
[2] Quoted in *Voice of Industry*, October 1, 1847.

That we will sign no contract to work more than ten hours per day;

That to the support of these resolutions we pledge our lives and sacred honor.[1]

The fears of the friends of the Ten-Hour Law were well founded. The Nashua Corporation had special contracts calling for the old hours, drawn up and presented to their employees, and those who refused to sign were discharged three days before the new law went into effect.[2] Discharge, of course, meant blacklist and the certainty of looking in vain for work in Lowell and elsewhere. But only from one third to one half the operatives signed the contracts and some mills and parts of mills had to close down. The mills, however, "were soon filled with fresh hands." [3]

At the present time [said the Manchester "Democrat,"] when the law of the State provides that the operative need not work more than ten hours unless he or she so pleases, one would hardly have supposed that we had among us men so devoid of humanity, so emphatically black-hearted as to blacklist any operative for exercising a right conferred by the statute. . . . Yet such is the fact. Operatives who have refused to sign the special contracts binding them to work "as long as the mills run" have been discharged and blacklisted. Yes, more than this. Operatives who have been to Lowell and engaged to work on the corporations have been refused work after word has been sent from Manchester that they had refused to take the new regulation papers.[4]

Yet this was the system of 'moral police' that aroused the enthusiasm of the Reverend Henry Miles and many others.

On September 28th, after the New Hampshire law had been in effect for two weeks, the Dover "Enquirer" made the astonishing admission:

The whole matter [of hours] is one which can best be regulated by those whom it most concerns — the employer and the employee. And such, we are happy to learn, has been the course pursued. The largest portion of those who are employed in our mills

---

[1] *Voice of Industry*, August 27, 1847.
[2] *Ibid.*, October 9, 1847.   [3] *Ibid.*, September 17, 1847.
[4] Quoted in *Voice of Industry*, September 17, 1847.

— working as they do by the job and piece — are desirous of working as many hours as they can. Those who take a different view of the matter seek other employers or different occupations. It is a free country.[1]

But [protested the "Tribune" in reply] if, as admitted, the laborers have the contracts presented for their signature under peril of ejection from employment if they see fit to refuse, while a secret agreement among the employers of the entire state and with others outside the state binds each not to employ any one who refuses to sign a contract to work as many hours per day as the employers see fit to exact, then it seems clear that the law is evaded and subverted.[2]

In April, 1847, the Lowell corporations reduced the hours of labor in the mills by an average of twenty minutes per day throughout the year, by adding fifteen minutes to the dinner hour for eight months in the year (January, February, and May, June, July, August, and November, December) and thirty minutes for the other four (March, April, and September, October). This, on the basis of Montgomery's computation, made the average working day throughout the year 11 hours, 58 minutes.[3] This reduction was made voluntarily, but was due in part to the growing protests and the fact that thirty minutes (during eight months of the year) was not sufficient time for the operatives to go to and from the boarding-houses and eat their dinners properly. It was claimed that instead of forty-five minutes, the new noon meal-time was actually only thirty-five, and even at that "many foolish girls were seen standing at the gates waiting for admission." [4] One of the men who had been an overseer and had spent eighteen years in the mills claimed that the mill time was 'fixed.'

[1] Quoted in the New York *Daily Tribune*, October 16, 1847.

[2] New York *Daily Tribune*, October 16, 1847. Laws similar to that of New Hampshire were passed in Pennsylvania, 1848; New Jersey, 1851; Ohio, 1852; and Rhode Island, 1853.

[3] Mass. House Doc. no. 153, 1850. Dr. Curtis said that the change involved only fifteen minutes addition to the dinner hour throughout the year. (Curtis, *Hygiene in Massachusetts*, p. 27.)

[4] *Voice of Industry*, May 7, 1847.

From November till March our time is from twenty minutes to half an hour too slow. So you see instead of getting out of the factory at half-past seven o'clock in the evening, it is really eight; and more than this, some of the clocks are so fixed as to lose ten minutes during the day and gain ten minutes during the night, thereby getting us into the mill five minutes before five in the morning and working us five minutes after seven at night.[1]

Another mechanic had observed a similar 'fixing' of the mill time in 1846:

My clock and watch will agree with the bell on the Middlesex Corporation at noon; at night, when the same bell rings at half-past seven to release the worn-out operatives, my clock and watch will agree, but will be five minutes too fast by the Middlesex bell; and in twenty-five minutes after the ringing of the half-past seven bell, it will strike for eight o'clock . . . and this, I believe, is the general practice of the corporations in this city. . . .[2]

The Pennsylvania Ten-Hour Law was passed March 28, 1848. It was like that of New Hampshire, allowing special contracts for more than ten hours a day in the case of persons over twelve years of age. After its passage the operatives in and about Philadelphia continued at the old hours, but held meetings and decided not to work more than ten hours a day after July 4th. On July 6th all the Fairmount mills went on the ten-hour schedule. At Manayunk and Delaware County the mill-owners shut down or reduced the wages one sixth, and some of the operatives continued at the old hours under special contracts. At Allegheny City the seven cotton mills closed down July 4th, shutting out two thousand employees. They remained out until August 18th when they resumed work on the ten-hour basis with a reduction of sixteen per cent in their wages. On July 31st the Penn Mills opened with contract hands at the old hours. This mill was fiercely attacked on August 1st.[3]

[1] *Voice of Industry*, March 26, 1847.   [2] *Ibid.*, February 27, 1846.
[3] A vivid description of this attack is given in the Pittsburgh *Daily Commercial Journal*, August 1, 1848.

CHAPTER IX

THE CHANGE OF PERSONNEL

THE chief characteristic of the early factory population was its extreme mobility. The mills were using up the available labor supply at an extraordinary rate. The New England girls who went into the cotton mills probably stayed, on an average, not more than a year. The estimates differ from nine months to four and five years. "From one room," said the Lowell "Citizen," "where the average number of girls employed is forty, there left the mill, during the year ending in August, fifty-two . . . and a large proportion of these had worked in the factory but a few months." [1]

The fact that the girls stayed so short a time in the mills was made one of the major defenses of the long-hour system. It was contended that the operatives did not stay long enough to endanger their health; that, unlike England, America had no permanent factory population. "The evils," said William Boott, "which constant employment and want of amusements are calculated to produce if persisted in too long, are, to a very great extent, counteracted by periodical visits to their friends." [2]

But the defenders of the factory system failed to understand that this tremendous labor turn-over could not go on indefinitely; that sooner or later a 'permanent factory population' was certain to appear; that the New England mill girls of whom every one was so justly proud were being driven from the factories and a class of operatives lower in the scale was replacing them. The mobility of the factory population was the result of an increasing pressure upon the

[1] *Corporations and Operatives*, p. 53.
[2] Mass. House Doc. no. 50, 1845, p. 24, and Senate Doc. no. 81, 1846.

operatives in the matters of hours, wages, discipline, and speed. This pressure drove the New England girls out, and their places were taken by immigrants who were more amenable to the new discipline. The immigrants did not drive the New England women from the mills. They simply took their places after the New England women had been driven out by the conditions in the industry.[1] After every strike there was the same story of the places of the strikers being filled by newcomers. The failure of the Ten-Hour movement, the reduction of wages, and the increase of speed and effort explain the change of the personnel of the mill forces during our period.[2]

In connection with the Lowell strike in 1836 against a reduction of wages, Mrs. Robinson, who was then in the mills, said:

After a time, as the wages became more and more reduced, the best portion of the girls left and went to their homes or to other employments that were fast opening to women, until there were very few of the old guard left; and thus the status of the factory population of New England gradually became what we know it to be to-day.[3]

The great scarcity of labor that gave endless trouble to the corporations was due largely to the rapidity of the turnover. There can be no doubt as to this scarcity in good times. The tightening-up that occurred about 1845–46, in the enforcement of the regulation that an operative must serve twelve months, was an indication of it. Another in-

[1] The fact that immigrant labor was available was of course responsible to some extent for these conditions.

[2] John Fitch found this to be true in the steel industry at a later period. The Irish, he said, were not driven from the blast furnaces by the immigrant, but by the conditions in the industry. (*The Steel Workers*, p. 146.)

The astonishing thesis of Carroll D. Wright, *Industrial Evolution*, that the destiny of the factories was to reach down and lift people out of lower into higher levels, is worth noting, if only for its speciousness. The problem of the factory population is one of the factory population, not of those who escaped the factories.

[3] *Loom and Spindle*, p. 86.

dication was the use made of the "slaver." From 1836 the corporations had been in the habit of sending agents into the country to recruit help. The agents were paid one dollar a head, and naturally they did not understate the case for factory employment. One girl was said to have been promised one dollar a week and her board to start, but at the end of five weeks she found herself with ten cents. Five girls from Lower Canada were sent by train with their fares paid, but no provision made for food on the way.[1] In 1846

a long, low, black wagon, termed a "slaver," makes trips to the north of the State cruising around in Vermont and New Hampshire with a commander who is paid $1 a head for all [the girls] he brings to the market and more in proportion to the distance — if they bring them from a distance they cannot easily get back. This is done by representing to the girls that they can tend more machinery than is possible and that the work is so very neat and wages such that they can dress in silks and spend half their time in reading.[2]

But these efforts were unavailing against the backflow from the mills, and the way was opened for the immigrant. The main stream of immigration into the mills during our period was Irish, with lesser streams of English, German, French, and Canadian. Many of them did not go direct to the mills, but went first to the farms where they took the places of the departed New-Englanders. The result was social cleavage, the accentuation of class, and a decline of position for both farm helper and factory worker.

The exodus of the New England native from the mills began in Rhode Island and Fall River. In the Fall River petition of 1842 the influx of foreigners was noted. Out of 612 operatives in Fall River in 1826, only 38 were foreigners. In 1846 Irish were found there in large numbers and by 1860 English and Irish operatives formed the major part of the working population. The Rhode Island constitution

---

[1] *Voice of Industry*, May 29, 1846.   [2] *Ibid.*, January 2, 1846.

did not allow a foreigner to vote unless he owned $134 worth of land. ". . . The result of this rule is to induce the manufacturers to turn off the native citizens and employ foreigners in their stead. . . . If the American citizen votes contrary to his employer he very quietly tells him, 'We want your tenement,' and he and his dependent family are driven into the streets to beg. . . ." [1]

The displacement of the native worker in the larger mills of Massachusetts and New Hampshire was more difficult because of the non-family system, but in the depression of 1848–51, when wages were reduced and the "streets were literally swarming with worthy females and laborers seeking employment," the exodus made great strides. In 1851 it was estimated that, in Massachusetts, 200,000 spindles were idle out of a total of 1,200,000, and in New England, 700,000 out of a total of 2,500,000. It was during this period that the change of personnel was most marked. The Amesbury strike in 1851 was typical of the character of the exodus, and of the tendency of the mills "to drive from our manufacturing villages the best portion of the native population and to fill their places with a vagrant, dependent, and irresponsible class." [2]

In 1849 the "New England Offering" had to call for contributions not only from those who "are," but from those "who have been," operatives, and Miss Farley lamented that "the good old times will not return even if the good old wages are again held out as an inducement." [3] "The discovery of gold in Colonel Sutter's mill-race in California in August, 1848 . . . wrought wonderful changes in the character of the operatives of the Lowell mills. The news of that event fell upon their ears with a seductive thrill. From that day a change began to work itself out in the people here.

---

[1] *Eleventh Annual Report*, Mass. Bureau of Labor Statistics, p. 13.
[2] *Voice of Industry*, September 18, 1846; *Eleventh Annual Report*, Mass. Bureau of Labor Statistics, 1880, pp. 9–14; McNeill, pp. 119–20.
[3] *New England Offering*, 1849.

The Americans started by scores for the land of gold. This Californian emigration, together with that of the Great West, deprived Lowell of some of the best elements in her varied population." [1] In 1850 the minority of the Ten-Hour committee of the Massachusetts Legislature noted that "the infusion of foreigners among the operatives has been rapid and is going on at a constantly increasing rate. ... It will be found that in a few years an entire modification and depression of the state of society in and about manufacturing places will be wrought by this cause." [2]

By 1850, the day of 'mind among the spindles,' the New England mind at least, had passed. The white-gowned girls who marched to welcome Presidents, who talked so intelligently to foreign visitors, who wrote poetry and stories filled with classical allusions, were no longer found in the cotton mills. They had been driven out by a prolonged and fruitless struggle to protect their standards. Their requiem was sounded by Cowley in his "History of Lowell":

On September 24th [1861] Prince Jerome Napoleon, with his consort, the Princess Clotilde ... visited Lowell, having doubtless been recommended to do so by his friend Michel Chevalier. More than a quarter of a century had elapsed since Chevalier's visit: the New England girls on whom he then gazed so admiringly had passed away, and their places were now filled by a motley crowd of Americans, English, Scotch, Irish, Dutch, and French Canadians, who were hardly likely to arouse that exquisite poetic sentiment which Chevalier felt for the factory girls of 1834. [3]

---

[1] Cowley, *History of Lowell*, p. 188.
[2] Minority Report, Mass. House Doc. 153, 1850.
[3] Cowley, p. 200.

CHAPTER X

THE TEN-HOUR MOVEMENT: POLITICAL
1850-60

THE New England Ten-Hour movement of the forties had
failed and in the depression in the cotton industry of 1848,
the working-class agitation died out. When the movement
revived in the fifties, it was of a different sort and under
new auspices, finding its leaders among the middle class and
its field of operations the political. Many of the new leaders
were in the Massachusetts Legislature. The ten-hour system had become a part of the platform of a political party.
In the fifties it was possible for the first time for the corporations to get up counter-petitions in the mills in support
of their opposition to hour legislation.

That which made possible the change in the character of
the Ten-Hour movement was the exodus of the New England operative from the mills, described in the last chapter.

One of the new leaders was Ben F. Butler, whose interest
in the Ten-Hour movement was less for the movement
itself than for the aid it might render his political career.
In 1851 Butler added a ten-hour plank to the platform of
the Coalition Party in Lowell and carried the election. Another of the new leaders was William S. Robinson, who had
married one of the old type of mill girl, the author of "Loom
and Spindle." Robinson went to Lowell in 1849, established
the Lowell "American," a Free-Soil paper, and took up the
ten-hour cause. He wrote the Minority Report of the Ten-
Hour Committee of 1852 and gave to the cause his considerable ability and disinterested service over many years.
The third leader of importance was James M. Stone, of
Charlestown, who, with Salmon Thomas, signed the Minority Report of 1850.

Up to 1850 the Ten-Hour movement had made little impression on the solidarity of the Massachusetts Legislature. The committees that were appointed after 1845 followed in routine fashion the lead given by Schouler, reporting consistently that they found no necessity for legislation. But in 1850, though the committee as usual reported unfavorably, a minority report was presented signed by James Stone and Salmon Thomas. This report used much of the material of Bartlett in a critical fashion and added thereto the findings of Dr. Curtis and some evidence of the working of the shorter day in English mills and manufacturing establishments. The point of view of the new minority is in marked contrast with that which dominated the older committees. Taking as their basis the time schedule of Montgomery, and allowing for the reductions made in 1847, the committee found that the hours of labor in the mills ran from 11 hours, 9 minutes, in December and January, to 13 hours, 1 minute, in April, an average of practically 12 hours a day (11 hours, 58⅓ minutes.) [1] The New England operatives, the committee pointed out, worked, on an average, fourteen hours a week longer than the English factory operatives and, part of the year, they worked twenty hours a week longer.

In 1851 an organization called the New England Industrial League, a revival of the reform associations of the forties, came into existence and summoned the Massachusetts workmen to organize and send delegates to a State convention to prepare for the fall elections. A convention was held in Boston in October with thirty-two delegates representing twenty-two organizations in Massachusetts. Resolutions were passed like those of the New England Workingmen's Association of the forties in support of Land Reform and the Ten-Hour System. A committee was ap-

[1] Mass. House Doc. 153, 1850, Minority Report. This was for the Lowell mills, but they were followed by the Manchester, Nashua, and Dover Companies. (*Voice of Industry,* May 7, 1845.)

pointed to interview candidates for political office, to pledge them to support the Ten-Hour movement, and publish their replies. Up to this point there was no essential difference between the methods of 1850 and those of the forties. The difference did not appear until the next year.

New Jersey, in 1851, passed a Ten-Hour Law like those of New Hampshire and Pennsylvania, and the mills at Paterson reduced the operatives' wages by one half to one day's pay per week. The operatives struck and a compromise was arranged upon wages of $1.50 to $2 a week for women and boys.[1] A meeting of three thousand operatives was held at Gloucester at which objection was made to the employment of children under twelve years of age.[2]

The Ten-Hour movement of the fifties in New England did not get properly started until 1852 when the mills had well recovered from the depression of 1848–51, and the reform forces had completed their organization. The new movement was confined to the ten-hour issue alone and to the State of Massachusetts. Out of the New England convention of 1851 there grew the Ten-Hour State Convention for Massachusetts which held its meetings in Boston, January 28 and September 30, 1852. Free Land, Free Soil, Free Labor, had been discarded, and in keeping with the special purpose, the attainment of a ten-hour law for Massachusetts, the organization was confined to that state. If anything could achieve the end in view, this organization had every right to consider itself the chosen instrument. It had strong friends within the legislature and outside, and, with the break-up of the Whig Party, the prospects of success seemed good.

The second meeting of the Massachusetts Ten-Hour State Convention was "large, harmonious, and enthusiastic." There were 196 delegates from sixteen cities and towns, sixty of whom came from Lowell. A State Central

[1] New York *Daily Tribune,* July 11, 1851.
[2] *Ibid.,* July 14, 1851.

Committee was formed as a permanent executive body to carry on the work of the convention during the year. The chairman of this committee was James Stone, and on it were Fletcher and Young, the only surviving members of the movement of the forties. The business of the Executive Committee was to prepare an address to the public; to pledge candidates for office to the Ten-Hour Law; to collect funds for propaganda; and to organize local societies.[1] This last suggests the difference between the old and the new movements. In the former, the local organizations sprang up and grew into State and New England associations; in the latter, the initiative came from the top and it was necessary to stimulate local organization.

No new party was intended. The convention decided to take the field "by organized political action," by securing written pledges from the candidates of all parties to support an effective law to reduce the hours of labor. They had no faith in the New Hampshire type of law. They sought "an abridgment of the hours of labor, not a new method of measuring the present hours," and proposed that it should apply only to corporations. They were not prepared to say that ten hours should be considered a minimum working day for all time to come. "If it be God's will to abridge man's daily labor to eight, six, or even a less number of hours, we ought cheerfully to submit."

Petitions to the legislature in previous years had failed and the petitioners "may well begin to suspect that the corporation power prevents, by some insidious wiles, the legislature from giving the subject the candid attention and examination which its importance deserves at their hands." [2] The public was warned against the non-effective type of law and advised to go to the nomination meetings and see that real ten-hour men were chosen. Warning was

[1] "The Hours of Labor." Address of the Ten-Hour State Convention, 1852.
[2] Ten-Hour State Convention, p. 6.

also issued against accepting as a compromise the voluntary reduction of hours to eleven. Many corporations in Maine, New Hampshire, and Massachusetts had reduced the hours of the men in the machine shops (who, of course, had votes) just before the election, but had left unchanged the hours of the non-voting women.[1]

Both candidates for governor, H. W. Bishop and William Claflin, signed the ten-hour pledge, as did Amasa Walker and Horace Mann for lieutenant-governor, and the whole Coalition ticket for the Senate. It thus became for the State in 1852 what it had been in Lowell in 1851, a part of the Coalition platform. The Whigs weakened and showed signs of a desire to follow the example of New Hampshire. "The Whig Party is desirous of the passage of a law ... establishing ten hours of labor to be a day's work, not for one class or division of society, but for all the people of the Commonwealth." [2] The 1852 elections turned on the ten-hour issue in the mill towns and the ten-hour men claimed control of one tenth of the lower house.[3]

As a result of the new movement, a further wave of petitions flooded the State Legislature in 1852 and 1853. In 1852 the petitions contained from 3500 to 5500 names. Considering the strength of the ten-hour organization and the influence it had in the legislature, the number of signatures to these petitions was disappointing, the whole number being no greater than Lowell itself had supplied in 1846. This indicated the popular weakness of the new movement and aroused criticism, and, in 1853, as a result of redoubled efforts, the highest record of the earlier movement was equaled with 10,000 petitioners from some thirty localities.[4]

The committee appointed by the 1852 legislature submitted three reports. The majority, as usual, found it in-

[1] Ten-Hour State Convention, pp. 7–8.
[2] Persons, *Labor Laws and Their Enforcement*, p. 69.
[3] *Ibid.*, p. 70.   [4] *Ibid.*, pp. 67–68.

expedient to legislate. The first minority report proposed a special contract law like that of New Hampshire, finding themselves unjustified in "absolutely prohibiting the employing of hands more than ten hours in a day." [1] The third report (minority report number two) was signed by William Robinson and recommended the progressive reduction of the hours of labor in corporations to ten. He noted the criticism of the small number of petitioners and said that it meant simply that the operatives did not want their wages reduced. [2]

In the investigation of 1852 into the irregularities of the Lowell elections of 1851, described in a previous chapter, William Southworth, agent for the Lawrence Corporation, gave the hours of labor as from 6:45 to 7:30 during the winter, less 45 minutes for dinner (breakfast was taken before going to work), which would mean a working day of 12 hours; and during the summer from 5 to 7, less 45 minutes for breakfast and 45 minutes for dinner, being 12 hours, 30 minutes. [3] This is more than the hours accepted by the minority report of 1850, based on Montgomery's figure, and casts further doubt upon the latter. By 'summer' Mr. Southworth must have meant eight months, because it was during eight summer months that time was allowed off for breakfast, and by 'winter' he must have meant the four months when no breakfast time was allowed. This would give an average day of 12 hours, 20 minutes, instead of 12 hours, and would correspond to the figure quoted by Dr. Curtis. It meant that at the Lawrence, at least, the hours were no fewer than those given by Montgomery in 1839. Jesse Farnsworth, an overseer of the Lawrence Company for sixteen years, said that that company had begun 'light-

---

[1] Linus Child, agent of the Boott Mill, said he "had no particular objection against the New Hampshire law, for then they could probably make an arrangement with their help, though it would put them to some inconvenience." Mass. House Doc. no. 230, 1852, p. 18.

[2] Mass. House Doc. no. 185, 1852.

[3] *Ibid.*, 230, 1852.

ing up' in the morning in 1851, "a thing we never did before at this season of the year" [1] (December).

The fact about the voluntary reductions of hours in 1847 seems to have been that some of the mills were slack and reduced the time rather than close down, but when business revived in 1851 they tried by various devices to recover the loss, and frequently they succeeded. In 1852 the hours of mechanics in the machine shops in Massachusetts, New Hampshire, and Maine were reduced to eleven, just before the fall elections.[2]

In 1853 Rhode Island passed a ten-hour law allowing special contracts for adults but compulsory for minors. "Thereupon the employers held a meeting and fixed the hours for adult labor at twelve per day for the first five secular days of the week and nine for Saturday." The operatives seem to have made no move in the matter.[3] In Delaware County, Pennsylvania, where the hours were still twelve per day, the workers sent a memorial to their employers asking for a conference. The employers appointed a committee to take up the matter and this committee decided to introduce the ten-hour system, to reduce wages correspondingly, and to ask the workers to try to get the ten-hour system adopted throughout the country.[4]

The years 1852 and 1853 saw the rise of the aggressive trade-union movement that was so successful in comparison with the defensive movement of the forties. Rising prices and active business conditions gave the skilled workers an opportunity they were not slow to grasp. Strikes were epidemic and the unrest reached the mechanics in the factories. In these years the long-delayed reduction of hours of labor for mechanics in New England was achieved. In 1851 the machinists of Boston gained a ten-hour day. In Worcester, the ten-hour day for mechanics was "all but universal." In

[1] Mass. House Doc. no. 230, 1852.
[2] Ten-Hour State Convention, 1852, p. 8.
[3] New York *Daily Tribune*, August 5, 1853.   [4] *Ibid.*

March, 1853, the mechanics in the Lowell Planing Mills struck for ten hours, but failed. The movement was helped by the news from Delaware County and the appearance in Massachusetts of two delegates from Pennsylvania, in compliance with the employers' request, to assist in the movement in other States.

On September 21, 1853, the Lowell and Lawrence corporations reduced the hours of labor to eleven per day and they were followed immediately by Salem, Newburyport, and other towns.[1]

In the same year, another legislative committee reported against the ten-hour law, with a minority report, as usual.[2] The hour movement began to die down at this point, partly as a result of the action of the corporations in voluntarily reducing hours to eleven, and partly because the corporations were able to purchase immunity. William Robinson was "literally starved out" of his position in Lowell. The Coalitionists lost the city to the Whigs.[3]

But in 1854 a ten-hour bill was introduced in the House and was ordered engrossed. Petitions were renewed and the corporations got up counter-petitions or "remonstrances" with over two thousand signatures from Lowell alone.[4] In Manchester, where the eleven-hour regulation had been adopted in 1853, an attempt was made again to increase the hours. Five thousand operatives struck and stayed out almost a month, winning their point.

In 1855 the Massachusetts legislative committee reported in favor of a compulsory ten-hour law. But, says Cowley:

The corporation managers in Boston adopted the policy of Walpole and killed the bill by secretly buying up some of the most influential of its advocates. The legislature of 1855 has been the subject of much opprobrium. It has often been compared to the Lack-Learning Parliament which sat in England in the reign of Henry the Fourth. But the "Lobby" which controlled that legis-

---

[1] Persons, p. 88.   [2] Mass. House Doc. no. 122, 1853.
[3] Persons, p. 88.   [4] Ibid.

lature was more remarkable still. There the men who, for years, had clamored for a ten-hour law and whose pockets had been lined with corporation gold, were seen "doing the heavy standing round" and suggesting to members that, as the operatives were satisfied with the eleven-hour rule, it was not worth while to carry the matter further. Accordingly, the bill failed.[1]

[1] Cowley, *History of Lowell*, p. 149.

CHAPTER XI

THE REFORMERS: ASSOCIATIONISTS

IN dealing with the industrial situation, 1840 to 1860, it is necessary to include in the picture three theories of reform and groups of reformers: the Associationists (also called Fourierists, Socialists, Labor Reformers); the Land Reformers (calling themselves National Reformers and sometimes called Agrarians); and the Coöperators (consumers' and producers' coöperation).

The first two of these groups began their activities under the impression that it was no difficult matter to stop the progress of the Industrial Revolution and revert to the simpler and freer days before the rise of capitalist industry. They were both slowly weaned away from this optimism and ended up with less pretentious claims and purposes. The third group, the coöperators, represented a more realistic approach to the industrial problem, seeking immediate gains of a practicable sort, but at the same time keeping in mind the larger objects of the other reformers as an ultimate goal.

In their earlier enthusiasm, the Associationists would have nothing to do with coöperative stores. At the Fall River Convention of the New England Workingmen's Association in 1845, J. G. Kaulback introduced a resolution to support the coöperative retail store that had just been organized in Boston. But L. W. Ryckman, of Brook Farm, scouted the suggestion and regretted that such a resolution should be urged, as the New England Association was organized upon a "broader and nobler basis — it aimed at something more fundamental, that shall not merely ameliorate the working classes, but disenthrall the laborer from the power of misused capital..."[1] But

[1] *Voice of Industry*, September 18, 1845.

Ryckman and others were to discover that coöperative stores were more feasible than disenthralling the working classes, and the Associationists went over to a more realistic point of view before the decade had closed. They eventually claimed for the coöperative store an Association origin and regarded the coöperative movement as part of their own.[1]

The doctrines of the Land Reformers were derived from the English Agrarianism of Thomas Spence. Spence's disciple, George Henry Evans, who brought the doctrine to America, believed in the early years that "all adults are entitled to equal property." [2] This was gradually watered down, first to cover only land property, later the public lands, and, finally, when the doctrine got into legislation, it had resolved itself into the Homestead Law of 1861.

Both Association and Land Reform were middle-class movements that attached themselves to the workers' agitations of the period, often to the detriment of the latter. On the whole, the Associationists seem to have interpreted the workers' protests more sympathetically than the others, though the Land Reformers were the more efficient organizers and used the workers with greater effect in the political field. The only truly working-class movements of the period were the Ten-Hour movement of the forties, and the Trade-Union movement of the fifties, with Coöperation lying in between.

Albert Brisbane, an American intellectual with no direct experience of industrial conditions or communities, educated in France and Germany under Guizot, Savigny, and Hegel, came readily under the influence of the grand scheme of Charles Fourier for social and economic reform. He returned to America in 1834 and engaged for six years in personal propaganda in the interest of Fourierism, without making any appreciable impression upon the community. In 1840 he published a translation of Fourier's work, en-

[1] *The New Era*, July 6. 1848.
[2] Commons, *Documentary History*, vol. 7, p. 30.

titled "The Social Destiny of Man, or Association and the Reorganization of Industry," and shortly after, "A Concise Exposition of the Doctrine of Association." He also published "The Future," a periodical devoted to Association propaganda.

It is doubtful if much more would have been heard of Brisbane but for the fact that at that time Horace Greeley came under the influence of his theories. Greeley had come to New York in the thirties and, after experimenting for a year or so with the "New Yorker," had begun the publication of the New York "Tribune" in 1841. In 1842 he gave up one column to Brisbane for the discussion of Association. From then on the movement grew rapidly. In the same year Parke Godwin began the publication of "The Pathfinder," and Brisbane and Macdaniel brought out "The Phalanx, or Journal of Social Science" as the official organ of the group. "The Phalanx" closed in 1845 when it was transferred to Brook Farm, just converted to Fourierism, and rechristened "The Harbinger." "The Harbinger" continued to represent the Associationists until 1849, when the movement practically ceased. There were some eight or ten other Association publications, books and periodicals.[1]

Most of the minor intellectuals of the time gathered about the Association publications. Propaganda flourished. Fourier clubs were organized and conventions — the inevitable conventions — of the Friends of Association were held in Boston in December, 1843, and in New York in April, 1844. In 1846 the American Union of Associations was formed to absorb the two conventions. It continued to meet until 1850.[2]

Brisbane labored under one great difficulty for which he was in no way responsible. His 'community' or 'phalanx' inevitably suggested the community that Robert Owen had

[1] See list in Commons, *History of Labor*, vol. 1, p. 502.
[2] *Ibid.*, pp. 496–503.

established at New Harmony, Indiana, in the thirties. Owen's galaxy of idiosyncrasies had broken up with such regularity that the community idea was at a discount in America. The reputed communism and infidelity of the Owenites did not add to their popularity. To counteract the charges of infidelity that were made against the Associationists, there was formed in Boston, by William H. Channing, in 1846, a "Religious Union of Associationists," later called the "Church of Humanity." One of these 'churches' sent delegates to the New York Industrial Congress in the fifties.

As a result of inquiries as to when and how a 'phalanx' was to be established, Brisbane — in August, 1842 — published in the "Tribune" a scheme for a large association, with ground plan and elevation complete,[1] and in the fall of the same year the sale of stock in the North American Phalanx began.[2] But the intellectuals and workers who were interested had little money and the capitalists who were solicited did not show any great enthusiasm. Brisbane insisted, with the tenacity of a prophet, that the first attempt must be done on a proper scale, but the new converts could not wait, and the Sylvania Phalanx was founded in western Pennsylvania by a group of workmen and their friends. Brisbane was not pleased with this precipitate action and would not recognize the Sylvania Phalanx as a proper test of Associationism. He went on with his plans for the North American, which he regarded as the major experiment of the movement. The North American Phalanx was founded in September, 1843, and in the fall of 1844 it had seventy-seven members and $28,000 worth of land and improvements. In eight years the property increased to $80,000 and the membership to 112. In 1853 a part of the membership seceded and formed the Raritan Bay Union at Perth Amboy, New Jersey. The original phalanx ceased

[1] New York *Tribune*, August 13, 1842.
[2] *Ibid.*, October 28, 1842.

operations in September, 1854, though the Association was not dissolved until 1856.[1] Between thirty-four and forty Fourierite communities were established in the forties. Macdonald's list of eighteen showed a total of 3136 members, though many of these were the same people in different associations. Noyes estimated that 8000 persons in all participated actively in the movement.[2]

Many people have been puzzled by the fact that so respectable a citizen and so successful an editor as Horace Greeley should have become involved in Utopias like that of Brisbane. It has been explained as a result of Greeley's personal eccentricity, his hard-working boyhood, and the 'bad times' of 1837–38 when he first went to New York. But the phenomenon is not very puzzling when the real, as opposed to the legendary, character of Fourierism is taken into account. Fourierism was itself a highly respectable doctrine, not at all revolutionary, but rather a back-fire for revolution. It was a conservative attempt to avoid, on the one hand, the dangers of the new industrialism and, on the other, the destructive forces of working-class revolt. The 'socialism' of Greeley was simply "the faith that the laws and usages regulating the social relations of mankind may be so modified as to enlarge the opportunities and improve the circumstances of the classes now relatively destitute and suffering."[3]

Greeley was a stanch conservative; the radical factor in the situation was the new industrial régime. To Greeley's generation the new industrialism seemed ruthless and destructive, a thing to be curbed lest it utterly destroy the old values of independence and security. Unless it were, red revolution would descend upon America as it had descended on France in 1830, and it was against red revolution as much as against the new industrialism, that Fourierism was directed.

[1] Commons, *History of Labor*, pp. 504–06.
[2] Noyes, *History of American Socialisms*, pp. 11–12.
[3] The New York *Tribune*, January 21, 1852.

The doctrines of Charles Fourier, as interpreted by Albert Brisbane and his followers, have been almost more misunderstood than any other social theory in America. This has been due primarily to the fact that attention has been riveted upon the Fourier communities or phalanxes, to the neglect of other and more significant elements of the theory. If a group of people go into a wilderness to experiment with certain ideas of living and working, the fact of their going into the wilderness may perhaps loom largest in the popular eye, but for the student at least it should not obscure the purposes involved in the experiment itself. People go into the wilderness for all sorts of reasons and the validity of their undertakings depends less upon the fact that they retire, than upon the purpose they have in mind. Fourierism, then, cannot be judged by the experience of the communities, but only by the purposes the communities were intended to try out. It is true, of course, that this idea of community or association was one of the elements of the Fourier doctrine itself and, in so far, the interpretation of Fourierism as a community movement is legitimate. But Fourierism was more than that. It was a theory of the reorganization of society and especially of industry, and this aspect, probably the most important aspect in the Associationists' minds, has been too often neglected.

Fourier was not primarily interested in phalanxes. He projected a reorganization of industry and life. He saw, as did many others of his time, that the Industrial Revolution had resulted in anarchy, had broken up old social units in which security and some freedom had existed. In this transition labor had become a commodity forced by hunger to unpleasant tasks of which it had no choosing. On the other hand, the Associationists found an industrial feudalism arising in the nineteenth century in the place of the old feudalism that had been overthrown, a new "commercial feudalism and the subjection of the producing classes to the absolute control and tyranny of capital." [1] And as a result of this condition they saw, with the experience of Paris fresh in their minds, an imminent revolution that would destroy the values and achievements of civilization. Being normal middle-class persons of intelligence, Fourier, and after him, Brisbane, Greeley, Parke Godwin, *et al*, had no love for class war and sought to avoid it, to ward off disaster by making industry efficient and pleasant.

Fourier's chief contribution both to the present and to his own time was that he sought to make industry efficient with the help of the progressive capitalist. This was the center of his theories, and to attend solely to the phalanxes is to miss the real meaning of the Association philosophy. Unfortunately for Fourier's reputation, business men were not then ready to make industry 'attractive.' Labor was cheap and plentiful, and the only ones who interested themselves in the matter were intellectuals and some workers.

Fourierism was in fact too conservative for America. It was in part the product of an alien fear of revolution and Americans had no such fear. It was more in line with middle-class liberalism than with the temper of the workers of the fifties.

The Fourier system is out and out commercial; it rests on a business basis and treats labor, capital, and talent as partners who are entitled to share the profits equally.[2] . . . According to the notions of the Fourierites, the working-man in the phalanx would do from inclination what, in his present work, he does to keep himself from hunger. It would become in a sense his religion to make the capitalist rich . . . but the greatest need of mankind, his need of equality, finds no consideration in Fourierism.[3]

It was, in part, this non-indigenous conservatism that caused the downfall of the Wisconsin Phalanx. When this

---

[1] *Voice of Industry*, September 4, 1845.
[2] The Fourierists proposed the division of the product of industry: Labor, five twelfths; Capital, four twelfths; Skill (talent), three twelfths.
[3] Kriege in *Volks Tribun*, September 26, 1846.

experiment came to be liquidated, a very positive conclusion remained with the survivors.

Our charter contains a radical error. It is not just nor expedient
to credit stock [capital] yearly with one fourth of the net increase
in the annual appraisement of the property. . . . We are now
firmly of the opinion that no dividend should be allowed to
capital.[1]

"All that Fourierism will agree to," said the Land Reformers, "is that a capitalist class — having its origin in
injustice — shall to all eternity live upon the toil of the
industrious." [2] John A. Collins, of the Skaneateles Community, a follower of Owen, visited the Sodus Bay Phalanx
at Rochester in 1846 and spoke to the discouraged Associationists, "proving to the satisfaction of most of them . . .
that Fourier's plan of distributing wealth was both arbitrary and superficial; that it was a useless effort to unite
two opposite and hostile elements, which had no more af-
finity than water and oil or fire and gun-powder. . . . Association is a great school for Communism." [3]

The 'alien origin' charge against Fourierism was equally
applicable to all the reforms of the period. "Niles's Register" noticed Fourierism, in 1843, among the "attempted
improvements of the times." "It would seem from his
writings that he knew nothing of the workings of society
under the republicanism of this country, and all his conclusions are drawn from premises of European, Asiatic,
and barbarian origin." [4]   Evans charged Owen with
proposals "calculated for the meridian of England." [5]
Macdaniel said of Evans, "that the idea that the root
of the evil is in a monopoly of the land comes from
England." [6] Wendell Phillips said of the Associationists,

[1] Spirit of the Age, December 8, 1849.
[2] Working Man's Advocate, August 31, 1844.
[3] Noyes, History of American Socialisms, p. 290.
[4] Niles's Register, May 6, 1843.
[5] Working Man's Advocate, July 20, 1844.
[6] The Phalanx, August 10, 1844, p. 229.

"that many of their errors on this point came from looking at American questions through European spectacles." The circle would have been complete had Owen suggested that the anti-slavery agitation was also of English origin — a reasonable charge.

The 'alien origin' cry was overdone. It was true enough, the ideas of the reformers were of alien origin. Most ideas are. It is its 'alien' origin that distinguishes idea from habit. But ideas, alien or native, do not germinate unless the soil is prepared. The movements that arose around these ideas were indigenous enough, the causes of unrest were American. And in their interpretation of the problem of the worker, the Associationists were more nearly at one with the working-class groups than any other of the reformers.

Scarcity of employment, low wages, and fourteen, sixteen hours of labor per day [they contended] are indeed grievances which the laborer does now and then muster courage to grumble about; but they are not fundamental. The laborer does not belong to himself, has no right to be, and exists upon sufferance. He is emphatically a wage slave. Herein is the fundamental evil to which he is subject . . . and it is to my mind clear that he can attain his rights only by democratic association with his brethren so that all may in their turn equally participate in the exercise of legislative power. . . .[1]

Up to a certain point, all the reformers and the workers themselves were in agreement. They claimed that the great mass of the population was going down in the scale, both as persons and as workers. Division arose when they began to discuss the cause of the difficulty and the remedies that should be sought. The Associationists asserted that the cause was to be found in the economic field: the Land Reformers, in the political. As to remedies, the Land Reformers sought safety in flight back into a local agricultural society: the Associationists sought the re-

[1] Letter of William West in reply to Devyr. New York *Tribune*, June 18, 1850.

form of industry by way of the phalanx or reorganized community.

Fourier's system, like many of the philosophies of the time, was on a grand scale, but it was grounded in a psychology which, while naïve enough in the light of present standards, was no more naïve than the one it opposed. It was not, strictly speaking, Fourier's psychology at all, but the common property of the age, the psychology which underlay the idealism of Europe and America. It was found in Rousseau as opposed to the theory of Hobbes, and as far back in philosophical thought as one cares to go.

Fourier denied the doctrine of the essential depravity of human nature and the conclusions based thereon that men must be disciplined and enslaved by an alien industrial power. He claimed that men were not necessarily lazy and of no account, but had impulses of a creative character that modern industry was especially adapted to destroy. He proposed the reorganization of industry on the basis of these creative impulses to permit their free expression, believing that in this way industry could be made attractive and efficient rather than repulsive and wasteful.

What the modern psychological industrial reformers call instincts, Fourier called 'passions,' and he found twelve of these basic passions to which the monotony and discipline of modern industry were ill-adapted. He concluded not that the passions should be suppressed as evil, but that industry should be recognized as inefficient.

Fourier had little or no interest in the problem of the distribution of the product of industry — the major concern of the Socialists proper. It is true that he laid down a plan for the distribution of the product: five twelfths to labor, four twelfths to capital, and three twelfths to talent.[1] But his main concern was with the productive processes themselves. He wished first to reorganize industry so as to call out the best that was in the worker, to gain his complete

[1] Brisbane, *The Social Destiny of Man*, p. 155, note.

allegiance and interest, in order to give to the worker the free exercise of his creative impulses and to industry a greater efficiency than "repulsive" labor could achieve. He claimed not to want the industrial worker regimented that he might be comfortable, but free that he might produce more and better and in a better way. Neither did he want the worker to free himself.

The man had a passion for economic efficiency that would make even the Fabians blush. He deplored the time lost in controversies "which confuse all subjects," in commotions [1] and even in social gatherings, as diversions from industry.

> If the overseer is away, the workmen stop; if they see a man or a cat pass, they all turn to look; leaning on their spades and gaping for diversion; forty or fifty times a day they lose in this way five minutes. Their week's work is hardly equal to four full days. . . . [2]
> Labor performed with apathy and indifference does not yield the half of what it would if the rivalry and enthusiasm which animate the groups could be communicated to it. . . . We find none of these inducements in civilization; pecuniary interest is the only stimulant of the laboring mass. [3]

But Fourier's belief in the possibilities of human nature led him beyond the defects of industrial organization into civilization itself with its separate family. In the separate family, in the work of the housewife, for instance, he found labor without rivalry, prosecuted alone, without variety or 'elegance.' [4] In the education of children, likewise, there was no system of developing the instincts and no training for industrial life. [5] All civilized society lacked order, harmony, efficient working.

By bringing order out of chaos Fourier and his followers hoped to reform industry and society. Along with much

---

[1] Brisbane, *The Social Destiny of Man*, p. 70.   [2] *Ibid.*, pp. 69–70.
[3] *Ibid.*, p. 65.   [4] *Ibid.*, p. 85.
[5] *Ibid.*, pp. 85–86.

that was wise, there was much that was fantastical. He claimed for his reform too much. He insisted that he not only had something to teach about labor management and the internal organization of industry, but that his plan would reform society. Charging that "the very foundation of our society is injustice and oppression," [1] he proposed to remove this injustice and oppression without conflict with the interest or prejudice of any portion of the community.[2] This was the claim of a charlatan. It should have been obvious to Fourier and to other conciliators that injustice can never be remedied without hurting some one's interest or prejudice, and it should have been obvious too that it is not likely to be removed without conflict of some sort. Men do not ordinarily relinquish privileges by being exhorted thereto. And it was at this point that working-class realism parted company with the romanticism of the Associationists.

The phalanxes failed within a few years. The longest-lived, the American Phalanx, existed eleven years, but most of the others broke up within a year or two of their founding. Innumerable reasons have been adduced for this failure by friends and enemies alike. The Associationists claimed that none of the phalanxes had been properly founded, and certainly none of them resembled Brisbane's gorgeous plan. But the obvious reason was their artificiality. A new society cannot be created overnight according to plans and specifications drawn up in the study. The very thing that Brisbane refused to do, being doctrinaire, to start in in a small way and work up, as the religious communities had done, was the one possible way of success. There was nothing artificial about the religious communities. They were composed mostly of peasants with one idea and that not of this world, who went into the wilderness to make themselves comfortable until death should take them. But it was the extreme of artificiality to try to plant in the wilderness a full-

[1] Brisbane, p. 104. [2] *Ibid.*, p. 105.

fledged, highly specialized, agricultural-industrial community and expect it to last.

Many instances of what happened to these experiments
were described with great detail and sympathy by Macdonald, a Scottish Owenite, who came to America to follow
the fortunes of his master and found nothing but ruins.
He faithfully performed the melancholy task of gathering
the survivors' stories of suffering, failure, and disillusion-
ment both for the Owenite and Fourier communities, but
died before he was ready to publish. Noyes has used this
material in his book "The History of American Socialisms."

Brook Farm

The little colony of idealists who gathered at Brook
Farm, Roxbury, near Boston, in the spring of 1841, had no
particular social or economic philosophy to work out. They
felt that Christianity was not sufficiently Christian and
modern competitive society not conducive to the development of the spiritual values they cherished.   Under these
circumstances they believed the thing to do was to withdraw from society and cherish the values they regarded in
their own way. They were not overanxious to propagate
their views or to gain converts, preferring rather to train
those children who might be sent to them for instruction,
in what they considered more humane and more reasonable
doctrines than those of their own youth.

In its religious aspect the Brook Farm movement was a
revolt against the externality and harshness of Calvinism
toward the idealism of the Hegelians, Swedenborg and
Carlyle. The original group out of which the exodus proceeded was composed entirely of intellectuals, many of
them clergymen. They began as a club in 1836, meeting in
the homes of the members. They accepted the name
"Transcendentalists" and in 1840 began to publish "The
Dial," a literary and critical magazine, to the first number

of which most of the literary lights of Massachusetts contributed, including: Emerson, Margaret Fuller, Channing, Dwight, Parker, Ripley, Alcott, Ward. "The Dial" proposed to be "one cheerful, rational voice amidst the din of mourners and polemics," measuring no hours but those of sunshine.

No one [said the editors in their introductory statement] can converse much with the different classes of society in New England without remarking the progress of a revolution. Those who share in it have no external organization, no badge, no creed, no name . . . without pomp, without trumpet, in lonely and obscure places, in solitude, in servitude, in compunctions and privations, trudging beside the team in the dusty road or drudging a hireling in other men's cornfields, schoolmasters who teach a few children rudiments for a pittance, ministers of small parishes of the obscurer sects, lone women in dependent condition, matrons and young maidens, rich and poor, beautiful and hard-favored, without concert or proclamation of any kind, they have silently given in their several adherence to a new hope and in all companies do signify a greater trust in the nature and resources of man than the laws or the popular opinions will well allow.[1]

George Ripley, a Unitarian minister in Boston, was one of the group. He was not satisfied with a 'revolution' that existed only in the idle longings of disappointed clergymen, teachers, elderly maidens, and tired farmhands. He felt that if labor were good and honorable, as every one agreed, then all men should labor. There had grown up in God-fearing Massachusetts, social and economic classes, ranks and distinctions that were un-Christian and unreal. The 'hired girl' had become the 'mere help.' This should be changed; the simpler realities of the past should be regained. The great fact was that of human equality before God.

I cannot behold [said Ripley in a letter to his Church in 1840] the degradation, the ignorance, the poverty, the vice, the ruin of the soul which is everywhere displayed in the very bosom of

---

[1] *The Dial*, vol. 1, July, 1840, p. 2.

Christian society without a shudder. I cannot witness the glaring inequalities of condition, the hollow pretentions of pride, the scornful apathy, with which many urge the prostration of man, the burning zeal with which they run the race of selfish competition with no thought for the elevation of their brethren, without the sad conviction that the spirit of Christ has well-nigh disappeared from our churches. . . .[1]

But the churches were not interested in Ripley's egalitarian Christianity and in the same year he resigned his charge.

The defense of humanity is sometimes considered an attack on society. . . . When a minister of the Gospel cannot show by his life and conduct, by his word and his works, that he is hostile to all oppression of man by man . . . and that all his sympathies are with the down-trodden and suffering poor, without impairing the influences of his labors, I feel that it is time to look at the foundation on which we stand, and see if it does not suffer from some defect which threatens its destruction.[2]

In the spring of 1841 George Ripley and a few friends started in a small way "The Institute of Agriculture and Education," commonly called "Brook Farm." He left behind him most of his Transcendentalist friends, including Emerson and Margaret Fuller. But Hawthorne joined him and some others who were more useful in the barnyard.

Ripley hoped to get in touch with the working classes, and the leaders of the Brook Farm group attached themselves to any labor movements that were going in the vicinity, with the frequent result that the labor movements died under their soaring periods. Brisbane went up to visit the Farm, as did most of the travelers of the time seeking thrills. He saw in Brook Farm a going concern to add to his string of phalanxes and set himself to convince Ripley of the value of the Fourier terminology and form of organization. In 1845 he was successful and

---

[1] Frothingham, *George Ripley*, p. 74.   [2] *Ibid.*, p. 75.

Brook Farm became a full-fledged phalanx so far as the name and a burdensome constitution could make it so. Unfortunately, some of the members who had expected to dignify labor by their adherence did not like the social promiscuity that the new departure would involve and deserted the sanctuary. Some of the pupils were withdrawn from the school and Emerson's sympathy was alienated.

The workers with a few exceptions were not involved in the phalanxes. The influence of the Associationists on the workers' movements was of a different sort, by way of their intellectual control in the conventions and assemblies of the workers' organizations. The Brook Farm group captured the New England Workingmen's Association before it was well begun, and Greeley was in constant touch with the New York workers' organizations. Unfortunately for the working-class movements of the forties, the intellectuals were always attempting to use them to advance their own plans.

Brook Farm came to an end in 1847 as a result of the burning of the new Phalanstery. Ripley shouldered its debts and spent some part of his life working them off as a journalist and author. But the enthusiasts of the movement did not consider that they had failed.

We write from the scene of one of the sublimest triumphs ever achieved by man [said D. H. Jaques in 1847]. We speak of triumph, though around us are what might seem to be signs of defeat. The "Eyrie" is nearly deserted. The "Cottage" and the "Pilgrim House" will soon be without tenants. The swarm which thronged "The Hive" is scattered, and yonder stands the blackened walls of what was dignified by the name of "Phalanstery"! Still there has been success — triumph. Do you ask wherein? In this: the great social problem has here been solved.[1]

Jaques was wrong, but it is not necessarily right to say that Brook Farm was a failure. The social aims of Brook Farm had originally to do almost entirely with the people

[1] *Voice of Industry*, October 22, 1847.

who entered it. These people, feeling uncomfortable in the life of their time, withdrew and set up a life of their own. This they seemed to find good.

The life we now lead [said "The Harbinger"], though to a hasty and superficial observer surrounded with so great imperfections and embarrassments, is far superior to what we have been able to attain under the most favorable circumstances in civilization. There is a freedom from the frivolities of fashion, from arbitrary restrictions, and from the frenzy of competition; we meet our fellow men in more hearty, sincere, and genial relations. Kindred spirits are not separated by artificial conventional barriers; there is more personal independence and a wider sphere for its exercise; the soul is warmed in the sunshine of a true social equality; we are not brought into the rough and disgusting contact with uncongenial persons which is such a general source of misery in the common intercourse of society; there is a greater variety of employment, a more constant demand for the exercise of all the faculties and a more exquisite pleasure in effort, from the consciousness that we are not working for personal ends, but for a holy principle.[1]

All this was very well if that was the sort of person one happened to be. There were people, however, who had no enthusiasm for "freedom from the frivolities of fashion." There were people who enjoyed the "frenzy of competition" and there were many groups in the community in which 'kindred spirits' found few conventional barriers dividing them. Any one who wished to estabish 'social equality' by eliminating 'uncongenial persons' had a right to do so, but when they went beyond their original intentions and set themselves up as a model for the reorganization of society, they left themselves open to criticism. The one thing the reformer never understood was that it takes all sorts of people to make a world. Brook Farm succeeded so long as it regarded itself as one sort of person trying to be happy and succeeding reasonably well. It failed when it became Fourierist and set out on the assumption that all people would be equally happy under similar arrangements.

[1] *The Harbinger*, December 20, 1845.

CHAPTER XII

LAND REFORM

LAND REFORM was no less intellectualist in its origins than was the Association movement, but it carried over from its earlier agrarian sentiments a less conciliatory point of view. It paraded as a class doctrine and had less fear of strife and less faith in harmony than the Fourierists. But it was no less transcendental and its proposals were no more realistic in their approach to the industrial problem. It sought not a solution, but an escape. It would have recalled the old localism, a localism that was doomed. It would have had every man to recline under his own vine and fig-tree. Each 'rural republican township' was to become a self-sustaining social and economic unit.

The Land Reformers hoped that the public domain could be equally divided among users of land and so kept that their peasant proprietor idyll might come true. Public lands were selling at $1.25 an acre, but they were remote, and it was no part of Evans's plans that the public land should be sold for little or much. The more cheaply the land sold the worse, so far as he was concerned, because it permitted greater inequalities and the monopoly of large tracts in the hands of speculators. The land should be given away to users in small holdings and made inalienable.

Land Reform watered down its proposals, but not its hopes. It continued to believe that it would undo the work of the Industrial Revolution, would tear apart the rising cities, "reconstruct the map of the earth," and "draw all the small holders of property in these large cities into the townships," leaving nothing but "warehouses, shipyards, and foundries to accommodate international commerce at the great sea and river ports of the earth." [1]

[1] Masquerier, *Sociology*, pp. 98–99.

In this reconstructed earth each township would be a complete, self-sustaining economic unit with its own farms, its own traders, and its own small mechanics and their shops. There would be no need for national or international trade, for centralized industrial production, and very little for railroads and canals. Artisans would again exchange their products directly with the farmers or through local traders in the village square.[1]

The central idea in the theory of Land Reform was the Rural Republican Township created out of the public lands. All the public lands of the United States were to be surveyed into townships of six miles square containing thirty-six sections, each of one square mile, and subdivided into 144 quarter-sections. The center section of each township was to be laid out in village lots averaging five acres each, with a thirty-acre park to contain the public buildings. Any landless man was to have the right to settle on a quarter-section farm or village lot, but he was to have no more land, and his farm or lot was to be inalienable. Every one coming of age was to have the same right.[2]

The Land Reformers saw the problem of their day as political and their ends attainable by political action. This tended to alienate them from the workers' movements that were still smarting under the recollection of the fiasco in which the Workingmen's Party of 1829 had ended. The purposes of the workers were not attainable by political action, and Land Reform, where it did not help to wreck the workers' movements, drifted apart, ending in the Republican Party and the Homestead Act.

George Henry Evans, an Englishman, who came to America as a child, started the "Working Man's Advocate" in 1829 in New York to propagate the agrarianism he had learned from his father, a disciple of Thomas Spence. After the failure of the Workingmen's Party he retired, in 1837,

---

[1] *Young America,* June 28, 1845.
[2] *Working Man's Advocate,* March 15, 1845.

to a New Jersey farm, and, with the improvement of business conditions, he returned to New York, March 16, 1844, and began to publish a second paper of the same name. In 1845 the name was changed to "Young America." On his return to New York in 1844 Evans called together half a dozen kindred spirits at John Windt's print-shop and proposed three principles for agitation and political action: (1) the freedom of the public lands to actual settlers: (2) exemption of the homestead from seizure for debt; and (3) the limitation of the amount of land that any one person might acquire. The charter members of this band of National Reformers, as they called themselves, were: John Windt, Thomas A. Devyr, James A. Pyne, James Maxwell, Lewis Masquerier, and George Evans. They organized themselves as a band of speakers and held meetings at the parks and street corners to catch the attention of the working-men. They held evening meetings in various halls in the city and finally settled on Croton Hall as their headquarters.[1]

Four days after his arrival in New York, Evans called a 'working-men's' meeting at Croton Hall and formed the National Reform Association. A paper organization was drawn up involving a Central Executive Committee in New York of one delegate from each ward for every six members of the ward organization. As there were no such ward organizations, the committee of fifteen was to be chosen at Croton Hall from among those who signed the National Reform pledge. Membership in the National Reformers meant signing the pledge and paying twenty-five cents initiation fee and two cents a month dues.[2] It is doubtful if this central committee were ever elected by any one but Evans, though some ward organizations were created.

Mike Walsh, the Tammany insurgent, with his 'Spartan

[1] Masquerier, pp. 95–96.
[2] *Working Man's Advocate*, March 30, 1844.

Band' of plug-uglies, welcomed Evans, and, after making one of his famous speeches at the first meeting of the Reformers, headed the list of pledgers and supported Land Reform in the 'Subterranean.' [1]

George Evans was the most rigid doctrinaire of a period of doctrinaires. "This is the first measure to be accomplished" was his position, "and it is as idle to attempt any great reforms without that as it is to go to work without tools. Place the surplus mechanics on their own land in the west in Rural Republican Townships with their large Public Square and Public Hall in the center of each, leaving full employment to those who remain in the cities . . ." [2] and all will be well. The Associationists were ready to welcome suggestions of reform from other quarters, did welcome Land Reform. The advocates of the Ten-Hour movement and the Coöperators did the same. Even Owen was willing to admit that there might be something in other plans, though not much. But Evans was immovable. Almost every line he wrote had the one refrain; every incident pointed the one moral. Owen's proposals were "calculated for the meridian of England," a futile attempt to harmonize conflicting interests.

According to our view the attempt is futile . . . the disparity we think must be removed by . . . an eradication of the cause that has produced it. . . . The cause . . . it can be hardly necessary for us to state, is the monopoly of the soil; it seems to us a pity that Mr. Owen's well-intentioned efforts have not been directed to the abolition of that monopoly rather than to fruitless appeals to the wisdom and justice of those who have profited by it.

The same criticism he applied to the Associationists. [3]

Evans's chief interest in the working-class movements

---

[1] *Working Man's Advocate*, March 30, 1844.

[2] *Ibid.*, July 20, 1844.

[3] *Ibid.* When Owen called a World Convention for the fall of 1845, Evans wrote to the *Voice of Industry*, "Please state in your columns" that the National Convention of Reformers (Evans's own convention) "is a distinct affair from the World's Convention . . . and will have nothing to do with theology." (*Voice of Industry*, August 28, 1845.) Evans did add the Ten-Hour measure to his programme.

of his time was to tie them to his programme. He failed to
get the New England Workingmen's Association to call a
national convention before they had properly organized
locally, and left the meeting before it was over, to call his
own national convention.[1] A mass meeting of the trades
was called in New York in 1845 to "organize the trades
into a great benefit society for coöperative purposes, to
bring the producer and consumer face to face and thereby
dispense in time with the services of the intermediate
employer and retail dealer." But Bovay, one of Evans's
lieutenants, had no faith in the plan and switched the
meeting off on to land reform. In 1846 Evans noticed the
coöperative movement of New England, "their object
merely to buy of the producer instead of the merchant."
As it was rare, he objected, that the workman could find
time for more than one society, such an organization would
do more harm than good because it did not take land
monopoly into consideration. The New York workmen, he
claimed, understood this so well that they were nonplussed
that the East was so dilatory. Evans accused the Boston
friends of ignoring the National Convention and of going
off on their own. "Our worst enemies could not adopt a
more effective course to put us back a year. . . ."[2] The
National Reformers started their own Coöperative Brotherhoods, called "Young Americas." They were identical
with the Industrial Brotherhoods of the National Industrial Congress except that the latter admitted none but
actual working-men, and Evans as an employer was thus
excluded, and had to start his own.[3]

[1] *Working Man's Advocate*, March 8, 1845.

[2] *Young America*, January 24, 1846; cf. *Voice of Industry*, February 20,
1846.

[3] *Ibid.*, December 13, 1845. The important thing about the Land Reformers was their activity in the labor movement rather than their theory.
With the Associationists the opposite was the case. This explains the
relatively little space given Land Reform in this chapter. The activities
of the Land Reformers have a large place in Chapters XIV and XV.

CHAPTER XIII

COÖPERATION

Some one group of reformers in all this welter of transcendentalism had to show a sense of realities. This was
left to the Coöperators. Some workers could of course for-
sake the world and enter a phalanx. Some could settle on a
quarter-section in the Western wilds. But most of them
had to stay where their work was being done. And unless
they were to continue to sink in the scale a realistic reform
had to be proposed. The coöperators understood this, and
set out to gain some of the benefits of Association without
its limitations. The workers' position was clearly put at a
meeting of the Laborers' Union of South Boston in 1845:
"Resolved, that as practical laborers who have not the
means or the inclination to withdraw from society, we
deem it incumbent on us to use all the means in our power
to remove existing evils from the present state of society." [1]
Their proposals might be 'tinkering,' as the Utopians
would insist, or they might not. It was at least better than
waiting for a millennium which might never appear.

The Coöperative movement grew out of the disillusion-
ment of one group of Associationists with large schemes of
reform and out of the despair of the workers over their
failures to increase their wages and shorten their hours of
labor. In January, 1845, there developed in Boston a plan
of producers' coöperation or self-employment under the
caption "Industrial Association," that was soon superseded by the more feasible consumers' coöperation of the
Protective Unions. A committee of the Mechanics and
Laborers' Association of Boston reported a plan for self-
employment that was Fourierism with a working-class
twist to it and without the phalanx.

[1] *Voice of Industry,* July 17, 1845.

The direction and profits of industry [they said] must be kept in the hands of the producers. Laborers must own their own shops and factories, work their own stock, sell their own merchandise, and enjoy the fruits of their own toil. Our Lowells must be owned by the artisans who build them and the operatives who run the machinery and do all the work. And the dividend, instead of being given to the idle parasites of a distant city, should be shared among those who perform the labor. . . .

It was proposed to form a joint-stock company, an industrial firm, in Boston, on a coöperative basis. Stock was to be sold in small units, a savings bank established, and a large 'unitary edifice' built to house, in the basement, a community store; in the second story, a hall for concerts, a library, art gallery, and school; and, in the third story, mechanical, artistic, and manufacturing operations (printing, shoemaking, etc.). Dividends were to be divided among the members in the proportion of: Labor, three fifths; skill, two fifths; capital, one fifth.[1] This was simply the Phalanstery adapted to Boston, with the division of the product changed slightly to benefit the worker at the expense of the capitalist.

This plan of the Industrial Association was taken up by the Lynn shoemakers in February, 1845, after the failure of their strike call of the previous year. A shoemaking shop was established, the capital paid up, the first lot of stock purchased, cut up, and given out to the members. There were thirty members, and the venture seems to have succeeded for a while.[2] In 1848 one of the Divisions of the Protective Union again reverted to the idea of producers' coöperation to prevent the "social, moral, and political degradation" of the small mechanic, who is "even obliged to surrender his business as a master mechanic with all its profits and enjoyments to the monied mechanic who is without the smallest knowledge of the trade."[3] As late

[1] The Awl, January 18, 1845.   [2] Ibid., February 8, 1845.
[3] The New Era, July 20, 1848.

as 1850 there was a coöperative bootmaking establishment at Randolph and a paper-mill at Hardwick, Massachusetts.[1]

But the distinctively Massachusetts development was to
be in the direction of consumers' coöperation. In New
York, under the ægis of Greeley and chiefly among the
seamstresses, tailors, and shoemakers, coöperative production was occasionally taken up, usually along philanthropic lines.

Consumers' coöperation began in Boston in October,
1845, when the "Workingmen's Protective Union" was
organized with Horace Seaver, president; C. C. Jones and
Henry P. Trask, secretaries; and J. G. Kaulback, treasurer.
The original purpose was much wider than that of a coöperative store; the latter was, in part, a bait to entice the
workers along the road to Association. "It was seen to be
impossible to introduce any system of complete coöperation at once, and it had been proved by sad experience that
without a degree of unity in some material interest no
union of workingmen could be made either permanent or
efficient." [2] The Protective Union was organized by five
or six 'friends of the workers' in the printery of A. J.
Wright. There was no capital and the organizers had had
no experience in business, but a constitution was drawn up
and the movement was ready to proceed.

The constitution of the new union declared in Fourierist
language: "Whereas, many evils arise from the isolated
way in which the laborer as a man of small means has to
purchase the necessaries of life: therefore to unite the little
fund of the producers and purchase in season, as do the
wealthy class, their fuel and groceries, would, it is obvious,
secure to them a larger share of their products." [3] In addition to the store, an employment bureau was contem-

[1] New York *Daily Tribune*, June 18, 1850.
[2] *Voice of Industry*, February 11, 1848.
[3] *Ibid.*, November 28, 1845.

plated, it being "the imperative duty we owe to one another and ourselves to give all the information in our power to the procurance of sure, steady and profitable employment." Further, they were to indulge "in deeds of genuine sympathy" by relieving the destitute and administering to the sick. These were not, however, regarded as ends in themselves, or as striking at the roots of their troubles. And there were added, as more radical purposes, the attainment of higher wages and shorter hours of labor, to "thereby in no ordinary degree remove the cause of poverty and sickness." [1] The original Protective Unionists expected to accumulate a fund for the purpose of starting self-employment workshops, combining in this way consumers' and producers' coöperation.[2] The initiation fee was three dollars and the dues twenty-five cents a month.

All early coöperators were involved in a conflict between the ambitious aims of the reformers and the desire of the workers for immediate returns. The Protective Union expected to satisfy both. They proposed to sell at wholesale prices, plus cost of handling, to meet the demands of the workers, and at the same time to set aside a fund to create self-employing workshops. This was obviously impossible and the larger plans were quietly forgotten. In England the Rochdale pioneers originated a compromise by selling at market prices and paying back a part of the profits in the form of dividends on purchases, the remainder being held for education, expansion, and protection in case of bad times. The American Coöperators had no knowledge of this plan and labored under a serious

---

[1] *Voice of Industry*, November 28, 1845.

[2] *Ibid.* The New York City Protective Union tried to unite all trades in a coöperative store and use the profits to start coöperative production. They organized a bakery and wheelwright shop. This movement was more closely connected with the Associationists than the Boston Coöperators. Ryckman, of Brook Farm, was business agent for the New York Coöperative until succeeded by Ira B. Davis. (New York *Daily Tribune*, June 1 and July 13, 15, 1850.)

financial handicap in making no provision for a reserve fund.

The Boston Division of the Protective Union was the first of a list of more than four hundred that grew up in New England before the decline began in 1851. It is significant of the close connection of the movement with the Associationists that Roxbury was the second division to be organized, in 1846. In January, 1847, a Supreme Division was created with R. L. Robbins, president, and Albert J. Wright, secretary-treasurer. At this time there were twelve divisions in the movement, and the Supreme Division was intended to unite them, much as the Wholesale unites the British retail stores. But the Supreme Division, unlike the English Wholesale, was a delegate body with legislative functions, composed of one delegate per twenty-five members from the constituent divisions. It had sole right to organize new divisions, to decide constitutional questions, and to deal with internal quarrels. Attached to the Supreme Division was a Board of Trade which employed a purchasing agent for all the divisions that were willing to make use of his services.[1]

An interesting departure was made in 1847 when the Boston Division sent an address to the Farmers of New York State suggesting that they organize and exchange their products directly with the workers to eliminate the charges of the middlemen. There were at that time forty divisions of the Protective Union and three thousand members.[2]

Signs of internal trouble appeared almost from the start. In 1847, Division No. 9 registered an objection to the highly centralized form of the organization. It claimed the right of local divisions to make their own constitutions

---

[1] *Voice of Industry*, October 15, 1847.

[2] *Ibid.*, December 17, 1847. In January, 1847, there were 12 divisions; October, 25; November, 34; December, 40; June, 1848, 42; July, 56 and 8000 members; July, 1849, 62 divisions.

and by-laws and wanted to be insured against losses to the subdivisions as a result of mismanagement on the part of agents of the Supreme Division.[1] Division No. 9 voted to dissolve its connection with the Supreme Division after January 1, 1848.[2] The chief objection of some of the stores to the constitution laid down by the central organization was the inclusion of benefit features. With the success of the store as a business undertaking, it tended to grow away from the reform purposes of the founders. The local groups had less interest in the principles of Association than in cheap groceries.[3]

The early success of the movement was very great. Plans were discussed for more ambitious things and the original dream of coöperative production appeared again. ". . . There are exchangers beyond the retailers who want looking after. The importer and the wholesale dealer are diving deeper into the pockets even than the retailer. . . . We have enough in the Union now to charter a small vessel to the West Indies for sugar and molasses."[4] The "subject of establishing furnishing stores among the seamstresses of the city upon humane principles" was introduced by a member of No. 3 Division. Coöperative home-building and a coöperative savings bank were suggested.[5]

To us there is nothing more interesting [said John Orvis] than to observe the growth of the principles of coöperation in the minds of the oldest friends of this movement. This is the third meeting of this body [Supreme Division] at which we have been a spectator, and we can truly say no one thing has struck us with more force than their constant expansion of thought, of power of ready and intelligent action and ability both to speak and understand each other. . . . This shows the Protective Union to be . . . a school in which the working classes are unconsciously fitting themselves for seats in other places now too exclusively filled by the myrmidons

---

[1] *Voice of Industry*, December 31, 1847.   [3] *Ibid.*, December 17, 1847.
[3] *Ibid.*, November 19, 1847.   [4] *Ibid.*, October 22, 1847.
[5] *Ibid.*, March 3, 1847; *The New Era*, July 6, 1848.

of a false, antagonistic industry and a destructive system of trade.[1]

The success of coöperation commanded the attention of the Associationists, though they had at first repudiated it. At the second annual convention, in January, 1849, the constitution of the W.M.P.U. was altered and its name changed to the New England Protective Union. The name of the Supreme Division was changed to Central Division.[2] Statistics show the growth of the movement as follows:[3]

Amount of business done per quarter:

1848 —	January 1 (preceding quarter)	$18,748.77
	April 1	24,359.02
	July 1	33,000.00
	October 1	36,400.00
1849 —	January 1	40,910.24
	April 1	49,601.14
	July 1	60,439.00
	October 1	69,851.22
1850 —	January 1	102,353.53
	April 1	126,301.92
	July 1	150,831.30
	October 1	155,851.81
1851 —	January 1	180,026.47

A growing distrust on the part of the local divisions toward the central purchasing agency is seen in the report of the committee on trade in 1851. Many of the sub-divisions failed to make use of the agent except for small purchases and those of the most difficult sort to make. But the movement continued to grow and, in 1852, there were 403 divisions reported, though many had undoubtedly failed. Talk of difficulties and failures and their causes increased. One of the greatest problems was to get good business men to handle the stores.

The future of the Protective Union depends upon men. . . . We

---

[1] *The New Era*, July 13, 1848.
[2] New York *Daily Tribune*, July 18, 1850.
[3] *Eighth Annual Report*, Mass. Bur. of Labor Statistics, p. 69.

want no more fanatics to lead us on to nothingness — persons who ridicule the plainest truths of political economy because above the reach of their mental vision, and deny the existence of the very stars because they cannot see them at noonday.[1]

In 1853 the "Tribune" noticed the difficulties of the movement and declared that among the obstacles to their success were: the benefit feature; the want of incorporation which deprived the divisions of their capital whenever members left the community; the inability to check fraud because the agent could not be criminally prosecuted; and the fact that the Central Division was a delegate body and did too much talking and too little administration. Only one third of the divisions were buying through the central agent because of distrust and quarrels.[2]

In the same year the growing complaints resulted in opposition to the renomination of the purchasing agent and another was appointed in his place. The old purchasing agent managed to get the Board of Trade to create a second purchasing position and have himself retained. The Committee on Trade refused to recognize this action, and a 'battle of circulars' ensued between the two factions to gain the allegiance of the local divisions.[3] The split remained unhealed and two organizations developed, the seceders calling themselves the American Protective Union. The American Protective Union had none of the reform purposes of the old organization and developed as a joint-stock company along purely commercial lines. The old Protective began, in 1853, to publish a "Journal of the P.U.," with only fifty divisions remaining on its list. The old principles were reasserted and the practice deplored of selling goods well beyond cost and declaring dividends among the shareholders. As a movement for the amelioration of the condition of the workers, the New England

[1] *Eighth Annual Report*, Mass. Bur. of Labor Statistics, p. 73.
[2] New York *Daily Tribune*, May 25, 1853.
[3] *Eighth Annual Report*, Mass. Bur. of Labor Statistics, p. 73.

Protective Union came to an end in 1853. It continued after that as a joint-stock undertaking until 1859.[1]

A few consumers' coöperation ventures were launched in New York City, but had very slight success. They were usually connected with schemes of producers' coöperation and under the wing of the Associationists. The New York Protective Union was organized in 1849 and at one time had four hundred members. It operated a coöperative bakery and smith and wheelwright shops in connection with its store, the Economical Exchange.[2] In 1850 the formation of a Coöperative Labor League was recommended to the New York Industrial Congress, for 'the reorganization of industry.' [3]

PRODUCERS' COÖPERATION

Coöperative production or self-employment began with the Lynn shoemakers' organization already described. In the same year, the seamstresses of New York established a coöperative shop with the aid of some philanthropic persons, under the title "The Ladies' Industrial Association." Little progress was made, however, in this direction until the end of the decade, when a number of attempts at self-employing workshops grew out of labor disputes. The most talked-of of these was that of the iron-moulders of Cincinnati in 1848. These men, who had failed in a strike the previous year, organized a "Journeyman Moulders' Union Foundry" with $2100 capital they collected among themselves. They bought a piece of land on the Ohio, eight miles below Cincinnati, and two friends of the undertaking put up the buildings. They elected directors, a foreman and a business agent, and opened a store in Cincinnati to buy stock and sell their products. Work began in August,

---

[1] *Eighth Annual Report*, Mass. Bur. of Labor Statistics, pp. 84-85.
[2] New York *Daily Tribune*, April 20, August 15, 1850, and January 20, 1851.
[3] *Ibid.*, December 12, 1850.

1848. Horace Greeley, who claimed to know something about castings, said there were no better to be seen and pointed the Association moral, "There is an obvious reason for this in the fact that every workman is a proprietor in the concern and it is to his interest to turn out not only his own work in the best order, but to take care that all the rest is of like quality." [1] The iron-moulders were wise enough to keep their profits in the business, and by January, 1850, they had added $5692 to their original capital.[2] They were, however, not able to weather the depression of the following winter and the underselling of their competitors, and the venture failed.

Similar attempts were made about Pittsburgh, and co-operation was discussed for the iron trade as a whole. At Wheeling and Steubenville, Ohio, and at Sharon, Pennsylvania, small shops were set up. In the latter place about one hundred iron-workers formed a partnership after a strike, subscribing fifty dollars each to establish a shop. Each shareholder had one vote, irrespective of the number of shares held. Some twenty shoemakers of Pittsburgh attempted a similar undertaking and were said to have met cut-throat competition from the regular concerns.[3] Even the Church took up the pen against them, the "Christian Advocate" characterizing their attempts as "absurd and blasphemous."

Quite recently the spirit of pretended anti-aristocracy and monopoly has revived and men are again attempting to mend the existing state of human society.... A foundry, I believe, is to be erected and each one is to give a certain proportion of money to its completion. What other things these men are going to do I know not, neither do I care. One thing seems very clear, and it is this: however much the enterprise may be lauded and however flattering its prospects for ultimate success may appear, no long time will

[1] New York *Weekly Tribune*, December 15, 1849.
[2] *Pittsburgh Post*, January 15, 1850.
[3] New York *Daily Tribune*, June 4, 1850.

elapse before the abettors will be scattered, confounded, and disappointed, and the whole affair itself swept from the community. The attempt to improve the Divine Law is not ridiculous simply; it is absurd and blasphemous. If men cannot live and get along as God ordained, they can get along in no other way. . . .[1]

After a three months' strike for wages in December, 1849, the Boston tailors decided on coöperation and formed the Boston Tailors Associative Union. Having learned from experience and the Associationists the futility of strikes, they concluded that "every effort of workingmen in Europe and America to improve and elevate their position in society by 'strikes' and 'trades' union combinations' has hitherto, after the expenditure of millions of dollars, failed, or at best afforded only temporary relief, while their position was daily becoming more wretched." Their balance sheet, published at the end of one year of operation, showed a net profit of $51.35 on an investment of $1,334.94. This was "not so bad for thirty or forty workmen with only $483 capital to commence. Every man has been paid regular wages" and a new store was to be opened.[2]

In the summer of 1850, as a result of a strike for a new scale of prices, the German tailors of New York City appealed for help to establish an association clothing establishment [3] and an attempt was made to include the American tailors in a Protective Union.[4]

The National Typographical Society, in 1850, considered coöperation and recommended the formation of joint-stock printing offices as "the ultimate and only radical cure . . . where every man shall feel that he is working for himself and not for another. . . ." [5]

---

[1] From the *Christian Advocate*, organ of the Methodist Evangelical Church, quoted by Commons, *History of Labor*, vol. 1, p. 571, from the *Quaker City*, July 7, 1849.

[2] New York *Daily Tribune*, January 14, 1850.

[3] *Ibid.*, July 19, 26; August 8, 1850.

[4] *Ibid.*, August 13, 1850.   [5] *Ibid.*, May 22, 1850.

The Shirt Sewers Coöperative Union Depot was set up at No. 9 Henry Street, New York City, in 1851, and implored the public to aid them as they were too poor to advertise, but were attempting to help women who "were sewing at once with a double stitch, a shroud as well as a shirt." [1] Over a month later the business was firmly established "in spite of pessimistic predictions of manufacturers and business men," [2] and after two years, with headquarters in Bleeker Street, it was "among the most successful combinative efforts at work in this city." [3]

The Union Bakery, which was established in 1848, with $400 capital, supplied bread to its members at cost. It also carried sickness insurance, paying $4 a week and a death benefit of $30 for a worker and $25 for his wife. The price of the bread was not changed with the changes in the price of flour, but the size of the loaf was increased or reduced. In 1850 it was employing 14 journeymen and paying as the highest wage $13.50 a week, and as the lowest (boys) $3.50. The total receipts from April 30, 1848, to April 30, 1850, were $49,010.48; expenditures, $48,656.53, leaving a credit balance of $353.95. [4]

Besides these, there were in New York City, in 1851, a Coöperative Boot and Shoe Store at 203 William Street and a Hat Finishers' Union at 11 Park Row. [5] The bookbinders, [6] the German carpenters, and the German cabinetmakers [7] of New York, and the tailors of Buffalo, had coöperative shops in 1850–51.

Many explanations have been attempted of the failure of Coöperation in America in contrast with its marked success in European countries. It has been attributed to the individualistic character of the people, their extravagance,

[1] New York *Daily Tribune*, July 31, 1850.
[2] *Ibid.*, September 11, 1850.
[3] *Ibid.*, June 8, 1853.   [4] *Ibid.*, May 6, 1850.
[5] *Ibid.*, April 23, 1851, and December 19, 1850.
[6] *Ibid.*, January 31, 1851.   [7] *Ibid.*, April 26, 1850.

the faults of the system of selling at the wholesale price plus cost, the inability of the movement to secure efficient and honest administration, and so on. All these things had something to do with it, but the underlying difficulty is probably to be found in the extreme mobility of the American industrial population. A people in the process of conquering a continent of the richness of America is not in a position to found institutions that require some class or vocational stability and length of residence in one place. With a constantly fluctuating population, it was impossible to maintain organizations like the coöperatives just as it was impossible to maintain trade unions.

CHAPTER XIV

THE LABOR MOVEMENT: DEFENSIVE
1840-50

THE term 'defensive' is used to indicate a state of mind and to suggest that the workers and intellectuals who participated in the labor movement of the forties had not emancipated themselves from the traditions of an earlier economic society and were simply trying to ward off the encroachments of the new power of capitalist industry. The history of trade-unionism is so involved with distinctions based on forms that it has seemed necessary to get back of these into the mental attitudes of the workers. The forms, of course, relate themselves to the attitudes, but in the present instance the latter have been regarded as of primary significance.

In the experience of the worker, the industrialism that grew up in the first half of the nineteenth century was a new thing. It tended to depress both his physical and social standards of life. It was aggressive, revolutionary and destructive. His primary reaction during this period was one of hesitating and uncertain protest and a vain endeavor to hold fast to the past. It was only as he saw the hopelessness of this protest and the inevitability of the new industrialism, that he either left the field or organized with others in small specialized unions for the attainment by aggressive action of limited ends.

In the first decade of our period, neither the workers nor the reformers who shared in their movements realized the inevitability of the new industrialism. They were unable to convince themselves that the old relationship of master and journeyman had to go. They saw that the condition and status of the worker were declining, but, underestimated the new forces at work, and, imbued with the optimism that characterized the period, they made a strong but ineffectual effort to stem the tide.

The economic depression that settled on the country from the panic of 1837 to 1842 left the standards of the industrial worker woefully reduced. In 1842–43 business conditions improved and, to the end of the decade, trade and industry flourished. But little or none of the new prosperity passed on to the worker. His position instead of improving tended to decline. In 1843 he began to attempt to better his condition, not in one concerted direction, but along many and often conflicting paths, and out of these grew and declined, as the decade advanced, the defensive labor movement.

It is neither possible nor desirable to keep the labor movement and the reform movement of this period apart. They arose separately, but came together as one. At the same time it is necessary to insist that the labor movement was a reality and not simply a bogey created by the reformers to promote their own ends. It existed in the numerous strikes, in ephemeral organizations, in an equally ephemeral press, largely in protests. So much attention has been paid, proportionately, to the reformers as to suggest that the labor movement of 1840–50 embraced only Evans, Brisbane, Owen, Ripley, etc.[1] This was not the case. These men, with their various reforms, were part of the same protest that created the workers' movements, but they were not the whole. Frequently they captured the workers' organizations and as frequently dropped them when they ceased to serve the purposes the reformers had in view.

The labor movement of the forties began with an organization of master and journeymen mechanics in New York State. On October 6, 1841, the first convention of

---

[1] This is the chief fault to be found with Hoagland's treatment of this period in Commons, *History of Labor*.

the New York State Mechanics' Association was held at Albany and a paper was published, the "New York State Mechanic," to further its aims. The movement was of a political character and represented the fag end of the political activities of the thirties. Its basis of organization was territorial and its strength was drawn chiefly from the little industrialized communities of the State. Its purpose was to elevate the mechanics' lot and character by education, temperance, 'self-improvement,' and to oppose the degradation that resulted from competition with prison labor.

Here was found the state of mind that was created and maintained by the old master-journeyman relationship. The idea of 'community of interest' was uppermost. They discussed the education of apprentices, with no understanding that the whole apprentice system was fast passing away, was already extinct in many places. Their attitude on the relation of employer and employed was typical of the older situation: "the whole intercourse between employer and employed should be characterized by a spirit of accommodation and good-will." [1]

A second convention was held in 1842, when Robert MacFarlane, a Scots dyer who had settled in Albany, became editor of the paper and organized a secret society at Buffalo, the Mechanics' Mutual Protection. The name of the paper was changed to "The Mechanics' Mirror." In 1847 the Mechanics' Mutual Protection had thirty-eight locals in New York State, seven in Ohio, three in Michigan, and one each in Pennsylvania and Wisconsin. In 1846 and 1847 it held State conventions in New York.

MacFarlane and his organization were opposed to strikes and combinations for wages. They advocated arbitration and stressed the social and mental improvement of the mechanic. Their major purpose was "the elevation of

[1] New York *State Mechanic*, June 4, 1842.

the mechanic to his true position in society." [1] The hope was expressed that every mechanic in the State and every employer would ultimately be a member of the society. A benefit feature was part of the scheme and only practical mechanics were admitted. Opposition to prison labor was the chief political plank. MacFarlane was made editor of the "Scientific American" in 1848. [2]

While this was not strictly a working-class movement in the modern sense — it included employer and employee — it was just that in the sense of the period that was passing away. The old workers, masters, journeymen, apprentices, when organized at all, were in one organization in opposition to their competitors or their customers. New times: new manners. This organization was already an anachronism in the industrialism that was growing up around it.

In 1843 there arose a different sort of agitation. Strikes became epidemic with the improvement of business conditions and the failure of wages to follow suit. "There are symptoms of rebellion among the operatives in all quarters. At Lowell, Pittsburgh, Philadelphia, Chicopee and elsewhere, strikes follow each other among different classes of mechanics." [3] A general assembly was held in Pittsburgh as a result of the strike of brickmakers and others. [4] In Cincinnati the printers succeeded in increasing their wages. Societies were formed among the shoemakers, tailors, cigar-makers. [5] The tailors struck for higher wages and paraded New York, two thousand strong, with two bands. The hand-loom weavers of Paterson struck for wages. [6]

Out of this ferment there grew up in the industrial towns of New England, almost overnight, at least a dozen

[1] *The Mechanics' Mirror*, August, 1846.
[2] Commons, *Documentary History*, vol. 8, pp. 249–62.
[3] *New York State Mechanic*, May 18, 1843, p. 205.
[4] *Ibid.*, May, 1843, p. 205.
[5] *Working Man's Advocate*, July 27, 1844, quoting *The People's Paper*, Cincinnati, October 14, 1843.
[6] *Ibid.*, July 27, 1844.

Mechanics' and Laborers' Associations, revivals of similar organizations of the thirties, that were to constitute the framework of the labor movement of the period. As is suggested by their names, these were general societies based on the neighborhood. They had no concerted plan or purpose, other than the desire to resist encroachment upon their standards. They were not revolutionary nor class-conscious, but loath to regard the interests of the employer and the employed as antagonistic.

In June, 1844, the Mechanics' and Laborers' Association of Fall River, Massachusetts, sent out a 'call' to the mechanics and laborers of New England, and to others who might be interested, to a convention for 'concerting measures' and to "find a more excellent system of labor than that which has so long prevailed and thus, under God, remove the heavy burdens which have long rested upon us and our children, and let the oppressed go free." [1] There was nothing very definite in their ideas of the nature of their burdens. The one specific complaint was against the length of the working day, "the twelve-to-fifteen-hour day" for mechanics and laborers. The thing that troubled them was that "we are fast approximating towards the disagreeable, servile, and degrading state of the English laborer." The time was ripe for "a general concert of action."

The present affords a favorable opportunity to all persons who feel at all interested in the general good of the whole people, for giving a free expression of their views and peculiar feelings on this subject and of securing joint efforts to carry forward a thorough and effective change in the present system of labor in New England. The time has never been since the adoption of the present system, when public sympathies have been awakened and when a general interest has been created to such an extent in behalf of the working classes. . . .[2]

The hours of labor for mechanics had been generally re-

---

[1] *Working Man's Advocate*, June 29, 1844.   [2] *Ibid.*

duced to ten a day in the thirties, except in New England,
and for this reason, because it was obvious, the mechanics
of Fall River made special mention of this reform. But
this did not make the resulting labor movement a ten-hour
movement. It was a general labor revolt, ready to welcome
suggestions from any quarter and anxious to gain, not a
specific reform, but 'a more excellent system of labor.'
No sooner was the 'call' issued than the reformers began
to make advances. On June 22d, George Henry Evans
sent an invitation to the Fall River mechanics to unite with
the Land Reformers, but received little encouragement.
They published his request in their paper, the Fall River
"Mechanic," but without comment. Evans consoled himself: "Of course the proposition is not disapproved of and
we may expect to hear from them soon." [1]

At the same time there were springing up all over New
England labor papers, organs of the various mechanics'
and laborers' associations. In all, about ten of these papers
seem to have come and gone in the space of four years.
The "New England Operative" of Lowell appeared "to
aid in the establishment of the ten-hour system and the
general improvement and elevation of all classes of laborers." [2] Associations were formed in Milford, Woburn,
Worcester, Newton Upper Falls, Taunton, South Manchester, Weymouth, Lowell, Marblehead, Salem, Boston,
Lynn, Portland, Dover, etc. The situation was electric,
vague, full of possibilities, rumors, and some dissension.

In Lowell the ranks were split, and a Workingmen's
Association was formed which issued the "Working Man's
Advocate" in competition with the Mechanics' and
Laborers' Association, publishing the "New England
Operative." It was said that the split was over personal

---

[1] *Working Man's Advocate*, June 22, 1844.

[2] *Ibid.* Others were: Boston *Laborer;* Manchester *Operative;* Lowell
Working Man's Advocate; Lynn *Awl; Voice of Industry,* Fitchburg and
Lowell; *The True Workingman,* Lynn; Essex *Factory Girls' Garland; The
Bee,* Boston.

matters,[1] but it is quite possible that the land reform propaganda had caused the difficulty. The division persisted and caused some trouble at the Lowell Convention of the New England Workingmen's Association later.

The first connection Evans made with the workers' movement was at Fall River where one of his agents, E. G. Buffum, "a young man from New York," met the Mechanics' Association and explained that land monopoly was the root of all their difficulties. The Fall River mechanics seem to have been hard to convince and, in October, Evans compromised and agreed that the ten-hour system was necessary to the operatives before the abolition of traffic in the public lands.[2]

Responses to the call of the Fall River mechanics for a New England Convention were received from Lowell, Boston, the New York shoemakers, the land reformers and the shoemakers of Lynn,[3] but, as no place or date had been specified, much time was lost before a settlement was made as to these details. On July 20th, the Lynn shoemakers concurred in the call and suggested that the convention should be held at Boston, Wednesday, August 21st, "for the purpose of taking into consideration the inadequate compensation of labor and to devise means whereby it can be improved." [4] The matter of wages had not been mentioned by the Fall River mechanics, but would undoubtedly have been included in their general statement of disabilities. This indicates the varied basis of complaint from which the movement grew, its spontaneous character, and the possibility of later disagreement. The date suggested by the shoemakers failed to satisfy, and Fall River offered September 18th as an alternative, so that the convention could be held in connection with the Mechanics' Fair. Lynn agreed and proposed to send one hundred delegates. Lowell,

[1] *Working Man's Advocate*, August 8, 1844.
[2] *Ibid.*, September 28, and October 5, 1844.
[3] *The Awl*, July 24, 1844.   [4] *Ibid.*

however, insisted on further delay, that more local associations might be formed, and the date was finally set
for October 16, 1844.[1] Meanwhile some of the first enthusiasm was lost.

This much-postponed New England Workingmen's Con-
vention was held in Boston, October 16, 1844, at Faneuil
Hall. There were two hundred delegates present represent-
ing not only the New England workers' organizations, but
the National Reformers and the Spartan Band of New
York (Evans, Devyr, and Mike Walsh), the Skaneateles
Community (Owenite), and Brook Farm. The New Eng-
land delegates came from Boston, South Boston, Fall River,
New Bedford, Worcester, South Andover, Newton Upper
Falls, Milton, Lowell, Lynn, Reading, Marblehead, Brook
Farm, Chelsea, and Chelmsford, Massachusetts; Paukatuck
and Stonington, Connecticut; Pawtucket, Rhode Island;
Manchester and Nashua, New Hampshire. The strongest
delegations were from Lynn, Lowell, and Fall River.[2]

This first convention was enthusiastic and representative and avoided falling under the domination of any one
group. Resolutions were passed [3] declaring that "by the
present system of labor the interests of capital and labor
are opposed, the former now securing the reward that
should only belong to the latter"; recommending petitions
to the legislature for a ten-hour law; further organization
among the mechanics "to investigate the causes of the
present fearful and still daily increasing disparities of social
condition"; the formation of associations for coöperative
production, "in which workingmen can use their own capital, work their own stock, establish their own hours and
their own price"; against the monopoly of the soil; for 'attractive industry,' the organization of labor; and a committee was appointed to draw up a constitution for a New

[1] *The Awl*, September 18, 1844.
[2] *Working Man's Advocate*, October 19, 1844.
[3] *The Awl*, October 23, 1844.

England Workingmen's Association and to fix a day and place for its first meeting.[1]

Evans, who had accepted half-heartedly the ten-hour proposal "as a temporary measure" and "as far as practicable," tried to rush the convention into a national organization without further local consolidation, but his proposal was so coolly received that it was withdrawn.[2]

No sooner was the convention over than signs of flagging interest began to appear. At Lynn it was said, in November, "the temporary excitement which attended our recent efforts on behalf of the cause of labor has, in a great measure, passed away and given place to a calmer and more steady but not less efficient plan of operations."[3] The enthusiasm of the shoemakers for a general labor movement was on the wane. "The Awl" insisted that the Lynn Society had two objects: the welfare of the shoemakers and that of the general laboring population, but the implication was strong that the tendency was to let the latter drop. In December, Allen of Boston went to Lynn to lecture and found his audience alarmingly small. "A crisis in the cause of humanity has arrived," "The Awl" protested. "Where were you all last Saturday evening?"[4]

The year 1845 was a gala year for the labor movement of America. Conventions multiplied and agitations grew. It is almost inconceivable that so many meetings could be held in one year, so many resolutions passed, and so little of real building actually achieved. The New England Workingmen's Convention met at Lowell, March 18th, reaching the high-water mark of the labor movement of New England. There were from fifteen hundred to two thousand delegates in attendance. The control of affairs at the opening was still in the hands of the workers and their spokesmen, but Mike Walsh, Evans, and a strong contin-

[1] *The Awl*, October 23, 1844.
[2] *Working Man's Advocate*, October 19, 1844.
[3] *The Awl*, November 16, 1844.   [4] *Ibid.*, December 7, 1844.

gent from Brook Farm were on the ground. John Spofford, of Lowell, was made president, William Phillips, of Lynn, T. D. Roberts, of Andover, and A. J. Wright, of Boston, vice-presidents; and L. Cox, Jr., S. Almy, and John Allen, secretaries. Non-delegates were refused permission to take part in the discussion, and the new Female Labor Reform Association of Lowell was welcomed and made a report of their doings. The women operatives of Lowell, in January, 1845, had formed an auxiliary to the Mechanics' and Laborers' Association. It had originally two members and thirteen officers, the chief of whom were Miss Sarah Bagley, president, and Miss H. J. Stone, secretary. After three or four months' existence, they claimed to have increased their membership to 304.[1]

As the Lowell Convention progressed, it passed out of the control of the originators of the movement and into the hands of the reformers, especially the Brook Farm delegation. The main business of the convention was the adoption of a constitution for the New England Workingmen's Association and L. W. Ryckman, of Brook Farm, was elected president.[2] A split occurred when J. C. Palmer, of Lowell, was refused a hearing on the ground that he did not represent a proper working-men's organization. A committee was appointed to pass on his credentials and reported against his admission.[3] But no committee passed on the credentials of Mike Walsh and others, with little claim to represent any one but themselves. The Workingmen's Association of Fitchburg later condemned this denial of freedom of speech.[4]

The membership of the New England Association was to be made up of delegates from all local associations paying twenty-five cents each into the general fund. The basis of representation was one delegate for every ten members up to fifty; one for every additional fifty up to five hundred;

[1] *The Awl*, April 12, 1845.
[3] *Ibid.*, May 3, 1845.
[2] *Ibid.*, March 29, 1845.
[4] *Ibid.*

and beyond that, one for every one hundred members.[1] A long list of resolutions was passed: in support of a ten-hour law; a lien law; against chartered monopolies which were 'contrary to the constitution,' "tending to gather the wealth of the community into the possession of the favored few, thereby establishing a dangerous, oppressive, moneyed oligarchy on the ruins of the constitution"; for political action; public education; labor representation in Congress; freedom of the public lands; and against prison labor and the high cost of legal proceedings.

The Lowell Convention, without waiting for the first meeting of the New England Association, decided to call a National Industrial Congress "to propose and adopt such measures as shall be found necessary to secure the rights and interests of honest industry and to hasten the accomplishment of the grand industrial revolution ["resolution" is used in the text, though no irony probably was intended] which is alike demanded by the nature of man, the mission of free America, the hopes of humanity and the law of eternal truth and justice." [2]

Brisbane presented a resolution that was a lecture on Fourierism, and Ryckman proposed the organization of a permanent Industrial Revolutionary Government, on the model of the Confederation of the States in 1776, to "destroy the hostile relations which at present prevail between capital and labor. ..." [3] Reform was in the saddle. Brook Farm led the wordy way.

On Thursday, April 17th, a meeting was held in Faneuil Hall preliminary to the first New England Association. The Lynn "Awl" was but little interested in it, satisfying itself with copying "a few of the long string of resolutions adopted by the meeting as an illustration of the objects and views of the movers in the affair." [4] From this point on, the attendance at the meetings declined and there were

[1] *The Awl*, April 5, 1845.   [2] *Ibid.*
[3] *Ibid.*   [4] *Ibid.*, April 19, 1845.

repeated complaints from the reformers of lack of interest on the part of the workers in their own welfare.

The first meeting of the New England Association [1] was held in Boston, May 28, 1845. The attendance was a disappointment, there being only ten or twelve organizations represented, and most of the delegates were reformers. They were, however, a brilliant crowd, including: Charles A. Dana, L. W. Ryckman, George Ripley, of Brook Farm; Horace Greeley, Albert Brisbane, of New York; A. J. Wright, Wendell Phillips, William Lloyd Garrison, W. H. Channing, and Marcus Morton, of Boston; Frederick Rob inson, of Charlestown; John A. Collins, of the Skaneateles Community, New York; and Robert Owen.

Greeley made a speech, to which the editor of "The Awl" did not listen as he was otherwise occupied, but he caught one sentence that made an impression. "It is much easier," said Greeley, "to get ten thousand to work for the laboring man than to get one to work for himself." [2]

The doors of the organization were thrown wide open, on the motion of President Ryckman, "to all those interested in the elevation of the producing classes and Industrial Reform and the extinction of slavery and servitude in all their forms." The main business seems to have been the advancement of the interests of Land Reform and Association. The proposal of the National Reformers for a convention in New York City "to draw up a reformative constitution for the United States" was seconded. It was out of this convention that the Industrial Congress grew, which drew away the reformers from the New England Association the next year, leaving it to the ten-hour people and the Coöperators. Addresses were made by Robert Owen on his plans for a World Convention, and by Brisbane and Dana on Association.

[1] The meetings already described were 'conventions' in preparation for this.
[2] *The Awl*, May 31, 1845.

An outsider's critical estimate of the convention was made by a friend of Greeley, signing himself "H. W.," who attended the meetings out of curiosity. He said there were only thirty delegates present, twenty men and ten women, and that a great deal of dissatisfaction was expressed by the members at the lack of interest among the workers. But H. W. was not surprised at this lack of interest when he took into consideration the absurdity of much of the talk.

A member from your city [Lowell] made a speech in which he said that capitalists and priests had joined hands to put down, grind and oppress the laboring man — that commerce, manufacturing and foreign emigration were killing them — that there was ten times more slavery in Lowell than on the Southern plantations — that Lowell manufactured the prostitutes of New York; and that the first thing we must do to elevate the workingmen was to collect and burn the Sunday-School books which were poisoning the minds of the young. . . . Albert Brisbane brought forward a plan which he said he had well matured . . . but it seemed to me one of the greatest pieces of folly I ever heard propounded by a man out of a mad-house.[1]

On July 4, 1845, a picnic of the New England Association was held at Woburn at which there was an attendance of two thousand. Speakers at this meeting deplored strikes and advised harmony. "My object," said Ryckman, "is not to array one class against another, but, by a glorious unity of interests, make all harmony and ensure universal intelligence, elevation and happiness." Hostilities, declared James Campbell, were foreign to the purposes of the Association; "the organization was not for strikes or more successful opposition to the capitalist . . . but to awaken from their lethargy those sordid devotees of wealth who . . . were unconsciously preying upon the ruin of their fellows."[2] It would seem a pity, if that were his object, that the attentions of Mr. Campbell and his friends should not have been directed to the unconsciously 'sordid devotees of

[1] *Voice of Industry*, July 3, 1845.   [2] *Ibid.*, July 10, 1845.

wealth' themselves, instead of wasting time on their 'prey.' The workers' revolt had become a farce or a tragedy in the hands of the harmonizers. And the farce-tragedy was carried a step further in September, at the Fall River convention, when Ryckman proposed a resolution that read:

Whereas, *We* the workingmen of New England can see no practical means of improving *their* condition . . .

Resolved, that we do hereby appeal to the wise and the good, the generous and the brave of all classes in behalf of this useful, suffering and numerous class of their fellow creatures. . . .[1]

At the Fall River Convention the few workers who were left began to show signs of unrest under the reign of the Associationists. The attendance was very small, so small that the meeting had to be adjourned to settle the difficulties that arose. Conflict came over two matters: a resolution in favor of coöperative stores, and one for political action. The former was vigorously opposed by the reformers; the latter was equally opposed by the rank and file. Coöperative production — self-employment — was a recognized part of the Associationist programme; consumers' coöperation was not. Kaulback, of Boston, proposed the endorsement of "concert of action in the purchase of the necessities of life, as the only means to unite the workers." He described the method adopted by the Boston group, of subscribing $2 each until $500 had been accumulated and taking $300 of that for the wholesale purchase of provisions. But his proposal was resolutely opposed. "Nothing short of an entire revolution in society," said Denton, of New Bedford, "can remedy the evils under which the laboring people suffer." [2]

A further difficulty arose over the method of procedure in the reduction of hours in factories. The Associationists supported the suggestion of political action to gain the

[1] *Voice of Industry*, September 18, 1845. (Italics mine.)
[2] *Ibid.*, September 18, 1845.

ten-hour system, and there was strong opposition. It would have meant, of course, that the women's delegation and their fight would be set aside.[1] The convention was adjourned to meet at Lowell, where it compromised both its difficulties by declaring, "that Protective Charity and concert of action in the purchase of the necessaries of life are *some* of the means, etc.," and that "a resort to the polls is *one* of the ... measures. ..."[2]

The Lowell Convention met October 29th and, after passing the usual resolutions, made the "Voice of Industry" its official organ.[3]

The "Voice of Industry" was the longest-lived of the labor papers of the period and its history parallels the labor movement of the forties. A number of labor papers had preceded it, among them "The Awl," Lynn, and its successor, "The True Working Man," "The Boston Laborer," "The Fall River Mechanic," and "The New England Operative" of Lowell. All of these had gone under by February, 1846. The "Voice of Industry" was a weekly, originally published in Fitchburg, Massachusetts, by the Workingmen's Association and edited by William F. Young, a mechanic of that place. It began publication May 29, 1845, taking over the subscription list of "The Lowell Operative." It had no panacea, but was established to promote the interests of the class that it represented. It favored land reform, supported the ten-hour movement, and, in its later years, labor reform and coöperation. It was interested, too, though less directly, in temperance, anti-slavery, and anti-war propaganda. In October, 1845, the paper was moved to Lowell and became the organ of the New England Association. It continued to be edited by Young, with the assistance of a publishing committee: Sa-

---

[1] *Voice of Industry*, September 18, 1845.
[2] *The True Working Man*, December 13, 1845. (Italics mine.)
[3] *Voice of Industry*, November 7, 1845.

rah Bagley and Joel Hatch. It was in constant financial difficulties in spite of a large and growing circulation. Its interests were widened and foreign news and Congressional reports began to appear. Young retired in April, 1846, on account of ill-health, but returned in November to find the paper in serious financial difficulties though it had two thousand subscribers. In his absence the editing had for a time been done by a committee: J. S. Fletcher, Sarah Bagley, and Joel Hatch, but in May, Miss Bagley, "a common-schooled New England female factory operative," took the editorial chair. The Female Labor Reform Association had bought the type and presses and carried on the undertaking with special attention to the ten-hour agitation. The task seems to have been too great for Miss Bagley and John Allen succeeded her in June. Allen was an Associationist and spent so much time lecturing that the paper suffered and Young returned. He remained nearly a year, but was unable to stave off disaster and the publication was discontinued in August, 1847. In October, the "Voice of Industry" appeared again as "An Organ of the People," edited by D. H. Jaques and primarily interested in Coöperation. John Orvis was added to the editorial staff in November, and in December it was moved to Boston, becoming an organ of Land Reform. It ceased publication a second time, April 14, 1848, for want of $350, and was revived by Orvis under the title "The New Era of Industry," June to August, 1848.

The absence of the National Reformers from the array of talent found at the Boston Convention in May is explained by the fact that they, in their impatience, had called a national convention of their own at Croton Hall, New York City, for May 5th, and were no longer interested in New England and its doings. The National Reform Convention attracted about thirty delegates including, besides the Land Reformers themselves, the Associationists and Robert Owen, and two of his disciples, Collins and Timms. The

main business of the gathering was to arrange for the calling of the Industrial Congress. When the usual speeches
had been made by the Land Reformers and the Associationists, Evans, as chairman, was asked to allow Mr. Owen
to present his plans. Evans objected that he had already
arranged for some one else, and in the mêlée that followed,
Timms called the Associationists 'Fourierists.' Brisbane
vehemently 'repudiated the name,' and Timms protested
that he had meant no reflection upon Brisbane and his
friends and would have called them 'Phalanzarians' if he
had thought the name would have been understood. Collins was given the floor and then Owen. The aged dreamer
(Owen was then nearly seventy-five) admitted that he
knew nothing about Land Reform, but he did not think
the plan was feasible, "the foundations were of sand and
the building would fall." [1]

Again, in July, the Land Reformers called a meeting at
Croton Hall of "mechanics, laborers, and useful persons."
They made a great parade of the craft character of the dele-
gation and declared that

in the City of New York are 65,000 paupers, that is, one-seventh
of the entire population; in the State, one in seventeen is a pauper,
and ratios in city and country are increasing year by year. The
compensation for labor is steadily sinking until thousands are now
reduced to the starvation point. Labor and laborer — it is useless
to deny it — are, in this Republican country even, subject to a
subtle, indirect slavery rarely acknowledged, but everywhere
felt. And in this respect the white laborer of the North is in a
worse state than the slave of the South, for while the condition of
the slave is pretty much the same from year to year, that of the
supposed free man is growing constantly worse. [2]

This Croton Hall meeting had grown out of a gathering
of mechanics at the National Hall to consider organizing
coöperatives. But Bovay, the secretary of the National
Reformers, had killed this proposal, asserting that the bal-

[1] *Young America*, May 10, 1845.
[2] *Voice of Industry*, July 17, 1845.

lot box was the only hope of the worker, and through the
ballot box the freedom of the public lands, "that the vir-
gin [soil], rich and wild as at the dawn of creation, should be
preserved, a free asylum for the oppressed and a safe re-
treat for the slaves of wages and all other slaves forever." [1]
The mechanics then proceeded to Croton Hall under the
Land Reformers' wing.

Robert Owen, the venerable and indefatigable English
reformer — philanthropist rather than Communist, as he
was called — had, after the failure of the New Harmony
Colony, spent his time trying to interest philanthropic capitalists in his plans for the reorganization of society by
means of joint-stock communities to be turned over to
workers at reasonable rates of interest. Having failed to
get the ear of the various working-class organizations that
had sprung up, he too called a convention of his own.
Owen was more ambitious than the rest of the reformers
and called his gathering a World Convention, whereas the
others had satisfied themselves with national affairs.

Owen's World Convention was held at Clinton Hall,
New York City, October 1, 1845. There were three hundred people present, of whom twenty-five or thirty were
said to be well-dressed women, but many of the men had
"a meager and melancholy cast of countenance," a sort of
"let's-all-be-unhappy-together style of face." The majority seemed intelligent enough. Among them were: Collins,
Ryckman, Evans, Bovay, Hooper, Smith, Davies, Brisbane, Hoyt, and Seller. Owen presided. Brisbane declined
office because he was opposed to Owen's plans. Ryckman
refused to serve without a guarantee that every kind of
view might be presented. Collins insisted that concrete
proposals be made, and so on. It was finally decided "that
every man and woman should have a right to get up and
advance any proposition for the benefit of the human
race." All the members were asked to sit together, but, as

[1] *Voice of Industry*, July 31, 1845.

the basis of membership had not been decided on, a Mr. Vale rose to ask:

"I came late and am ignorant . . ."

Collins, the chairman: "If the gentleman had been in time . . ."

Vale: "I should have found out, I suppose."

Collins: "Y-e-s."

Vale: "And that's the answer. That'll do. I'm satisfied."

General James A. Bennett said he was worth $50,000 and was ready to go into a division of property with the whole Union to-morrow. But unless all did, he would quit the camp. And he quit.

A resolution was presented that the object of the convention was to "emancipate the human race from Sin, Misery, and all kinds of Slavery." One delegate wanted to know what the others meant by 'sin' and 'misery,' and after some debate a substitute resolution was passed, "for the best practical measures for improving the moral and physical well-being of man." [1] Owen let every one bring forward his or her proposals thus to redeem the race, and, after all had had their say, he presented his own.

"I have given them a fair and full opportunity of placing their ideas, *crude as they are*, before the world, where they must sink or swim. . . . I have now to propose . . . etc.," [2] his own plan which needed $3,000,000 and 3000 persons to start.

Robert Owen had no connection with or influence upon the labor movement of the period. His final appearance in the American scene was at the Hopedale Community, a month or so after the World's Convention, where he was described as nearly seventy-five years of age, with vast schemes for establishing a great model of the new state. "He insists," wrote a Hopedale resident, "on obtaining a

[1] *Voice of Industry*, October 9, 1845.

[2] *Young America*, October 11, 1845. (Italics mine.)

million dollars capital for lands, buildings, etc., for his
model community, all to be finished and in perfect order
before he introduces to their home the well-selected population who are to inhabit it. He flatters himself he shall be
able by some means to induce capitalists, or perhaps Congress, to furnish a million dollars for this object. We were
obliged to shake an incredulous head . . . and tell him how
groundless all such great hopes were." But Owen "took it
all in good part and declared his confidence unshaken and
his hopes undiscourageable by any man's unbelief. . . ." [1]

So we may take leave of this amazing man, who turned
aside, though successful, from the path of his generation,
declaring that path crooked, wrong and cruel; who astonished the world with the magnitude of his impossible plans
and at seventy-five would not be discouraged by repeated
failures or by any man's unbelief.

The National Industrial Convention met in New York,
October 14, 1845, to arrange for the calling of a permanent
Industrial Congress to unite all reformers throughout the
country. A constitution for the Congress was drawn up and
the call issued. The Industrial Congress was to be a permanent body similar to Congress, meeting annually and
representing the interests of the industrial classes. Members were to be elected from the local societies: one representative for from five to fifty members, and one additional
representative for every additional fifty. It was decided to
hold the first Congress in Boston, the second in New York,
the third in Philadelphia, and the fourth in Cincinnati.
The body was to be purely advisory.[2] 'Industrial Brotherhoods' were to be organized for political action and, to attract the workers, sickness and burial insurance were added.
No employer, overseer, or superintendent was to belong to
these brotherhoods, only practical farmers, mechanics, operatives, or other workingmen. The Brook Farm group

[1] *Voice of Industry*, December 19, 1845.
[2] *Ibid.*, November 7, 1845.

could get in as 'practical farmers,' but Evans as an employer was excluded, and he in his turn established 'Young Americas' with a constitution identical with that of the Brotherhoods, except that it omitted the provision excluding employers.[1] Both these organizations seem to have failed completely.

One result of the Reformers' change of venue was a return of working-class control in the New England Association. In 1846 there was a revival of practical measures, such as ten-hour legislation and coöperation. The first meeting of the year was held at Lynn, January 16th, where two subjects of national import received attention, one of which was slowly making its way into first place against considerable inertia. A protest, based on rumors of a war with England, elicited what was an early American advance toward internationalism. "So far as regarding the laboring man on the other side of the water as our enemy and shooting him as such, we regard him as our friend and will do all in our power to better his condition." The other national matter was that of slavery and a resolution was proposed that "while we are willing to pledge ourselves to use all the means in our power . . . to put down wars, insurrections, and mobs . . . we will never take up arms to sustain the Southern slaveholder in robbing one fifth of our countrymen of their liberty." This resolution, in spite of the energetic opposition of Kaulback, who probably feared for working-class reform if the slavery issue should be injected into their discussions, was passed unanimously.[2]

At Manchester, in March, was held "one of the best and most spirited conventions ever held in New England." Seth Luther appeared, but was corrected when he wanted to make the ten-hour system a stepping-stone to something

[1] *Voice of Industry*, November 7, 1845; also *Young America*, December 13, 1845.
[2] *The True Workingman*, January 31 and February 7, 1846.

bigger, and it was emphatically asserted that the reduction of the hours of labor was "the great, prominent object of the workingmen of New England." [1]

A new constitution had been drawn up in January for the Lowell Female Reform Association, disapproving of "all hostile measures, strikes, and turn-outs *until* all pacific measures prove abortive, and then it is the imperious duty of every one to assist and maintain that independence which our brave ancestors bequeathed and sealed with their blood." [2] There was some talk of a Declaration of Independence, "to take the work into our own hands and declare our independence on the Fourth of July next." [3]

At the Nashua Convention, September, 1846, the name — the New England Workingmen's Association — was changed to the Labor Reform League of New England, showing the influence of the women's organization and the further specialization upon the ten-hour programme. A procession of one thousand persons was held to further the Ten-Hour movement which resulted in a 'turn-out' of the Nashua operatives against 'lighting up.' [4] The Protective Unions were strongly supported.[5]

In the fall election of 1846 the ten-hour and the land reform issues were prominent. A pledge [6] was sent to the candidates by the Lowell Industrial Reform Association and the replies printed in the "Voice of Industry." Most of the replies were typical politicians' evasions buried in mountains of words. One or two replied favorably to both measures, and Joseph T. Buckingham opposed them both.[7] The Land Reformers had nominated a complete ticket for Massachusetts, with David Bryant for governor and John Allen for lieutenant-governor. But the results were disap-

[1] *Voice of Industry*, April 3 and 10, 1846.
[2] *Ibid.*, February 27, 1846. (Italics mine.)
[3] *The True Workingman*, February 7, 1846.
[4] *Voice of Industry*, September 25, and October 9, 1846.
[5] *Ibid.*, October 2, 1846.   [6] *Ibid.*, November 13, 1846.
[7] *Ibid.*, November 6, 1846.

pointing.   Even Colonel Schouler was returned from
Lowell.

> The contest is over [lamented the "Voice of Industry"], and a
> more mongrel, conscience-elastic, conformatory set of voters
> than Massachusetts contains, we do not know where to look for.
> They have swallowed Texas, the Mexican War, and the whole of
> Cottondom with all their abominations. . . . The Whigs of Mas-
> sachusetts talk of their abhorrence of slavery and the present war
> and then walk up to the Ballot Box and sanction the same.[1]

In 1847 the Lowell Female Labor League decided that its
objects were not sufficiently attractive to the operatives,
and mutual aid or benefit features were added, similar to
those of the Protective Unions. Its name was changed to
the Lowell Female Industrial Reform and Mutual Aid Society. A sick-fund was established and Sisters of Charity
appointed to administer it.[2] The old organization had been
entirely reformist, but, with the changing character of the
mill personnel, it was losing its grip and felt the need of
"something more definite," something "in the present," to
appeal to the "self-love of the operatives as well as to their
higher natures." [3]
Again the New England movement passed into the hands
of other than working-class leaders at the Boston Convention of the New England Labor Reform League, January,
1847. The new leadership was not reformist like the old,
but philanthropic like that which was to dominate the Ten-
Hour movement of the fifties. Among the Boston leaders
were: Amasa Walker, Reverend Burton, William A. White.
and Dr. Channing. A resolution typical of the new influence was passed for cheap homes for the workers, "the best
safeguards against vice, crime, and immorality." Boston
was fatal to the New England working-class movements of
the period and the convention wound up as a Free-Soil and
Anti-Slavery affair. "American slavery," declared a reso-

---

[1] *Voice of Industry*, November 13, 1846.
[2] *Ibid.*, January 8, 1847.   [3] *Ibid.*, February 19, 1847.

lution which was a direct denial of the workers' earlier position, "American slavery must be uprooted *before* the elevation sought by the laboring classes can be effected." The
Associationists, too, reëmerged to assert that "the evils
which oppress and burden the men and women of New England arise from a vicious social organization." [1] Resolutions were also passed in favor of land reform, free trade,
direct taxation for revenue, the reduction of hours of labor,
and protective unions.[2]

The peak of the swing away from working-class purposes
and methods came at the adjourned meeting at Lowell,
March 30, 1847, when Dr. Tukesbury protested against the
usual measures proposed as visionary and foolish. There
was no reason, he said, why laborers should get up such
meetings and stir up discontent among the work-people
who were well enough off. If they got only ten cents a piece
for making shirts, they had better do that than nothing;
they were usually glad to get that. As for dividing the land
and giving every 'vagabond' a part of it without payment,
it was the height of folly and would only encourage idleness
and vice. The factory operatives, said the Doctor, were the
happiest members of the community. The capitalists too
worked long hours, in fact, "the human system was peculiarly adapted to these long and irregular hours of labor." [3]
Mrs. Townshend presented the matter of votes for
women.

In July a meeting was held at Dover. The attendance
was small and interest slack. A court was in possession of
the meeting-place and the Reformers, unable to secure the
place specified in their handbills, were considered by some
of the townspeople a 'humbug.' Mr. Trask spoke for the
Protective Unions and Cluer followed him, "seeming not
to understand the gentleman who preceded him, and as
they seemed not likely to end the argument, an adjourn-

---

[1] *Voice of Industry*, February 19, 1847. (Italics mine.)
[2] *Ibid.*, January 22, 1847.   [3] *Ibid.*, April 9, 1847.

ment was proposed." The choice of a place for the next meeting was left to the board of directors.[1]

Another meeting was called for Boston in January, 1848.

We are at times strongly made to feel [said the "Voice of Industry"] that the workingmen never will do anything for themselves. They are so half-hearted in whatever they attempt, so servile under capital, and so inconsistent in their course, that we cannot hope for much. If a meeting is called to promote objects dear to their interests, it is sparsely attended, is without a sustained enthusiasm, and comes so lonely off that the whole affair is a matter of ridicule and contempt on the part of their oppressors, and the workingmen themselves go home in shame-facedness and despair.[2]

The Boston meeting was held and the usual resolutions passed. "The report of this meeting," said Jaques, "will do instead of any extended remarks. We do not feel disposed to say much about it. We would be glad, under the circumstances, to say nothing." It was the first meeting of the New England Association that Jaques had attended, and he was not impressed.

Self-respect, order, decorum, a sincere and generous enthusiasm were but too much needed. We have only to say that if some of the workingmen, whom we heard make large claims to intelligence and high sense of honor, can give no better evidence of their possession than they displayed at that meeting, we humbly think they will do well to leave the work of reforming public abuses until they have experienced ... grace. ...[3]

The New England organization came to an end at Lowell, March 22, 1848. Nothing was done but appoint delegates to the Industrial Congress. The meeting adjourned *sine die*.[4]

THE NATIONAL MOVEMENT

In 1845 the Land Reformers and the Associationists deserted the New England movement for the larger national

---

[1] *Voice of Industry*, July 30, 1847. [2] *Ibid.*, January 14, 1848.
[3] *Ibid.*, January 28, 1848. [4] *Ibid.*, March 31, 1848.

field. We have followed their activities to the October convention for the organization of the Industrial Congress. This latter pretentious gathering came together in June, 1846, at Boston. It included practically all the Reformers of the time, with the Land Reformers predominating. There was little agreement among them as to what the Industrial Congress was to be. Horace Greeley conceived it as a congress of employers and employees in equal numbers to arrange, by agreement, uniform conditions of labor, including the ten-hour day, for the whole country.[1] At that time he was opposed to hour legislation, considering it "surrounded with difficulty," but believed "some reform in that particular desirable and practicable." Later he proposed limiting the hours of minors and "defining a day's work, when no other terms were stated in the bargain, to be ten hours."[2] But the employers did not respond and Greeley refused to consider the Boston affair a true Industrial Congress. He consoled himself with the reflection that the work to be done was so urgent that it was better begun "by any, rather than neglected by all."[3]

Most of the Reformers saw in the Congress a chance to promote their pet schemes. Evans, who was largely instrumental in its creation, expected to make it, as he did, a purely Land Reform organization. His idea was that "no time should be spent in discussing these hackneyed, threadbare and mystified topics [banks, tariffs, internal improvements] till the land is restored to the people."[4] Brisbane hoped to reconcile all differences. Ryckman wanted a revolutionary congress to free industry as the Continental Congress had freed the colonies.

The Land Reformers, who were much the best manipulators of popular bodies among the Reformers, dominated

[1] New York *Daily Tribune*, September 30, 1845.
[2] *Voice of Industry*, April 9, 1847.
[3] New York *Daily Tribune*, October 21, 1845.
[4] *Working Man's Advocate*, July 20, 1845.

the congresses from the first. David Bryant was made president and Evans, secretary. They insisted that members be pledged to "a reasonable limitation of the quantity of land that any individual may acquire possession of hereafter; exemption of the homestead from mortgage or debt hereafter; the freedom of the public lands to actual settlers; the limitation of the hours of daily labor for wages in all public works and in all establishments authorized by law, to ten." [1]

It was decided to form an auxiliary national reform association in every electoral district of the Union for political action, and to present memorials to Congress. [2] It was recommended that the National Reform Association "adopt the most democratic mode it can devise for nominating candidates for the President and Vice-President of the United States pledged to the freedom of the public lands," and that all national reformers and friends of Free Soil cooperate to secure their election. [3]

At the second Industrial Congress at New York, in 1847, a suggestion was made to inquire into the trade-union movement, "several members spoke of the inutility of trade unions," and Evans was asked if he had belonged to the General Trades Union of New York in the thirties. "Mr. Evans replied that his position as an employer at the time had prevented his being a member." [4] Mr. Ryckman proposed an address to working-men "evincing intimate knowledge of their condition." [5]

At New York, too, Bovay, as a member of the Committee on Presidential Candidates, recommended that the Industrial Congress should support the candidate of the Liberty Convention then in session at Macedon, if he should subscribe to the four land reform measures. [6] The Liberty League, a secession from the Liberty Party on the ground

---

[1] *Voice of Industry*, June 19, 1846.
[2] *Ibid.*
[3] *Ibid.*   [4] *Ibid.*, June 18, 1847.
[5] *Ibid.*
[6] *Ibid.*, June 25, 1847.

that "equal rights" meant more than freeing the slave and the belief that nothing was to be expected from the old parties, nominated for President, at the Macedon Convention, Gerrit Smith, and for Vice-President, Elihu Burritt,[1] and, in 1848, the Industrial Congress endorsed Gerrit Smith and substituted William S. Wait, of Illinois, for Burritt.[2]

Another matter that came before the New York Congress was Ryckman's scheme for a constitution for a free state based on the idea of "the entire good of the whole" in place of the "greatest good of the greatest number."[3]

But neither Ryckman nor any other reformer could make headway against the rising power of anti-slavery.

The question of slavery [declared the "Voice of Industry"] is in truth the question of labor. Wherever the rights of laborers are discussed or upon whatever department of labor reform we insist, the influence of slavery is arrayed against us. Do we ask for a Free Soil, a land limitation law, or any other measure which looks to the protection and elevation of the laboring classes, we are told by the McDuffies and the Calhouns that slavery is the natural and necessary condition of the producing classes. . . .[4]

In 1848 it was seen that

every succeeding day only renders this question of slavery more vexing. . . . Its ugly face peers up to view from every cranny and dog-hole into which it is attempted to hide it. There is now but one issue. Either slavery must have full liberty and sweep to expand itself in infinity or else it must meet in fell encounter with death. You cannot touch a single question of general policy in which slavery does not get some moral thrust. It cannot be avoided. Slavery must be extinguished. If the question of cheap postage comes up, it is alleged that the peculiar institutions of the

---

[1] *Voice of Industry*, May 21 and July 23, 1847.

[2] *The New Era*, June 15 and 29, 1848.

[3] *Voice of Industry*, October 8, 1847.

[4] *Ibid.*, November 26, 1847. Only three months before the *Voice of Industry* had said: "Whether the extinction of chattel slavery is to precede other reforms . . . remains to be seen. God grant its extinction may be speedy. But there are some who . . . deem it possible that the abolition of slavery may come after another reform." (*Voice of Industry*, August 13, 1847.)

South render such a reform impracticable. . . . Whether the question be of free trade, direct taxation, internal improvements — or of peace as a national policy — whether it be conquering or annexing territory or of organizing territorial governments — or whether it be of freeing the soil to actual settlers and limiting the quantity any man may acquire — whatever may be the question . . . this enormous dragon has something at stake. . . . We go for direct and internecine war with the monster. . . .[1]

In 1848 the Industrial Congress held in Philadelphia confined itself almost exclusively to land reform and other political measures. Other congresses met in Cincinnati in 1849, and in Chicago in 1850, "not very numerously attended, but a marked degree of talent characterizing their members." [2] It was an army of officers.

At the Albany Congress, 1851, Isaac P. Walker, United States Senator from Wisconsin, was nominated for the Presidency and an address was prepared to the people of the United States. Later meetings were held at Washington, in 1852, and at various other places until 1856, when the organization expired with only eleven delegates.[3]

The State Industrial Congresses were offshoots of the national organization. The first was the New Jersey Congress at Trenton in 1851.[4] The New York Congress met at Albany in the same year and passed resolutions for the ten-hour day, trade and agricultural schools, land reform, and against prison labor.[5] They spread as far west as Illinois.

---

[1] *The New Era,* July 27, 1848.
[2] New York *Daily Tribune,* June 13, 1850.
[3] Commons, *History of Labor,* vol. 1, pp. 550–51.
[4] New York *Daily Tribune,* February 8, 1851.
[5] *Ibid.,* September 5 and 6, 1851.

CHAPTER XV

THE LABOR MOVEMENT: AGGRESSIVE
1850–60

THE defensive labor movement of the forties had centered in New England and was organized on territorial rather than on occupational lines. It represented the worker as a citizen of a community rather than a member of a craft. This was the natural formation for a movement whose purpose was not primarily to seize new positions, but to defend old ones. But the defensive movement had failed, was doomed to failure from the start. And out of its failure there emerged a new point of view, new purposes, and a new form of organization.

The labor movement of the fifties achieved the emancipation of the worker from the tradition of 'community of interest' between employer and employed; the explicit acceptance of his trade status; the limitation of his purposes; and a compacted form of organization suitable to aggressive action. It was natural that this craft or trade-union movement should center chiefly in the cities where the old ideas and attitudes of citizenry were most readily broken down; and the craft organizations in the cities in the forties graduated from purely benefit unions into bargaining organizations, experimenting with producers' coöperation and political action on the way. By 1853 they had accepted the inevitable loss of status involved in the Industrial Revolution and had organized to demand, in lieu of that status, wages, hours, and conditions of work, not for the workers as a whole, but for their own crafts.

The depression of 1837–39 left nothing of trade-unionism in New York but a few benevolent organizations that, because they were small and had funds, were able to weather the storm. To these were added in the beginning of our period some others of a similar character, like the "New York Benevolent Association of Bookbinders" which was incorporated in 1839. The bookbinders represented one of the best trades in the city. They were "contented, respectable, and industrious mechanics." There were only about seven hundred of them, and they were paid, in the forties, from $8 to $15 a week. Most of them were Americans with constant employment during the seasons which ran from September to January and March to July. They had few grievances except the employment of 'rats' in some of the shops at lower than the accepted wages.[1]

In 1843 and 1844 an epidemic of strikes swept the country in the wake of improved business conditions and, in 1845, there were formed a number of unions, often miscalled 'protective,' of truly aggressive nature, seeking 'trade' ends. An organization of this sort was formed by the bookbinders, called "The Bookbinders' Union," which grew rapidly to three hundred members and presented a new scale of prices to the employers.[2] The "New York Upholsterers' Society," of mixed racial character, American, French, German, Irish, and English, also presented a new list of prices advancing their wages from $7 to $9 a week.[3] In July, 1845, a general trade meeting was held in New York, but was immediately captured by the Land Reformers and carried to Croton Hall, with a band. Two measures were proposed, and the committee, which was mostly Land Reform, agreed that both should be presented to the meeting. "Mr. Davis proposed and advocated," said Evans in reporting the affair, "a plan of coöperation which we shall publish hereafter, if furnished with a copy. . . . Mr. Bovay then proposed the freedom of the public lands and in a speech. . . ." The speech was given two columns. Finally, "the hour being late, the meeting then adjourned, with the

---

[1] New York *Tribune*, August 22, 1845.
[2] *Ibid.*, August 28, September 11, 1845.   [3] *Ibid.*, April 20, 1845.

understanding [informal] that the subject for which the meeting had been convened should be considered at the next meeting of the National Reform Association." [1]

In 1846 there was a renewed outbreak of strikes in the cities and, in 1847, as a result of rising prices, strikes for wages were "of almost daily occurrence." [2] The machinists of Boston held a meeting at Faneuil Hall in May and sent out a circular to their employers asking for the adoption of the ten-hour day. Only two of the forty employers replied and the machinists decided to strike. A proposal was made by a clergyman that they subscribe $100 each and start a workshop of their own. This was rejected, and the meeting broke up with "a feeling that the machinists must protect themselves, if they wished to be protected at all." [3]

Slowly and hesitatingly the workers in special crafts were disentangling themselves from the general mass and developing a technique and purpose of their own. The remarkable labor activity of the spring of 1850 was of a mixed sort in which the struggle between the defensive and the aggressive attitudes became acute. Nearly the last of the protests against the social and professional degradation of the craftsman was made by the Bricklayers' and Plasterers' Union in this year. They had no complaint to make of "legitimate employers" and were willing to unite with them to protect the trade from "innovation and reproach." They complained of the "tyranny" of those employers who were "butchers and tinkers who have never learned the trade, usurping the place of legitimate mechanics" and

[1] *Young America*, July 19, 1845. A previous meeting called by the Land Reformers in June had been instrumental in calling this meeting of the trades. (*Young America*, June 14, 1845.)

[2] Among the tailors of Cincinnati, the coal miners of Pennsylvania, the weavers of Philadelphia, the shoemakers of New York, the painters of Boston. In 1847: boot and shoemakers, tobacconists, and tailors of Pennsylvania, cabinet-makers of Pittsburgh, laborers near Boston, iron-workers of Cincinnati, carpenters and painters of Nashville. (*Voice of Industry*, March 13 and 20, 1846, and June 11, June 18, 1847.)

[3] *Voice of Industry*, May 28, 1847.

making the name of 'journeyman' "a by-word and reproach," by manufacturing annually "hordes of unfinished
workmen piling brick together, unsightly to the eye and
disgraceful to the trade — driving men like slaves that
they may enrich themselves from the blood and sweat of
those whose necessity knows no law . . ." [1] The Philadelphia carpenters, on the other hand, organized to "place
ourselves in a position successfully to combat capital"; [2]
and the National Typographical Society declared: "It is
useless for us to disguise the fact that under the present arrangement of things, there exists a perpetual antagonism
between labor and capital."

It was this new realistic attitude that alienated Greeley
and the rest of the Reformers. "The jours are all for more
wages," protested the editor of the "Tribune," "a strike is
the thing. . . . Just see, say the jours, how the employers in
almost every trade come and pay the wages demanded." [3]
But this would not last, Greeley thought; "The jours are
fatally misled if they suppose the employers can pay good
wages whenever they please. Just now they can. California is drawing away our labor and pouring in gold." [4]

Greeley was thinking here in terms of the economic determinism that dominated his generation. Wages could not
rise except from 'natural' causes. It is one of the little iro-
nies of history that those who most vigorously asserted the
inviolability of the 'natural' law of supply and demand in
relation to wages were the first to override it in relation to
prices. Beginning with laws of incorporation and the tariff,
Greeley, and those for whom he spoke, worked indefati-
gably for the curtailment of the field of competition. But
when the skilled workers attempted the same thing they
were regarded as deluded and misled.

The mixed character of the unionism of 1850 is seen in
the case of the shoemakers. The "United Society of Jour-

---

[1] New York *Tribune*, June 13, 1850.   [2] *Ibid.*, August 6, 1850.
[3] *Ibid.*, April 24, 1850.   [4] *Ibid.*

neymen Cordwainers" was an old benefit society in the
'men's branch' organized in 1803.[1] It was purely benevolent and its constitution disclaimed any intention of interfering with the regulation of trade or wages.[2] In March,
1850, this society had only eighty members.[3] A new constitution was drawn up and a price list presented to the employers. The journeymen claimed that they had often to
work eighteen hours a day and earned an average of only
five dollars a week. The new price list set seven dollars per
week as a minimum; a committee was appointed to present
the list to the employers, and preparations were made for a
strike. The new society was called the "United Society of
Operative Cordwainers of the City of New York." It was
both benefit and bargaining. It continued the boycott of
non-union men, declaring "that any member who shall
board or work with any man not belonging to this society" would be fined one dollar and compelled to leave.
Women were not to be allowed to work in any shop controlled by the society unless they were wives or daughters
of members.

The new society increased its membership to three hundred. A strike was called that lasted three weeks and only
two employers refused to accept the scale.[4] The German
cordwainers coöperated with the Americans to the extent
of refusing to allow their members to act as 'scabs' and by
maintaining the same wage scale.[5] The strike was considered a great success and a procession was held to celebrate
the victory.[6] But with "some exceptions the rates were not
afterward sustained," and many of the members dropped
out of the organization.[7]

During the cordwainers' strike, a proposal was made to
establish a coöperative workshop (Association shop) for the

---

[1] New York *Daily Tribune*, April 9, 1850; *ibid.*, June 6.
[2] *Ibid.*, June 6, 1850.   [3] *Ibid.*, April 23, 1850.
[4] *Ibid.*, April 23, 1850.   [5] *Ibid.*, April 16, 1850.
[6] *Ibid.*, April 23, 1850.   [7] *Ibid.*, May 3, 1853.

journeymen who were out of work. A "Shoemakers' Working Union" was established, including both branches of the trade, to secure "independence of the tyrannical dictation and extortion of the intermediate capitalists alias bosses." Greeley and Ryckman were on the board of trustees.[1]

In May the Ladies' Branch organized and presented a new scale of prices. They enrolled one hundred and fifty members, and at their meeting a "Tribune" reporter suggested "the name of a gentleman to address them," evidently paving the way for Ryckman or Greeley and coöperative production. But the shoemakers declined the honor.[2] Again, in 1853, the shoemakers demanded increased prices and considered self-employment.[3]

This mixed character of the shoemakers' activities — benefit, coöperation, trade agreement, strike, closed shop, and boycott — was characteristic of the unionism of the period from 1847 to 1853. The skilled worker was in process of extricating himself from the larger purposes of the past and of confining his attention to ends of an exclusively trade character and methods adapted to those ends.

The New York carpenters struck on March 11, 1850, for $1.75 a day. They formed a procession four deep and one quarter of a mile long, and were warned by Greeley that strikes would not help them. But "if all the carpenters who may be thrown out of work by this strike were to form promptly a coöperative union, choose a thoroughly competent business agent and a foreman, get together a capital of $20,000 to $30,000 and appeal to the public, especially to workingmen for contracts . . . that would be a decided step toward the emancipation of labor. . . ."[4] A Joint-Stock Building Association seems to have been formed with a capital of five thousand dollars. The strike was only partially successful, some of the contractors agreeing to

[1] New York *Daily Tribune*, April 9, April 17, 1850.
[2] *Ibid.*, May 7, 1850.   [3] *Ibid.*, May 3, 1853.
[4] *Ibid.*, March 12, 1850.

fourteen shillings and many of the workers returning at thirteen.[1]

A benefit union, "The Pioneer Temple No. 1, House Carpenters' Protective Association," with members in the principal shops in the city, was then in existence, having been organized in 1844. Its avowed purpose was to promote brotherly feeling, relieve distress, assist unemployed members, and advance craft knowledge and skill. It was a secret order having passwords, grips and so on. It had been organized by seven men who had had a long experience of carpenters' societies that seldom lasted more than six months. To keep together, they had adopted the principle that "the interests of the employer and the employed are one and the same." Some of the most active of their members were boss carpenters.[2] Toward the end of April this society joined the younger organization and, in May, when some of the bosses who had agreed to fourteen shillings went back to thirteen, both organizations "began to arouse themselves from the listless state into which they had fallen since the strike," [3] and entered the political arena with a platform of city measures. This platform, "to be agitated at the ensuing fall elections," [4] comprised: a legal minimum wage for mechanics and laborers on public works; relief from the payment of rent for tenements condemned by the health officer; a decent public cemetery for free burial; free dispensaries in each ward; free night lodging-houses for the homeless, to be erected and supported by the city; and the inspection of buildings being erected or taken down. In the fall the carpenters struck against a reduction of wages and for the eight-hour day.[5] In 1854 they struck for increased wages for the fourth successive spring, asking an advance of one shilling on sixteen and seventeen per day. Some of them were receiving as high as $2.25 a

[1] New York *Daily Tribune*, April 8, 1850.
[2] *Ibid.*, May 13 and 17, 1850.   [3] *Ibid.*, May 6, 1850.
[4] *Ibid.*, May 25, 1850.   [5] *Ibid.*, October 19, 1850.

day. It was decided to form a "permanent organization" because it was understood that the bosses had combined. In June, 1853, a national organization was proposed.[1]

In the spring of 1850 trade-union organization in New York reached a high point. The house painters organized a "Practical Benefit Protection Society" with three hundred members, both employers and journeymen approving of its purposes.[2] The "Confectioners' Benefit Society" (German) proposed a coöperative shop and bank to take care of union funds, and a labor exchange for meetings and to secure employment.[3] The German tailors and German locksmiths organized. The "Laborers' United Benevolent Society" was formed. The watchcase-makers organized and advanced their wages forty per cent.[4] The shipwrights and calkers had a society.[5] The German cabinet-makers, with some French and English, had eight hundred members, half of whom were in favor of coöperation. The American society, however, would not make the venture and the proposal was dropped.[6] The upholsterers struck and cautioned the journeymen of Boston against advertisements of work to be had in New York. The employers were notified that they could procure workers by applying to the Union.[7] The New York printers prepared a report on the state of the trade.[8]

The tendency of these various trade organizations to come together in city trades' unions was implicit in the purposes that had brought them into existence. A tentative movement was made in this direction in 1845, but was immediately absorbed by the Land Reformers. Again in 1850 the trades began to come together, but their attempt to form a purely trades' union was forestalled and the City Industrial Congresses resulted. The first of these congresses

---

[1] New York *Daily Tribune*, June 27, 1854.
[2] *Ibid.*, April 16, 1850.   [3] *Ibid.*, April 18, 1850.
[4] *Ibid.*, April 19, 1850.   [5] *Ibid.*
[6] *Ibid.*, April 26, 1850.   [7] *Ibid.*, April 29, 1850.
[8] *Ibid.*, April 22, 1850.

was formed in Pittsburgh and they later spread to New
York, Boston, Philadelphia, Baltimore, Albany, Auburn,
Buffalo, Trenton, Cleveland, and Cincinnati. The term
'Industrial Congress' indicates the relationship of these organizations to the National and State Industrial Congresses under the control of the Land Reformers, but there
was a difference. In the case of the City Congresses the
organization had a real basis in local trade societies, while
the State and National organizations were reformist pure
and simple. The City Congresses — the New York City
Congress at least — represented a legitimate industrial
movement dominated early in its life and increasingly by
intellectuals and politicians.

The Pittsburgh Congress came into existence as a result
of the decline of the iron-workers. In November, 1849, the
iron-masters of the United States held a convention in
Pittsburgh in the interest of further protection of their
trade, but, deciding that their chances were not bright, and
needing a month or so to make shop repairs, the Pittsburgh employers cut wages, claiming that it was necessary
because of lack of protection. A strike resulted which
lasted until February, when the masters began to bring in
immigrants to take the place of the strikers. A workingmen's congress was then called by representatives of fourteen trades.[1] In April a delegate convention met as "The
United Trades and Labor Organizations of Allegheny
County." [2] They demanded an incorporation law so that
the workers could better start coöperative shops, the exemption of the homestead from debt, and freedom of the
public lands.[3] They discussed the tariff, the banking system, coöperation, and separate political organization for
the workers.[4]

In Boston, the Congress developed out of coöperative ac-

[1] Commons, *History of Labor*, vol. 1, p. 552, and note.
[2] New York *Daily Tribune*, April 22, 26, 1850.
[3] *Ibid.*, May 14, 1850.   [4] *Ibid.*, May 28, 1850.

tivity. The shoemakers proposed to form a coöperative society "to emancipate themselves from the system of wage slavery and become their own masters." The tinsmiths had been 'aroused' by Brisbane and expected further instruction from Dwight, Trask, Hibbard, Treanor. A meeting was held in the Associationists' rooms of delegates from the various trade and reform societies in the city. Out of this activity grew the New England Industrial League [1] that gave place, in 1852, to the Massachusetts Ten-Hour State Convention.

In New York the German unions had established a Central Committee to correspond to the Pittsburgh Congress,[2] and on June 5–6, the first meetings were held of the New York City Industrial Congress, with eighty-three delegates, representing fifty benevolent and protective societies.[3]

At first the Land Reformers were unsympathetic, and Evans protested against the use of the name:

> The trades of Pittsburgh have organized what they call a Congress composed of delegates from each, who meet weekly to discuss their affairs. The term thus used by them has already been appropriated by a national organization, the Industrial Congress, now four years old, which has recommended the organization of Industrial Legislatures in each State. Two have already been organized, in Ohio and Illinois, and it would be well for the trades of Pittsburgh, New York, and other cities to take measures to organize legislatures for their respective States.[4]

But Evans, finding that the name of his organization had been appropriated by the City Congresses, proceeded shortly to appropriate the latter to himself. The Associationists, however, were well represented in the early stages and probably controlled a majority of the delegates. The New York "Herald" said of the undertaking:

[1] New York *Daily Tribune,* April 23 and June 3, 1850.
[2] *Ibid.,* May 28, 1850.   [3] *Ibid.,* June 6, 1850.
[4] *Ibid.,* May 25, 1850.

The great error in this movement is that it did not begin right; it did not originate with the trades, but with a knot of political tricksters, and hence the peculiar composition of the body. What are its constituent parts? — Horace Greeley, his two reporters, Johnasson and Ottarson, and his printer's devil, Henderson, represent a party paper, the New York "Tribune," the organ of Free Soil, Whiggery, and Socialism. Then there is, on the other hand, Mr. Daniel B. Taylor, a well-known politician, once a member of the Assembly and mixed up with every election for years. Ostensibly he represents the hodmen, but really the Democrats. . . . Mr. Bailey, the chairman; Mr. Crate, the secretary. The former represents . . . What? (Don't laugh, readers!). He represents the Church of Humanity! The latter represents some other body of men, but they are not a body of tradesmen.[1]

A contest developed immediately over the qualifications for the admission of delegates. Objection was made to the admission of those of benevolent organizations, and it was claimed that all sorts of secret fraternities, such as the Odd Fellows, Free Masons, and Sons of Temperance, might come in under such a classification.[2] The delegate of the bricklayers claimed that non-working-men could and did get in under the cloak of benevolent societies and that a secret society in the city was intriguing to gain control of the Congress. The bricklayers proposed that a General Trades' Union should be formed, but the "Tribune" reporter told them that the Congress was "opposed to spending their money in supporting other trades in striking against their employers."[3]

The guiding hand of the Associationists was further seen in the preamble of the constitution which defined the purpose of the Congress, "to devise means to reconcile the interests of Labor and Capital, to secure the laborer the full product of his toil — to promote union, harmony, and brotherly feeling among workmen."[4]

[1] New York *Herald*, July 16, 1850.
[2] New York *Tribune*, July 3, 1850.
[3] *Ibid.*
[4] *Ibid.*

Trade interests having been eliminated from the agenda, the Congress was free to listen to reformers of every stripe. In response to the plea of the German tailors for aid in establishing a coöperative shop, it extended its sympathy, but had no funds to lend. It refused to ask the State for aid for the seamstresses in a similar undertaking and failed to aid them privately. It discussed the eight- and ten-hour day, the collection of debts through the courts, recommended the workers to patronize the Economical Exchange, and appointed a board of managers for the Coöperative Labor League. It discussed Kellog's "Labor and Other Capital" and glanced at Stephen Pearl Andrews's "Declaration of Fundamental Truths." This was too much for the trade societies and many of them withdrew.

But the Associationists were children in comparison with the Land Reformers in the matter of manipulating popular bodies, and Evans, having recovered from his pique at the appropriation of the name he considered his own, proceeded to take the organization in hand and launch it upon a political career. In 1851 the Land Reformers had become so strongly entrenched that a change of name was considered to "The New York Industrial Council," corresponding to the City Council, as the National Industrial Congress corresponded to the United States Congress and the State Industrial Legislatures to the State Legislatures.

The political policy of the Land Reformers soon led to Tammany. In June, 1853, the Industrial Congress accepted an invitation to participate in a grand mass meeting at Tammany Hall.[1] The basis of representation was changed to the wards and the Congress took the shape that Evans had planned in 1843 for the National Reformers.

Thus slowly and uncertainly, hindered more by friend than foe, the skilled crafts were creating their own technique to achieve their limited but practicable trade ends. As they proceeded, they and the Reformers drew apart.

[1] Commons, *History of Labor*, vol. 1, pp. 550–62.

So long as the labor movement was defensive, a general attempt to ward off encroachment on the standards of the
workers, Greeley and others were sympathetic, though perhaps not very helpful. But when the movement became aggressive, the Reformers became cold. "We cannot believe
it wise," said Greeley in 1853, "for men who are offered
two dollars a day to strike for an *advance* of only a shilling.
If it were to *maintain* a long-established rate, a strike might
be justified." [1] This was the turning-point and here Greeley
parted with the enthusiasm of his youth as did many another.

In August, 1853, the New York painters struck to maintain their rate of two dollars a day that had been granted
them in the spring and upon which some employers had
gone back.[2] A demonstration was held in the Metropolitan
Hall of two thousand mechanics to aid their brethren. The
Laborers Society contributed five hundred dollars and it was
decided to form a General Trades' Union.[3] In September,
1853, the Amalgamated Trades' Convention met with three
delegates from every trade association, the delegates being
required to be journeymen working at their trades; a delegate from every shop employing from twenty to one hundred men; two from shops with one hundred to two hundred men; and three from shops with more than two hundred. The Printers Coöperative Union objected to the regulation that only journeymen might be delegated, but the
other organizations insisted that "it had been a too common practice among workingmen to admit wire-pullers and
such designing persons as would make these workingmen's
associations mere tools for the furtherance of their personal
or party interest." No delegates were admitted from benevolent or secret societies.[4] This organization met on Tues-
day, October 18th, and was evidently in existence in June,

[1] New York *Daily Tribune,* April 1, 1853. (Italics mine.)
[2] *Ibid.*, August 25, 1853.   [3] *Ibid.*, September 1, 1853.
[4] *Ibid.*, September 21 and 28, 1853.

1854, as the carpenters were then given credentials to a Trades' Union.[1] It was the culmination of the aggressive movement. But nothing more is known of its activities.

Toward the end of the decade a number of national craft organizations were formed, but few of them survived the Civil War. They belong rather to the beginning of the labor movement of the sixties than to ours. The labor movement in America finished the period 1840–60 as it had begun — practically in nothingness.

[1] New York *Daily Tribune,* June 27, 1854.

SELECTED BIBLIOGRAPHY

SELECTED BIBLIOGRAPHY

Abbott, Edith, "Harriet Martineau and the Employment of Women in 1836." *Journal of Political Economy*, vol. 14, 1906, pp. 614 ff.

Abbott, Edith, "The Wages of Unskilled Labor in the United States, 1850–1900." *Journal of Political Economy*, June, 1905, vol. 13, p. 321.

Abbott, Edith, *Women in Industry*. New York, 1910.

Aiken, John, *Labor and Wages at Home and Abroad*. Lowell, 1849.

Appleton, Nathan, *Introduction of the Power Loom*. Lowell, 1858.

Awl, The. Lynn. 1844–45. Published by an Association of Cordwainers.

Ayer, J. C., *Some of the Usages and Abuses in the Management of Our Manufacturing Corporations*. Lowell, 1863.

Bagnall, Wm. R., *Textile Industry of the United States*. Cambridge, 1893. 2 vols.

Barnett, George E., *The Printers*. Publications of the American Economic Association, vol. 10, 3d Series, 1909, pp. 433–820.

Bartlett, Dr. Elisha, *Vindication of the Character and Conditions of the Females employed in the Lowell Mills against the Charges contained in the Boston Times and Boston Quarterly Review*. Lowell, 1841.

Batchelder, Samuel, *Introduction and Early Progress of Cotton Manufacture in the United States*. Boston, 1863.

Bemis, Edward, *Coöperation in New England*. Publications of the American Economic Association, vol. 1, no. 5, 1886.

Bishop, J. L., *History of American Manufactures, 1608–1860*. Philadelphia, 1868.

Bogart, E. L., *Economic History of the United States*. New York, 1912.

Boston Daily Times, July 13, 15, 16, 17, 18, 19, 22, 25, 26, and 29, 1839.

Boston Quarterly Review (O. A. Brownson, Editor). "The Laboring Classes," July, 1840, vol. 3; "Conversations with a Radical," January and April, 1841, vol. 4; "Address to Workingmen," January, 1841, vol. 4; "Letter to the Editor of the 'Lowell Offering,'" April, 1841, vol. 4.

Brisbane, Albert, *The Social Destiny of Man*. 1840.

Bromwell, Wm. J., *History of Immigration to the United States.* New York, 1856.

Burton, T. E., *Financial Crises.* New York, 1902.

Butler, Benj. F., *Butler's Book, Autobiography and Personal Reminiscences.* Boston, 1892.

Carey, Mathew, *Tariff Pamphlets.* Philadelphia, 1826.

Carey, Thos. G., *Profits on Manufactures at Lowell.* Boston, 1845.

Carey, Thos. G., *Gold from California and Its Effect on Prices.* New York, 1856.

Carlton, F. T., "The Workingmen's Party of New York," *Political Science Quarterly,* vol. 22, 1907, p. 401.

Carlton, F. T., "An American Utopia," *Quarterly Journal of Economics,* vol. 24, pp. 428–33.

Chevalier, Michel, *Society, Manners and Politics in the United States.* Boston, 1839.

Chronotype, The Daily. Boston, 1848.

City of Boston, Doc. no. 66, 1849, "Report of Committee on Internal Health."

Clark, Victor S., *History of Manufactures in the United States, 1607–1860.* Washington, 1916.

Coburn, Frederick W., *History of Lowell and Its People.* New York, 1920. 2 vols.

Codman, J. T., *Brook Farm,* 1894.

Coman, K., *The Industrial History of the United States.* New York, 1911.

Commons, John R., *A Documentary History of American Industrial Society.* Cleveland, 1910. 10 vols.

Commons, John R., "Labor Organization and Labor Politics," *Quarterly Journal of Economics,* vol. 21, pp. 323–29.

Commons, John R., "American Shoemakers, 1648–1895," *Quarterly Journal of Economics,* vol. 24, pp. 39–81.

Commons, John R., "Horace Greeley and the Working-Class Origins of the Republican Party," *Political Science Quarterly,* vol. 24, 1909, pp. 468 ff.

Commons, and associates, *History of Labor in the United States.* New York, 1918. 2 vols.

Corporations and Operatives; Being an exposition of the condition of factory operatives and a Review of the 'Vindication' by Elisha Bartlett, M.D. Published at Lowell, 1841, by a Citizen of Lowell in the *Vox Populi.* (Published as a pamphlet by Samuel J. Varney, 1843.)

Cowley, Chas., *History of Lowell.* Boston, 1868.

Cowley, Chas., *Handbook of Business in Lowell, with a History of the City.* Lowell, 1856.

Curtis, *The Republican Party.* New York, 1904. 2 vols.

Curtis, Dr. Josiah, *Brief Remarks on the Hygiene of Massachusetts, more particularly of the Cities of Boston and Lowell.* Philadelphia, 1840. (Reprint from *Transactions of Am. Med. Ass'n,* vol. II.)

Desmond, H. J., *The Know-Nothing Party.* Washington, 1905.

Dewey, *Financial History of the United States.*

Dial, The. Boston. July, 1840–April, 1844.

Evans, F. W., *The Shakers.* New York, 1859.

Fenner, H. M., *History of Fall River, Mass.* 1911.

Freedley, E. T., *Philadelphia and Its Manufactures in 1867.* Philadelphia, 1867.

Frothingham, O. B., *Transcendentalism in New England.* Boston, 1876.

Frothingham, O. B., *Gerrit Smith.* New York, 1876.

Frothingham, O. B., *George Ripley.* Boston, 1882.

Greeley, Horace. *Hints Toward Reforms.* New York, 1850.

Grund, Francis J., *The Americans.* London, 1837. 2 vols.

Hall, P. F., *Immigration.* New York, 1906.

Harbinger, The. June 14, 1845–October 30, 1847.

Hazzard, "The Boot and Shoe Industry in Massachusetts," *Quarterly Journal of Economics,* vol. 27, February, 1913.

Higginson, Thos. W., "The Sunny Side of the Transcendental Period," *Atlantic Monthly,* January, 1904, pp. 6 ff.

Higginson, Thos. W., "Part of a Man's Life," *Atlantic Monthly,* January, 1904.

Hillquit, Morris, *The History of Socialism in the United States.* New York, 1906.

Hours of Labor, The. An address of the Ten Hours' State Convention, held in Boston, September 30, 1852, to the people of Massachusetts, together with a report and bill submitted to the Legislature of Massachusetts, Session of 1852, by the Minority of the Committee on Hours of Labor.

Johnson, David N., *Sketches of Lynn.* Lynn, 1880.

Levasseur, *The American Workmen.* Johns Hopkins Press, 1900.

Lockwood, G. B., *The New Harmony Movement.* New York, 1907.

Lowell, Handbook of. Lowell, 1848.

Lowell Offering, The. A repository of original articles written exclusively by females actively employed in the mills. Lowell, Mass., 1840–45. 5 vols.

Luther, Seth, *An Address on the Origin and Progress of Avarice* . . . Boston, 1834.

Martineau, Harriet, *Society in America.* 2 vols. 3d ed. New York, 1837.

Masquerier, Lewis, *Sociology, or the Reconstruction of Society, Government and Property.* New York, 1877.

Massachusetts: *History of the Bureau of Statistics of Labor of Massachusetts and Labor Legislation of that State — 1833 to 1876.* Boston, 1876.

Massachusetts: *Eighth Annual Report*, Bureau of Statistics of Labor, 1877, no. 31, "Coöperation in Massachusetts."

Massachusetts: *Eleventh Annual Report*, Bureau of Statistics of Labor, January, 1880, no. 15, "Strikes in Massachusetts."

Massachusetts: *Sixteenth Annual Report*, Bureau of Statistics of Labor, August, 1885. Pub. Doc. no. 15, "Historical Review of Wages and Prices, 1752–1860."

Massachusetts House Doc. 21, 1840, Horace Mann, *Third Annual Report*, Board of Education.

Massachusetts House Doc. 4, 1842.

Massachusetts House Doc. 48, 1844.

Massachusetts House Doc. 50, 1845.

Massachusetts House Doc. 153, 1850.

Massachusetts House Doc. 185, 1852.

Massachusetts House Doc. 230, 1852.

Massachusetts House Doc. 122, 1853.

Massachusetts House Doc. 80, 1855.

Massachusetts House Doc. 98, 1866, "Hours of Labor and Condition of the Industrial Classes."

Massachusetts Senate Doc. 81, 1846.

Massachusetts Senate Doc. 21, 1868, Oliver Report.

Massachusetts Senate Doc. 50, 1875, "Report on Child Labor," by George E. McNeill.

McNeill, Geo. E., *The Labor Movement: The Problem of To-day.* New York, 1888.

McNeill, Geo. E., *Argument on the Hours of Labor before the Labor Committee of the Massachusetts Legislature.* 1871.

Mechanics' Mirror, The. 1843.

Miles, Rev. Henry A., *Lowell As It Was and As It Is.* Lowell, 1845.

Montgomery, James, *A Practical Detail of the Cotton Manufacture of the United States of America.* Glasgow, 1840.

Myers, *History of Tammany Hall.* New York, 1917.

National Association of Wool Manufacturers. *Bulletin*, "New England Wool Manufacture," vol. XXIX. Boston, 1899.

New England Offering, The. (Editor, Harriet Farley.) 1848–49. 1 vol.

New Era of Industry, The, 1848 (June 2 to August 3). Boston.

New York State Mechanic, 1841–43.

New York Daily Tribune.

New York Weekly Tribune.

New Yorker, The, 1837–38.

Niles's National Register, 1840–44.

Nordhoff, Chas., *Communistic Societies of the United States.* New York, 1875.

North American Review: Miles' Review of Baines, and the "Slater Memoir," January, 1841, pp. 31 ff.; "The Future of Labor," vol. LXXIV, 1852, pp. 445 ff.; "Dwellings and Schools for the Poor," vol. LXXIV, 1852, pp. 464 ff.; "Free Trades, Wages, Rent," vol. LXXIV, 1852, p. 216.

Noyes, J. H., *History of American Socialisms.* Philadelphia, 1870.

Operatives Reply to Hon. Jere Clemens. (Harriet Farley.) Lowell, 1850.

Parton, James, *The Life of Horace Greeley.* New York, 1855.

Pennsylvania: Bureau of Industrial Statistics, *Annual Report,* 1880–81. Leg. Doc. 8.

Pennsylvania: Bureau of Industrial Statistics, *Annual Report,* 1882. Leg. Doc. 8, "Labor Troubles in Pennsylvania," pp. 262 ff.

Persons, C. E., "The Early History of Factory Legislation in Massachusetts"; in Kingsbury, S. M., *Labor Laws and Their Enforcement.* New York, 1911.

Phalanx, The. October 9, 1843–May 28, 1845. New York.

Pidgeon, Daniel, *Old World Questions and New World Answers.* New York, 1885.

Proceedings of the Convention of the Manufacturers, Dealers, and Operatives in the Shoe and Leather Trade in the State of Massachusetts. Boston, 1842.

Rhode Island: Report of the Commissioner appointed to ascertain the numbers, ages, hours of labor and opportunities for education of children employed in the manufacturing establishments of Rhode Island to the General Assembly, January Session, 1853. (W. B. Sayles.)

Robinson, Harriet H., *Loom and Spindle.* New York, 1898.

Schulter, *Lincoln, Labor and Slavery.* New York, 1913.

Scoresby, Rev. Wm., *American Factories and Their Female Operatives.* London, 1845.

Sorge, "Die Arbeiterbewegung in den Vereinigten Staaten, 1850–60," *Die Neue Zeit,* 1890–91, pp. 193 ff. and 232 ff.

Sotheran, Chas., *Horace Greeley and Other Pioneers of American Socialism*. New York, 1892.

Sumner, *Protection in the United States*. New York, 1877.

Swank, James M., *History of the Manufacture of Iron in All Ages*. Philadelphia, 1892.

Swift, Lindsay, *Brook Farm*. New York, 1904.

Taussig, *Tariff History of the United States*. New York, 1907.

Towles, "Labor Legislation of Rhode Island," *American Economic Association Quarterly*, 3d Series, vol. ix, no. 3.

True Workingman, The, 1845 (October 22)–1846 (February 7). Lynn.

U.S. Exec. Doc. 1, part 5, 50th Congress, 1st Session, 1887, pp. 1027–1108, "Strikes and Lock-outs in United States prior to 1881"; also, *Sixteenth Annual Report*, Commissioner of Labor, 1091. House Doc. 18, 57th Congress, 1st Session.

U.S. House Doc. Misc. 42, part 2, 47th Congress, 2d Session. Carroll D. Wright, "Report on the Factory System of the United States."

U.S. House Doc., 49th Congress, 1st Session, 1, part 5. Report of the Secretary of the Interior, 1885.

U.S. House Doc. 353, part 1, 54th Congress, 2d Session, p. 137. Davis Murray, "The Anti-Rent Episode in the State of New York." *Annual Report*, American Historical Association.

U.S. House Doc. 353, part 1, 54th Congress, 2d Session, p. 175. G. H. Haynes, "A Know-Nothing Legislature." *Annual Report*, American Historical Association.

U.S. House Doc. 386, part 4, 58th Congress, 3d Session. *Bulletin*, Bureau of Labor, no. 59, "Documentary History of Early Organizations of Printers."

U.S. Senate Doc. Report 1394, 4 vols., 52d Congress, 2d Session. "Wholesale Prices, Wages and Transportation." (Aldrich Report.)

U.S. Senate Doc. 645, 61st Congress, 2d Session. *Report on the Condition of Women and Child Wage-Earners in the United States*, vol. ix. Helen Sumner, "History of Women in Industry in the United States."

U.S. Senate Doc. 645, 61st Congress, 2d Session. *Report on Condition of Women and Child Wage-Earners in the United States*, vol. x. Andrews and Bliss, "History of Women in Trade Unions."

U.S. Senate Doc. 72, parts 1, 2, and 3, 62d Congress, 1st Session. Tariff Proceedings and Documents, 1829–57.

U.S. Senate Committee Investigation, 1885. 5 vols. *Labor and Capital*. Committee on Education and Labor.

Voice of Industry, Fitchburg, Lowell, and Boston, 1845–48.

White, Geo. S., *Memoir of Samuel Slater*. Philadelphia, 1836.

Woollen, Evans, "Labor Troubles between 1834 and 1837," *Yale Review*, May, 1892.

Working Man's Advocate, The, 1844–45. New York.

Young America, 1845–46. New York.

INDEX

Abbott, Edith, 119

Agrarians. *See* Land Reformers.

Aldrich Report, 34, 119, 129

Allegheny, mass meeting and strike, 141

Allen, John, 213, 219,

Amalgamated Trades Convention, 239

American (Lowell), 154

American Factories and Their Female Operatives (Scoresby), 95 *fn* 110, *fn* 113

American Phalanx, 174

American Protective Union, 192

American Statesman, 24

American Union of Associations 165

Amesbury, 94; strike, 152

Associationists, 163-179; slavery, 94; influence on workers' movements, 178, 221; criticized by Evans, 183; Cooperative movement, 185

Awl (Lynn), 41, 206, 208, 209

Bagley, Sarah, 90, 115, 125, 139, 213

Banks, Governor, 104

Bartlett, Dr. Elisha, 82-83, 85, 132, 136, 155; compares Lowell to Portsmouth, 86-88; estimates savings of Lowell operatives, 97

Basting machine, 1

Battle of Books, 77, 88

Bean, B. W., 1

Bigelow power loom, 64

Bishop, H. W., 158

Blacklist, 107-109

Board of Trade. *See* Protective Union, Board of Trade.

Boarding-house, 72; regulations, 107

Boilers, strike, 27-30

Bookbinders, cooperative shops, 196; unions and strikes, 228

Boston Division. *See* Protective Union, Boston Division.

Boston machinists, ten-hour day, 160

Boston Manufacturing Company (Waltham), wage reductions, 116

Boston Tailors Associative Union, 195

Bovay, 184, 224

Brisbane, Albert, 164-167; labor movement, 208, 209

Brook Farm, 163, 175-179, 207, 208, 218; burning of Phalanstery, 178; *Harbinger*, 165

Brownson, Orestes, 20, 23

Buckingham, Dr. C. E., 14

Buffalo tailors, cooperative shops, 196

Building trades, wages, 33; hire workers for trade, 35

Bureaus of Labor, 133

Burritt, Elihu, 225

Burton, Reverend, 220

Butler, Benjamin F., 102, 126, 154

Cabinet-makers, working con-
    ditions and wages, 66-67
California, 38
Campbell, James, 210
Capital investment, increase
    from 1840 to 1860, 2-9
Carle, James, 134
Carpenters, unions and
    strikes, 232-233
Carpet weavers, strikes, 64;
    power loom, 110
Channing, Dr. William H.,
    21, 166, 220
Chevalier, Michel, 153
Chicopee Mills, wage reduc-
    tion, 118; strike, 122
Child, Linus, 103; blacklist,
    108
Child labor, Rhode Island,
    74, 75-76; Massachusetts
    laws, 126; Gloucester, 156
Christian Advocate, 194
Chronotype (Boston),
    "Mechanic" letter, 93
Church of Humanity. See
    Religious Union of Asso-
    ciationists.
"Citizen of Lowell," criticizes
    factory system, 83-85, 86-87
City Congress, 236
City of Spindles. See Lowell.
Claflin, William, 158
Clark, Dr. Henry, 74, 123;
    Half-Moon Place, 13
Clark, Samuel, 134, 137
"Clock fixing," 147
Cluer, John C., 10, 139-141,
    221
Coalition Party Massachu-
    setts, 102-103, 158; ten-
    hour plank, 154; loses
    Lowell to Whigs, 161

Collins, John A., 170
Committee on Internal
    Health, 14
Congress, Southerners attack
    New England Mills, 94
Consumers cooperation, 187
Cooperative Labor League,
    193
Cooperative stores, Associa-
    tionists, 163; Massachu-
    setts, 187; iron shops, 194;
    Cooperative Boot and Shoe
    Store, 196
Cooperators, 163, 185-197;
    financial problems of, 188;
    failure of, 196
Cordwainers, New York, 44-
    47
Corporations, combination
    among, 107, 109-110
Cost of living, rise after
    1843, 31
Cotton industry, 71, 74; in-
    crease in spindles, 2
Cotton Manufacture in
    Great Britain (Baines),
    132
Courier (Lowell), 82, 85, 88,
    101, 127
Cozzens, Benjamin, 35
Crompton Mills, 35
Croton Hall, 182
Curtis, Harriot, 89
Curtis, Dr. Josiah, 98-100,
    155

Daily Times (Boston), 80-81,
    82, 88, 132
Daily Tribune (New York),
    33, 118, 165, 166; "Dens
    of Death," 15; "A Visit to
    Lowell," 95

Democrat (Manchester), 144, 146

Devyr, Thomas A., 182

Dial (Brook Farm), 175, 176

Division Number 9. *See* Protective Union, Division Number 9.

Dressmakers. *See* Needle trades.

Economical Exchange, 193

Emerson, Ralph Waldo, 176, 178

England, holidays, 136; factory population, 149; cooperators, 188

English Agrarianism, 164

Enquirer (Dover), 146

Evans, George Henry, 23, 27, 164, 180, 181, 182, 183-184, 214, 236, 238; criticizes Owen, 170, 183; New England Workingmen's Convention, 206; Industrial Congress, 223-224

Factory controversy, 71-100

Factory Girls' Garland (Exeter), 134

Factory operatives, protection, 72; discipline, 78; treatment in Lowell, 80-88; estimated savings, 83; health, 98-100; regulations, 107; reductions in wages, 111-119; speed and effort, 120-124; hours worked, 128-132; characteristics, 149-153

Factory Tracts, 142

Fall River, contrasted with Lowell, 76-78; wage reductions and strikes, 116-118; union formed, 117; exodus of native mill workers, 151; mechanics labor movement, 202-204

Farley, Harriet, 82, 89-92, 152; replies to "Mechanic's" letter, 93; replies to Clemens, 94

Farnsworth, Jesse, 159

Female Industry Association, 53

Fletcher, 23, 157

Fourier, Charles, 164; doctrines, 168-169, 172-174

Fourier clubs, 165

Fourierism, 164, 167, 169

Fourierists. *See* Associationists.

Friends of Association, 165

Future (Brisbane), 165

General Trades Union, 239

Germans, cooperative cabinet shops, 196; cooperative carpentry shops, 196; unions, 236

Goddard, Abby A., 89

Godwin, Parke, 165

Gold discoveries, 37, 152

Government employees, ten-hour day, 126

Gray, Elizabeth, 53

Greeley, Horace, 27, 30, 31, 33, 36; place in labor movement, 21-22; printers, 56; Brisbane, 165, 167; cooperative production, 187; iron moulders, 194; New England Association, 209;

economic determinism, 230, 239

Gregory, John, 134

Half-Moon Place, 13
Hall, Lydia S., 89
Hand-loom weavers, working conditions and wages, 61-64
Harbinger (Brook Farm), 165, 179
Hatch, G. W., 141
Hatch, Joel, 213
Hat Finishers' Union, 196
Hat Finishers' Protective Society, 64
Hatters, working conditions and wages, 65-66
Health problems, factory population, 149
Herald (New York), 53
History of American Socialisms (Noyes), 175
History of Lowell (Cowley), 153
Holidays, 136
Homestead Act (1861), 164, 181
Housing, squalid conditions, 13-17
Housepainters, unionism, 234
Howe, Elias, 1
Hygiene in Massachusetts (Curtis), 98

Immigrants, increase in, 10-13; factory workers, 150-151
Independent Democrat (New Hampshire), 145
Industrial Association, 185
Industrial Commissions, 133

Industrial Congress, 209; Boston, 223; New York, 224; Philadelphia, 226; Albany, 226
Industrial revolution, dissatisfaction with, 20-25
Industry profits (1840-1860), 4-6
Institute of Agriculture and Education. *See* Brook Farm.
Irish immigrants, 36
Iron industry, increase in production, 4, 6; ore price reductions, 27
Ironworkers, cooperative efforts, 194

Jaques, D. H., 178, 213, 222
Jones, C. C., 187
Journal (Lowell), 93
Journeyman Cordwainers' Society, 41
Journeyman Moulders' Union Foundry, 193

Kaulback, J. G., 163, 187, 211, 218
King, W. I., 34

Labor, scarcity, 150
Laborers, working conditions and wages, 7, 67-70
Laborers Society, 239
Laborers' Union Benevolent Association, 68
Laborers' Union of South Boston, 185
Labor movement, defensive, 119-226; aggressive, 227-240
Labor papers, 203

Labor Reformers. *See* Associationists.

Ladies Industrial Association, 193

Laissez-faire, 74-76

Land Reformers, 18, 163, 164, 171, 180; Cluer, 139; Fourierism, 170, 180; desert New England movement, 219, 223; Croton Hall convention, 214

Lawrence, Abbott, 30

Lawrence Manufacturing Company, 103

Liberty Party, 224

Loom and Spindle (Robinson), 154

Lowell, dividend payments, 5; profits, 7-9; increase in population, 14; contrasted with Fall River, 76-82; estimated savings by operatives, 83, 97; treatment of female operatives, 80-88; compared to Portsmouth, 86-88; as viewed by Scoresby and Miles, 95-97; corporation control, 101-103; internal changes, 103-105; regulations for operatives, 107; wage reductions, 114; petitions to Massachusetts legislature, 133-135, 143; visited by Schouler committee, 137; hours' reductions, 147; strike, 150; California emigration, 153; eleven-hour day, 161; mechanics' labor movement, 203

Lowell Association, 141

Lowell corporations. *See* Lowell.

Lowell Female Reform Association, 138, 207; constitution, 218

Lowell Offering, 83, 85, 88, 89, 90, 92

Lowell Planing Mills, mechanics strike, 161

Luther, Seth, 218

Lynn Massachusetts, shoemakers, 39-44; wage complaints, 34-35

Macdaniel, George Evans, 165, 170

Macdonald, 167, 175

MacFarlane, Robert, 200, 201

Manchester, eleven-hour law, 161

Manchester of America. *See* Lowell.

Mann, Horace, 126, 158

Martineau, Harriet, 42, 72-73

Masquerier, Lewis, 182

Massachusetts, cotton industry, 71-74; Schouler committee, 135-138; displacement of native mill workers, 152; ten-hour movement, 125, 126-128, 131, 154-155, 156, 161; Ten-Hour State Convention, 156-157; consumers' cooperation, 187

Maxwell, James, 182

McKay machine, 2, 47

Mechanics, labor movement, 200

Mechanics and Laborers' Associations, 202; Boston, 185

Mechanics Mirror, 200
Mechanics Mutual Protection, 200
Merrimack Mill, 80; studied by Curtis, 98-100
Middlesex Corporation, blacklist, 107; strike, 112; visited by Schouler committee, 137
"Middle system," 54
Miles, Reverend Henry, 95-97, 113, 131-132, 136, 146; blacklist, 108, 109
Mills, classes of workers, 111; exodus of native workers, 151
Mobility, factory population, 149
Montgomery, James, 130, 137, 147, 155, 159
Mortality rates, 86-87, 99

Nashua Convention, 109, 219
Nashua Corporation, strike, 144-146
National craft organizations, 240
National Industrial Convention, 217
National Reform Association, 224
National Reformers, 182; Croton Hall Convention, 213. *See also* Land Reformers.
National Typographical Society, 56, 195, 230
Needle trades, 49-55
Nepotism, 105
Newburyport, wage reductions, 113; eleven-hour day, 161

New England Association, Boston meeting, 209; Woburn picnic, 210; Fall River Convention, 211; Lowell Convention, 212; working-class control, 218
New England Industrial League, 155
New England Offering, 89, 92, 152
New England Operative, 79, 203
New England Protective Union, end of, 191-192. *See also* Workingmen's Protective Union.
New England Workingmen's Association, 184; Fall River Convention, 163; Brook Farm, 178
New England Workingmen's Convention, Boston meeting, 205; Lowell meeting, 206; constitution, 207
New Era of Industry. *See Voice of Industry*, history.
New Hampshire, ten-hour law, 144-146, 157, 159; displacement of native mill workers, 152
New Harmony (Indiana), 166
New Jersey, ten-hour law, 156
New York City, population growth, 12; unemployment, 26; mass meeting of trades, 184; cooperative production, 187; cooperative stores, 193, 196
New Yorker, 165

New York Printers' Union, 57

New York Protective Union, 193

New York State Mechanic, 200

New York Typographical Society, 56, 57

Niles' Register, 3; Fourierism, 170

North American Phalanx, 166

Organ of the People. See Voice of Industry, history.

Owen, Robert, 18, 165; Land Reform, 214; World Convention, 209, 215; Utopian proposals, 216-217

Owenites, 166

Paternalism, 101-105; Lowell, 76-77

Paterson New Jersey, mill wage cuts, 156

Pathfinder, 165

Pauperism, 27

Pennsylvania, ten-hour law, 148

Petitions, to Massachusetts legislature, 132-135, 143, 158

Phalanstery, Boston, 186

Phalanx, 165, 185; Fourier, 168; failures of, 174; Brook Farm, 178

Phalanx, or Journal of Social Science, 165

Philadelphia, population growth, 12

Phillips, Wendell, 170

Phillips, William, 207

Pitkins Statistics, 76

Pittsburgh, strike, 141

Portsmouth, compared to Lowell, 86-88

Principles of Labor Legislation (Commons and Andrews), *fn* 127

Printers, unemployment, 7; working conditions and wages, 55-56, unionization, 57-61

Printers Cooperative Union, 239

Protective Union, 185; Board of Trade, 189, 192; Boston Division, 189; Central Division, 192; Division Number 9, 189-190; Roxbury Division, 189; Supreme Division, 189

Pyne, James A., 182

Railroad industry, increase in mileage, 4

Raritan Bay Union, 166

Ready-made clothing, 48

Reform, labor movement, 208

"Regulation paper," 135

Religious Union of Associationists, 166

Republican Party, 181

Rhode Island, cotton industry, 74-76; exodus of native mill workers, 151; ten-hour law, 160

Ripley, George 176-178

Robbins, R. L., 189

Robinson, William S., 126, 154, 159, 161

Robinson, Mrs., 89, 154

Rochdale (England), 188

Roxbury Division.
See Protective Union,
Roxbury Division.
Rural Republican Township,
181
Ryckman, L. W., 163, 209,
224-225

Salem corporation,
eleven-hour day
Sargent, Amelia, 90
Schouler, William, 85, 88, 89,
101, 127, 155; attacked by
Cluer, 140
Schouler committee. *See*
Massachusetts, Schouler
committee.
Scoresby, Dr., enthusiasm for
Lowell mills, 95
Seamstresses, New York co-
operative shop, 193. *See
also* Needle trades.
Sewing machine, 1
Seaver, Horace, 187
Sharon (Pennsylvania),
cooperative iron shops, 194
Shirt Sewers Cooperative
Union Depot, 196
Shoemakers, wage reductions,
7; working conditions and
wages, 39-44; strikes by,
44-49; Lynn cooperative,
187, 193, 204; Pittsburgh
cooperatives, 194; union-
ism, 232
Shoemakers' Working Union,
232
"Shop clothing," 48
Sketch of Lowell, 85
"Slaver," 151
Slavery, 93, 225
Smith, Gerritt, 225

Socialists. *See* Association-
ists.
Society for the Improvement
of the Condition of the
Poor, 16
Sodus Bay Phalanx, 170
Sons of Vulcan, 30
Southworth, William, 159
Spence, Thomas, 164, 181
Spinners strike, 37
Spofford, John, 207
Steubenville (Ohio), cooper-
ative iron shops, 195
Stock division bill, 104
Stone, James M., 154, 155, 157
Store-order system, 41
Supreme Division. *See*
Protective Union, Supreme
Division
"Sweating System," 54
Sylvania Phalanx, 166

Tailors, Boston Tailors Asso-
ciative Union, 195; Buffalo
cooperative shops, 196;
Germans strike in New
York City, 195
Ten-Hour Committee, 131
Ten-hour movement,
obstructed by blacklist, 107,
109; 1840's, 125-148, 164.
See also specific states,
cities, and corporations.
Textile mills, new industrial-
ism, 71
Thayer, John Quincy Adams,
134
Thayer, Reverend Thomas B.,
88
Thomas, Reverend Abel C,,
88
Thomas, Salmon, 154, 155

Times (Boston). *See Daily Times.*

Trades Union and Fall River Weavers' Journal, 117

Trade unions, 1850's, 164; formation, 228-240; history, 198-218

Transcendentalists, 19, 175

Trask, Henry P., 187, 221

Tribune (New York). *See Daily Tribune.*

Tukesbury, Dr., 221

Typhoid, 100

Union Bakery, 196

Union Society of Operative Cordwainers, 231

Usages and Abuses . . . of Manufacturing Corporations (Ayer), *fn*, 104

Van Buren, Martin, 126

Venereal diseases, 82

Voice of Industry, 11, 123, 125, 140; history, 212

Vox Populi (Lowell), 8, 83, 98

Wages (1840-1860), 119-120

Walker, Amasa, 40, 158, 220

Walker, Isaac P., 226

Walsh, Mike, 182, 206

Waltham system, 72

Watchcase makers, unionism, 234

Watuppa Corporation (Fall River), 117

Westward expansion, 36

Wheeling, cooperative iron shops, 194

Whig Party (Massachusetts), 102, 156, 158; factory controversy, 80

Whig clubs, 103

White, William A., 220

Wholesale (English cooperative union), 189

Women's Union of Manchester, 124

Windt, John, 182

Wisconsin Phalanx, 169

W.M.P.U. *See* Workingmen's Protective Union.

Wood, Reverend Henry, 15

Worcester mechanics, ten-hour day, 160

Working day, length of, 125, 128-132. *See also* Ten-hour movement and specific states, cities, and corporations.

Working Man's Advocate (Lowell), 181, 203

Workingmen's Association, 203

Workingmen's Party of 1829, 181

Workingmen's Protective Union, 187-191

World Convention. *See* Owen, Robert, World Convention.

Wright, Albert J., 187, 189, 207

York Company (Saco, Maine), working hours, 131

Young, William F., 23, 140, 157

Young America, 182

Young Americas, 184